RUSS CRANDALL

PHOTOGRAPHY BY RUSS CRANDALL AND GIANG CAO
COVER ILLUSTRATION BY ALEX BOAKE

"He that takes medicine and neglects diet, wastes the skills of the physician."
—Chinese proverb

VICTORY BELT PUBLISHING, INC.
LAS VEGAS

First Published in 2015 by Victory Belt Publishing Inc.

ISBN-13: 978-1-628600-87-2

Photography: Russ Crandall and Giang Cao
Design: Yordan Terziev and Boryana Yordanova
Cover Illustration: Alex Boake

Printed in the U.S.A.
RRD 0115

TABLE OF CONTENTS

INTRODUCTION / 7

CHINESE KITCHEN / 43

Japanese and Korean Favorites / 106

Southeast Asia and Beyond / 156

AMERICAN CLASSICS / 212

SAUCES, CONDIMENTS, AND SIDES / 260

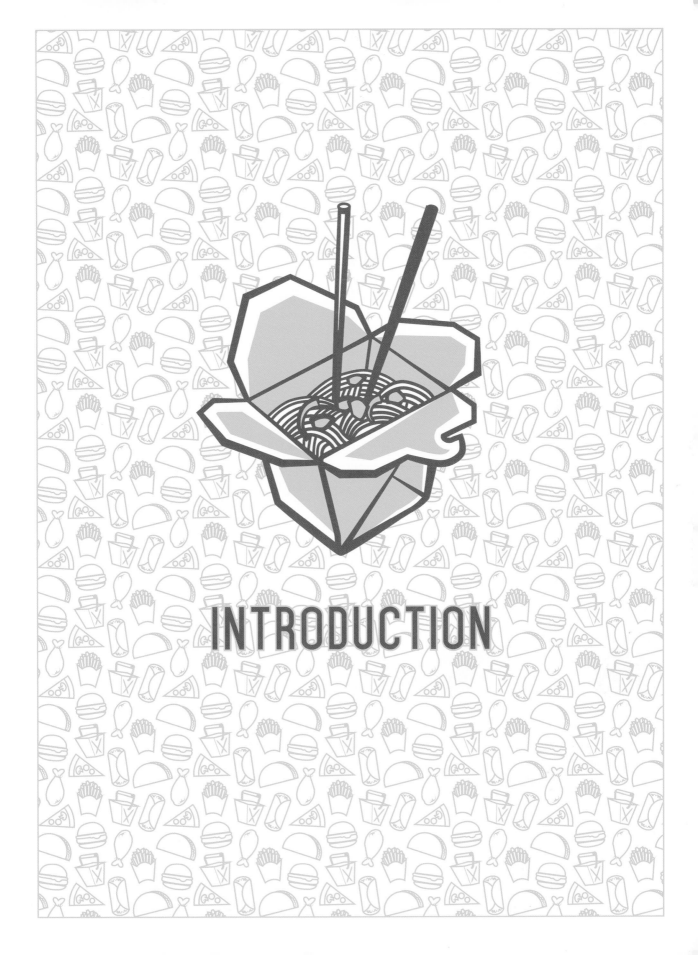

INTRODUCTION

MY STORY

SO HOW DOES A REGULAR GUY END UP WRITING A PALEO-MINDED COOKBOOK? GREAT QUESTION. I'D SAY IT PROBABLY STARTED WHEN I HAD A STROKE JUST A FEW DAYS BEFORE TURNING 25. BUT LET ME BACK UP A BIT.

I grew up in a small town (Yelm, Washington), doing the usual things that small-town boys did: playing in punk rock bands, chasing girls, and tipping cows (actually, I've never been cow-tipping, but the option was always there). When I turned 16, I got my first job working at our local Burger King. I later moved on to work in a pizza parlor, and then I worked as a dinner chef in a small, family-owned restaurant, where I learned the fundamentals of cooking that I still use today. By age 20, I needed a break—cooking just wasn't covering my college bills—so I joined the U.S. Navy in 2000, and I've been serving as a Russian and Indonesian translator ever since. One cool thing about my current job is that I've had the opportunity to travel, see the world, and try new cuisines—many of which are represented in this book.

So, back to the whole "stroke" thing. One afternoon, the left side of my body stopped behaving the way I wanted it to. I went to the hospital and, yep, I'd had a stroke in the right side of my pons (part of the brain stem), which was causing my left-sided weakness. One advantage to having a stroke at a young age is that the brain recovers quickly, so within six months I felt like I was basically back to normal. Learning how to walk, write, and drive again turned out to be pretty easy, in the grand scheme of things.

But then a year later I started feeling like I was constantly sick, and I had a hard time exercising and catching my breath. Figuring something was amiss, I went to see a doctor—who hospitalized me for a month to run the gamut of tests available to modern medicine. Turns out that my shortness of breath was caused by a narrowing of my pulmonary arteries due to inflammation. I was diagnosed with the rare autoimmune disease Takayasu's arteritis, and I then spent a year on heavy immunosuppressant therapy. We tried a combination of steroids and other heavy-duty drugs, and they worked, for the most part. Unfortunately, the medications had some hefty side effects, so I quickly started looking for alternative solutions to my predicament.

In the fall of 2007 I volunteered to undergo a pulmonary resectioning surgery. The doctors removed the inflamed tissue surrounding my pulmonary arteries and enlarged the arteries using parts of a cow's pericardium. The procedure is called a standstill operation—in order to get to the arteries, they had to perform a full cardiopulmonary bypass, deep hypothermia, and full cardiac arrest. In layman's terms, that means they rerouted my vital organs through a machine, drained a lot of blood out of my body in order to reach my pulmonary arteries, and lowered my body temperature to about 60 degrees to keep my brain alive. I had a 10 percent chance of not making it off the table alive due to the inherent complications associated with the surgery. It lasted about ten hours—and no, I didn't see a bright light at the end of any tunnel, or my childhood dog, Davey (miss you, buddy). I did make it out okay, and now I have a killer scar and some crazy stories. Unfortunately, the surgery didn't ease my symptoms—I was on the same amount of medication and saw little or no improvement.

So life went on. My continuous steroid and immunosuppressant medication therapy was starting to take its toll. I felt lousy most of the time, and worse still was the fact that I couldn't imagine it getting any better. I started developing kidney stones (youch!) and spent a month suffering through a serious bout of shingles. Basically, I felt elderly by the age of 28. I started to believe that the medications were going to kill me well before the disease ever could.

In 2010, at the age of 30, I happened across an article that mentioned the Paleo diet, which focuses on whole foods and has a good track record of helping to reverse autoimmune symptoms. Within a week I had devoured just about every Paleo resource I could find and switched my diet. My inflammation markers decreased significantly within a month.

Since then things have been much better. I'm not cured—there's no mistaking that I still have a serious autoimmune condition—but changing my eating habits allowed me to restore my health at a time when I thought it was "game over" for me. I started exercising for the first time in years. I was able to get off of steroid therapy, which was the most harmful of my medications, and since then I have weaned off nearly all my medications—from over a dozen a day at my worst to just one as of this writing.

In December 2010, I started thedomesticman.com, my little chunk of the Internet. I use the website to archive my favorite recipes and to chronicle my health journey. In February 2014, I released my first cookbook, *The Ancestral Table*, which focuses on traditional recipes and techniques. And here we are with *Paleo Takeout*!

THE STORY BEHIND *PALEO TAKEOUT*

I was inspired to write this book after thinking about an everyday challenge we all face: avoiding fast food restaurants. These places have become so convenient that it's hard not to fall back on them. There's a reason that you can find fast food restaurants in every town—letting someone else cook your food for you is easy and increasingly cheap, as many restaurants cut corners to improve their profits. The comparatively high cost of eating right (in terms of both money and time) just can't compete with a dollar menu or a takeout menu featuring over 100 offerings.

I realized early on in my health journey that it would be impossible to convince the entire world to eat better. After all, humans are hardwired to seek convenience (just open a SkyMall catalog to see what I mean). So instead I decided to challenge the notion of restaurant culture. What if I could write a cookbook that features the same dishes we know and love from our favorite restaurants, that are just as simple, fun, and fast to prepare as ordering takeout? And so the idea behind *Paleo Takeout* was born.

First, I decided to focus my recipe development on dishes that are difficult to re-create; as you know, a burger isn't rocket science. So I initially set my sights on one of the most popular and mystifying restaurant cuisines in the world—Chinese food. Did you know that there are more Chinese restaurants in the United States than all the McDonald's, Burger Kings, Wendy's, Domino's, and Pizza Huts combined—over 41,000 in total? That's a lot, yet it's surprisingly difficult for home cooks to replicate those tastes. From there, I expanded the book to include Japanese, Korean, Vietnamese, Thai, Indian, Mexican, Italian, Greek, and American favorites, all through the lens of America's tragically robust takeout restaurant culture.

THESE RECIPES ARE MY FAVORITE TO WRITE

There are two types of recipes that I love to write—Asian dishes and Paleo-friendly re-creations of popular foods. I lived on the Hawaiian island of O'ahu for most of my twenties, and my family still considers it home. I also spent several years traveling throughout Asia, sampling new flavors along the way. So to me, developing these recipes felt more natural than making a book based on any other cuisine.

I love the challenge of capturing familiar tastes using healthy ingredients. I did a ton of research and consulted with a few local restaurants to make sure that my techniques were solid. I'm very happy with the results, and I think you will be, too.

THE RECIPES IN *PALEO TAKEOUT* ARE SIMPLE AND EASY

I pride myself on focusing on traditional dishes, those that cultures have perfected over hundreds of years. The problem is, some of those dishes take a long time to cook—after all, if it's worth doing, it's worth doing right. The dishes I chose for this book are not all modeled after traditional or historic dishes; instead, they are meant to replicate and replace the sugar-filled, MSG-laden takeout foods that predominate in many Western countries (think shopping mall food court rather than an authentic, high-quality Chinatown restaurant).

It is always difficult for a cookbook author to strike a balance between convenience and authenticity. For this book in particular, I erred on the side of convenience; my thought process was that a recipe is good only if you are motivated to make it. Some recipes call for a marinating period, but for the most part I kept the recipes under an hour in total prep and cooking time. Additionally, I tried my best to design these dishes to serve four—perfect for a small family or for leftovers!

PALEO TAKEOUT MAY HELP
KICK-START YOUR HEALTH

Since adopting a Paleo-style diet in 2010, I have noticed that one of the main reasons people have a hard time jumping into a new dietary lifestyle is because they are unwilling to give up the foods they rely on the most. It's intimidating to have to give up your favorite staples.

It makes sense—most people, myself included, have an emotional connection to certain flavors. I grew up at a time when we were rewarded with pizza for meeting our grade school reading goals.

So, in my mind, creating a book of healthy alternatives to favorite dishes may give you the push you need to adopt an improved lifestyle, knowing that you don't have to abandon some of your favorite foods.

Many people are able to switch to a new diet overnight, especially in the face of health problems. But for everyone else, easing into new foods may be more prudent, and that's where *Paleo Takeout* really shines.

PALEO 101

WHILE *PALEO TAKEOUT* IS FOUNDED ON THE PRINCIPLES OF THE PALEO DIET, MY TAKE ON HEALTH AND NUTRITION ALSO DRAWS FROM OTHER POPULAR AND EMERGING FOOD MOVEMENTS. SO LET'S DIG INTO WHAT EXACTLY "PALEO" MEANS AND LOOK AT SOME LIKE-MINDED CONCEPTS.

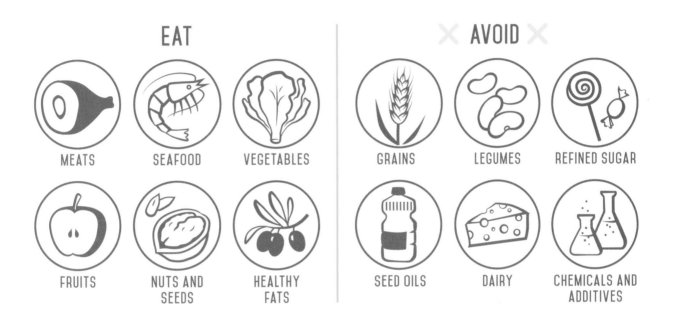

EAT | ✕ AVOID ✕

MEATS — SEAFOOD — VEGETABLES

FRUITS — NUTS AND SEEDS — HEALTHY FATS

GRAINS — LEGUMES — REFINED SUGAR

SEED OILS — DAIRY — CHEMICALS AND ADDITIVES

THE PALEO DIET

The Paleo diet is gaining in popularity daily. In a nutshell, it combines evolutionary science (looking at the foods humans ate historically) and modern nutritional studies to find an optimal way of eating. The conclusion: Eat plenty of meats, seafood, vegetables, fruits, and nuts—and avoid foods that are toxic (sugar, processed foods, and seed oils) and foods that may be problematic for digestion (legumes, dairy, and grains). There are some subtleties beyond those hard-and-fast rules, which I'll explain later (see "Gray-Area Foods" on page 16).

THE PERFECT HEALTH DIET

The Perfect Health Diet is founded on similar principles as the Paleo diet but encourages the consumption of "safe starches" (those that are low in toxicity) like potatoes and white rice in proportions that are similar to traditional practices. The diet also treats healthy forms of dairy (mostly butter and cream) as pleasure foods that should be used to season and enrich dishes—provided that they are well tolerated.

WESTON A. PRICE FOUNDATION

The Weston A. Price Foundation (WAPF) supports the use of traditional foods and food preparation techniques. WAPF encourages the consumption of raw dairy and the soaking or sprouting of certain foods (grains and legumes) to reduce their toxicity, and fermenting others (namely vegetables and dairy) to increase their digestibility.

A WHOLE FOODS APPROACH

A whole foods approach to eating is just like it sounds: Eat only foods that come from whole food sources. In other words, if you can find it in nature or prepare it in your own kitchen from scratch, then it's a whole food. While you probably aren't making your own olive oil, you could conceivably make it at home (quick tutorial: squeeze some olives). But could you make corn oil? Not without the use of chemical solvents—therefore it's not a whole food.

Everyone's journey is different—in the end, it's up to you to find what works for your particular health needs. Here are a few resources to help get you there:

- *The Paleo Cure, by Chris Kresser*

- *Perfect Health Diet, by Paul Jaminet, PhD, and Shou-Ching Jaminet, PhD*

- *Eat the Yolks, by Liz Wolfe*

JUST EAT REAL FOOD—"JERF"

My eating style is a combination of all these principles. I eat real foods from healthy plants and animals. I favor foods that are nutrient dense (meats, seafood, vegetables) over foods that are calorie dense but devoid of nutrients (processed grains). And I try to balance my macronutrients (carbs, fats, and proteins) in the way that makes me feel my best (see "The Four Corners Plate," page 19).

RICE

First and foremost, if you don't eat rice, don't worry—every dish in this book can be made without white rice or rice flour. Refer to my Substitution Guide on pages 304–305.

The use of rice in a Paleo-minded book seems counterintuitive, since rice is a grain. But hear me out, and maybe you'll join #teamwhiterice too. Historians estimate that the progenitor of rice existed some 130 million years ago—127 million years before humans first appeared! It's so old that similar strains were found in both Africa and Asia, indicating that it was around before the continents shifted to where they are today. Wild rice was eaten by prehistoric peoples, and it was first domesticated around 13,000 years ago, before the end of the Paleolithic era and a couple thousand years before wheat was domesticated. Rice also has a reputation among many traditional cultures as being a safe food for digestion.

Here's something that may surprise you: Throw out your "healthy" brown rice. True, the bran surrounding brown rice has more nutrients than white rice, but it is also significantly higher in inorganic arsenic (the bad kind) and toxins like phytic acid. Phytic acid, by the way, binds to the nutrients that are already present in your digestive tract, preventing you from absorbing them; in other words, eating brown rice could result in you digesting fewer nutrients than when eating white rice. White rice has the lowest toxicity, by far, of all the cereal grains. There are concerns that white rice still contains some phytic acid, but white rice actually has less phytic acid than many foods approved by common Paleo diet standards, such as coconut, avocados, walnuts, almonds, and coriander seeds. Finally, the vast majority of the toxins that remain in white rice are destroyed in the cooking process. White rice is not nutrient dense, so it's a good idea to cook it in broth and eat it as part of a nutrient-packed meal. In my family, we often top our rice with furikake (see page 32).

TYPES OF RICE

- **Calrose**, *a medium-grain rice, is your quintessential Asian-style white rice. It's the default rice in my kitchen. I prefer Nishiki brand Calrose rice, which is grown in California and of excellent quality.*

- **Basmati**, *a long-grain rice most prominent in India, carries a very low glycemic load and has the lowest arsenic content. It is best when soaked and steamed (see Steamed Basmati Rice, page 287). I prefer Lundberg brand basmati rice, grown in California.*

- **Mochi** *(also called sweet or glutinous rice) is a starchy short-grain rice used in making mochi and served in curries as "sticky rice" (see Thai Sticky Rice, page 287). I prefer the Hakubai brand, grown in California.*

- **Jasmine** *is a fragrant long-grain rice that is digested very quickly and therefore carries a higher glycemic load; I tend to avoid regular cooking with it, but my family does enjoy it from time to time. Jasmine is a good rice solution for folks with small intestinal bacterial overgrowth (SIBO); since it digests quickly, it prohibits bacteria growth.*

× **Parboiled rice** *is partially cooked in its bran before being polished. It has a higher nutrient profile and a lower glycemic index than white rice, but it retains more antinutrients. It is also mostly grown in the southern U.S., where arsenic-based pesticides were historically used, so it has a very high arsenic content (but not as high as brown rice). I avoid it!*

It's true that, like water and vegetables, rice contains arsenic. But most of the concerning statistics come from brown rice, not white rice. Also, white rice grown in California, India, and Pakistan (as opposed to East Asia and the southern United States) contains lower concentrations of arsenic; California-grown white basmati rice has about 1.5 micrograms per serving before being rinsed and cooked (which further reduces its arsenic content); by comparison, brown rice grown in the southern

U.S. can contain up to 8.5 micrograms per serving, and drinking water can legally contain up to 10 micrograms per liter (which is the amount the average person drinks in a day). So as long as you're sticking with white rice grown in California or South Asia, you should be okay. More information on arsenic and rice can be found through the references below.

RESOURCES:

"Rice," *Cambridge History of Food*, 2000. Available online at http://tdman.us/RiceHistory

"Living with Phytic Acid," The Weston A. Price Foundation, March 2010. Available online at http://tdman.us/PhyticAcid

"Arsenic in Your Food," *Consumer Reports*, November 2012. Available online at http://tdman.us/ArsenicStudy

POTATOES

White potatoes are also a source of controversy in the Paleo and ancestral communities, despite the widespread acknowledgment that underground storage organs, otherwise known as tubers, are important staple foods for nearly every indigenous culture on the planet. White potatoes are slowly gaining acceptance (the little tubers that could!) and were adopted into the Whole30 program, a fairly strict, no-nonsense Paleo eating regimen, in 2014.

Potatoes have a fair amount of nutrients, including potassium, magnesium, and vitamin C. They are also relatively free of toxins. Glycoalkaloids, their most prominent toxin, are significantly reduced when the potatoes are peeled and cooked gently (most traditional cultures peeled their potatoes). Modern potatoes were also cultivated over time to reduce glycoalkaloids and improve digestibility; russet potatoes have some of the lowest levels of toxins in potatoes today. There are studies showing that potatoes increase inflammation markers in some people, and the potato's status as being pro-inflammatory is due to its glycoalkaloid content. This effect may be more attributable to the form (fried potato chips) or skin content of the potatoes used in these studies. In other words, eating peeled and boiled potatoes is less inflammatory than eating fried potatoes or potato skins.

Some forms of potatoes encourage overeating, which gives potatoes in general a bad reputation. Scientists have developed what they call the Satiety Index, which rates foods by how good they are at satisfying hunger. Boiled potatoes were the most satiating, far outpacing and nearly doubling the next foods on the list, fish and beef. Potato chips and French fries, however, were only one-third as satisfying as boiled potatoes, which means that you could eat three times as many potatoes in the form of French fries or chips before feeling full. This is why you can eat a whole basket of fries or an entire bag of chips and not feel satisfied, but can barely make it through one or two boiled potatoes. For this reason, I prefer to eat boiled potatoes, but still indulge in some tasty fries (page 290) from time to time.

White potatoes were absent from the original list of "approved" Paleo foods when the diet was first emerging, most likely because white potatoes have a higher toxin profile and contain slightly fewer nutrients when compared to sweet potatoes. Sweet potatoes have nearly the same carb content and glycemic load as white potatoes. Today, many Paleo nutritionists concede that when cooked properly, white potatoes can have a place on the dinner table equal to sweet potatoes.

Potato starch is a prominent ingredient in this book, as it is used often in Asian cuisine to make a crispy breading. This starch is extracted from crushed potatoes, then washed and dried. Potato starch is a source of resistant starch, an indigestible fiber that has been found to feed gut bacteria and in many cases to help stimulate weight loss.

RESOURCES:

S. H. Holt, J. C. Miller, P. Petocz, and E. Farmakalidis, "A Satiety Index of Common Foods," *European Journal of Clinical Nutrition*, September 1995. Available online at http://tdman.us/SatietyStudy (chart: http://tdman.us/SatietyChart)

"Resistant Starch 101: Everything You Need to Know," *Authority Nutrition*, 2014. Available online at http://tdman.us/RSlink

DAIRY

Dairy is used sparingly and judiciously in this book, usually in the form of ghee, butter, cream, cheese, or yogurt. But let's talk about why dairy is in this book in the first place. Dairy is an excellent source of calcium and vitamins A, D, and K2, the latter being nutrients that are sometimes difficult to find in other foods. While conventional wisdom associates high-fat dairy with obesity, cardiovascular disease, and metabolic disease, observational studies have found the opposite to be true.

From a culinary perspective, dairy products are essential in any respectable kitchen. Butter and ghee impart richness. Cream adds body and depth of flavor, and cheese is overwhelmingly delicious. So I believe that there are nutritional and culinary reasons to find out how to prudently incorporate dairy into our diets.

The major reason people have issues with digesting dairy is that they lack an enzyme called lactase, which allows the body to digest lactose. It is highly dependent on ancestry; only about 40 percent of us maintain this enzyme past childhood. It's also highly dependent on the state of bacteria growth in an individual's digestive system. Ghee is a form of clarified butter (see page 29) that is lactose-free and approved by the Whole30 program.

Not all forms of dairy are equal. Many people who have adverse reactions to pasteurized dairy don't have issues with raw (unpasteurized) dairy. If you don't have access to raw dairy, try to find pasteurized dairy from grass-fed cows; grass-fed dairy products contain a significant amount of vitamin K2. Fermented dairy products like yogurt, kefir, sour cream, and hard (aged) cheeses are often better tolerated than milk. Butter and cream also contain less lactose since they have a higher fat content than milk. All the same, you'll find that the dairy amounts in most of my recipes are negligible or easily substituted; every recipe in this book that calls for dairy has a dairy-free alternative included.

Experimenting with cheese and yogurt made from the milks of other mammals (for example, goat's or sheep's milk) is another option.

RESOURCE:
M. Kratz, T. Baars, and S. Guyenet, "The Relationship Between High-Fat Dairy Consumption and Obesity, Cardiovascular, and Metabolic Disease," *European Journal of Nutrition*, February 2013. Available online at http://tdman.us/DairyStudyFat

LEGUMES

While legumes in general are high in some seriously disruptive toxins, some legumes aren't so bad. Peas and green beans in particular have been cultivated for so long that their toxicity is negligible. So I think they're fine to eat, and most Paleo folks agree. My personal philosophy is that if the bean is edible in its raw state (like snow peas, sugar snap peas, green peas, and green beans are), then it's good to go. I consider bean sprouts to be okay, too.

Make no bones about it—soy is pretty terrible for you. It has been linked to malnutrition, thyroid dysfunction, cognitive decline, reproductive disorders, and even heart disease and cancer. It has one of the highest toxin profiles of any legume, and it's baffling that we feed this stuff to our children via infant formula. But there's a bright spot in all this doom and gloom; fermenting soy, especially through the long, slow process of making tamari (a wheat-free soy sauce) and miso (a paste most commonly used in soups), eliminates its phytic acid and other digestive inhibitors. However, the fermentation process doesn't totally destroy phytoestrogen, another bad guy, although it does reduce it by up to 90 percent; you're likely ingesting more phytoestrogen through sesame seeds and garlic than through fermented soy.

THE FOUR CORNERS PLATE

PROTEIN ABOUT 1LB PER DAY

STARCHY FOODS ABOUT 1LB PER DAY

LEAFY VEG OR SALADS TO TASTE

HARDY VEG ABOUT 1LB PER DAY

There is no one way to eat that is perfect for everyone, but there are definitely some steps we can take to get closer to an optimal formula. I developed this "Four Corners Plate" over the past several years as a template to ensure that my meals are healthful, diverse, and satisfying. This plate is based on traditional and historic cuisines (what I would expect to see on a plate during an episode of *Leave It to Beaver*) and in portions that humans seem to naturally gravitate toward. Always keep in mind that variety is the key to ensuring that you are getting the right nutrients and preventing you from getting bored with certain foods.

PROTEIN	STARCHY FOOD
SEAFOOD, FISH, BEEF, BISON, LAMB, WILD GAME, PORK, CHICKEN, DUCK, TURKEY, EGGS	RICE, POTATOES, SWEET POTATOES, BEETS, PARSNIPS, PLANTAINS, YUCA, TARO, WINTER SQUASH (PUMPKIN, ACORN SQUASH, ETC.)

LEAFY VEG	HARDY VEG
LETTUCE, CABBAGE, KALE, SPINACH, GREENS, HERBS (SIDE SALAD OR BRAISED GREENS)	BROCCOLI, CAULIFLOWER, CUCUMBERS, RADISHES, TURNIPS, CARROTS, GREEN BEANS, EGGPLANT, SUMMER SQUASH (ZUCCHINI AND YELLOW SQUASH)

Dividing your meals into four equal-sized portions can help you balance your macronutrient ratios (carbs, fats, and proteins) as well as ensure that you are getting adequate micronutrients (vitamins and minerals) to improve and maintain your health. Arrange your plate as shown above.

Fruits, berries, nuts, and chocolate should be eaten seasonally and sparingly and should not be factored into meal planning. This approach is similar to the "pleasure foods" concept highlighted in the *Perfect Health Diet* book.

You may have noticed that this book doesn't contain any dessert recipes. The main reason for this is that there are already plenty of Paleo-fied dessert recipes out there; a quick Google search for "Paleo cookies" yields over *14 million* results, and chances are that a few of them are pretty good. My personal take is that post-meal treats don't necessarily need to be an involved process (berries drizzled with a bit of coconut milk and honey are delicious and satisfying). I prefer to keep desserts as rare, spontaneous moments—just as they have been throughout most of history.

SEASON WITH FATS AND ACIDS

Fats and acids have been used for thousands of years to improve the flavor of foods, and they do more than just make foods taste good—they improve their digestibility as well as the bioavailability of vitamins and nutrients. For example, adding olive oil to a salad enables the body to better absorb the fat-soluble vitamins A, D, and K found in leafy greens. Fats and acids also temper the glycemic load of starchy foods, potentially reducing blood sugar spikes.

Healthy fats include olive oil, coconut oil, lard, tallow, duck fat, butter, and ghee. Acids include citrus fruits, vinegars, alcohol, and acidic vegetables like tomatoes. Fats and acids should be incorporated naturally during the cooking process—for example, use oil to prevent food from sticking to the pan and a squeeze of lemon juice to brighten up a dish before serving.

PORTION SIZING

I prefer to eat two large meals a day (see "Beyond the Book," page 300). So eating in alignment with the Four Corners Plate is easy math; I generally eat half a pound of meat, starches, and hardy veggies at each meal. The portion sizes in this book are generally set to 8 ounces of protein per person, which takes the guesswork out of portion sizing.

A pound of starches a day sounds like a ton of food, but it's really not, since starchy foods are pretty dense and heavy. In general, a diet of up to 150 grams of carbs a day is still considered moderate to low-carb, while athletes can afford to eat 150 to 200 grams of carbs. As an example, a pound of white basmati rice contains 114 grams of carbs, a pound of boiled potatoes contains 91 grams of carbs, and a pound of winter squash contains 48 grams of carbs. Bear in mind that processed starchy foods like noodles are much higher in carbs per pound (since they are significantly less heavy), so adjust accordingly: A pound of sweet potato noodles contains 390 grams of carbs, and a pound of tapioca starch contains 353 grams of carbs. But again, it would be close to impossible to eat an entire pound of these foods anyway.

In the end, it will take some tweaking to find what works for you, since the consumption of starchy foods is very individualized and complex. But overall, I think this template is an excellent standard for healthy, satisfying, and sustainable eating.

DINNER IN AN HOUR

ONE OF THE BIGGEST CHALLENGES OF EATING AT HOME IS FIGURING OUT HOW TO SERVE A VARIETY OF FOODS IN A SHORT PERIOD. NOBODY HAS TIME TO CREATE A FULL-COURSE MEAL EVERY NIGHT, RIGHT? WELL, I'M HERE TO TELL YOU THAT WITH A LITTLE FORETHOUGHT, TIMING, AND MULTITASKING, YOU CAN KNOCK OUT A DELICIOUS DINNER IN AN HOUR OR LESS.

The chart you see to the right illustrates a meal from the Chinese Kitchen chapter and features Egg Drop Soup (page 46), Sweet and Sour Chicken (page 64), Vegetables in White Sauce (page 102), and Baked Cauliflower Rice (page 288). The chicken dish can be replaced with any number of meat dishes from that chapter, since they all take about the same amount of time to prepare and follow a similar method.

The most important tactics in planning a meal are reading through and understanding each recipe and finding a way to have its directions complement the other recipes you're preparing. As you can see in the chart, there is never a moment when you're doing two things at the same time; instead, you fill your hands-off time on one dish with some hands-on time on another dish. In general, the only time you'll be working on all the dishes at once is when you're preparing and chopping ingredients at the beginning.

Keep in mind that it doesn't matter how long a dish takes to make—10 minutes or 45 minutes—what's more important is to finish all the dishes you are serving at the same time. When wrapping your mind around preparing meals, think about the final product and work your way backward. This is what restaurants do; they want to plate all the components of a meal at the same time.

So here's my challenge to you: Try preparing this meal exactly as specified in the recipe directions and on this chart, and time yourself. Were you able to knock it out in an hour? If not, where did you get hung up? Then try it again, but maybe make it with Orange Chicken (page 66) instead of Sweet and Sour Chicken. Did your timing improve? Now imagine how much easier it'll be after following this method for a month or two!

Another possible solution is to bring your family on board for the challenge. Let your significant other (or a child who can read) act as your point person, and have them handle the instructions while you do the work. It's fun to time yourselves and see if you can beat your "PR."

Once you've got the method down, try it out in different contexts. If you eat rice, try using a rice cooker to essentially eliminate one of the processes. Or you could roast some vegetables while you bake the cauliflower rice—just toss some carrots, Brussels sprouts, or other vegetables in olive oil, salt, and pepper and then roast until crispy—that will eliminate another process. By shortening your other processes, you'll have more time (and confidence) to tackle some of the more challenging dishes in this book and in other cookbooks. Good luck! And above all, have fun.

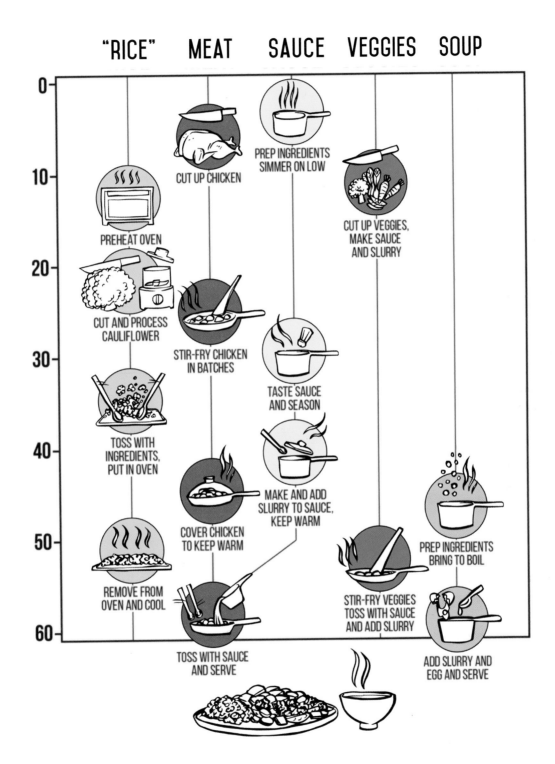

"RICE" MEAT SAUCE VEGGIES SOUP

PREP INGREDIENTS SIMMER ON LOW

CUT UP CHICKEN

CUT UP VEGGIES, MAKE SAUCE AND SLURRY

PREHEAT OVEN

CUT AND PROCESS CAULIFLOWER

STIR-FRY CHICKEN IN BATCHES

TASTE SAUCE AND SEASON

TOSS WITH INGREDIENTS, PUT IN OVEN

MAKE AND ADD SLURRY TO SAUCE, KEEP WARM

COVER CHICKEN TO KEEP WARM

PREP INGREDIENTS BRING TO BOIL

REMOVE FROM OVEN AND COOL

STIR-FRY VEGGIES TOSS WITH SAUCE AND ADD SLURRY

TOSS WITH SAUCE AND SERVE

ADD SLURRY AND EGG AND SERVE

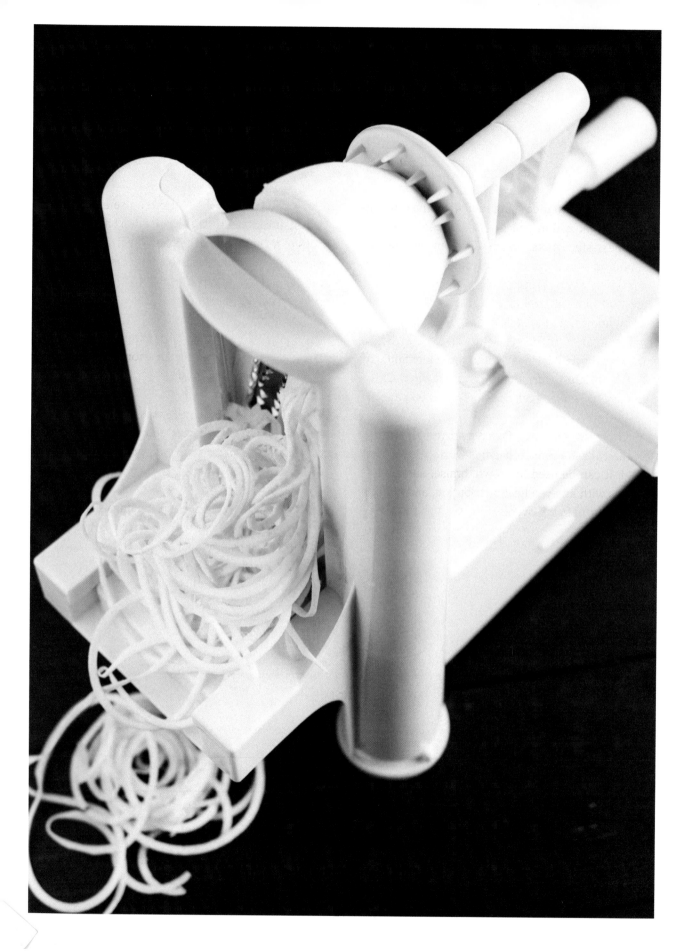

ESSENTIAL TOOLS

POTS AND PANS

WOK: An essential cooking tool when making stir-fries, a wok is thin and heats (and cools) quickly. Stainless-steel woks are standard but require seasoning to prevent sticking; if you have the money, some European brands make nonstick woks that are 100 percent free of PFOA and PFOS toxins, are made from recycled metals, and can be used with metal utensils. My favorites are SCANPAN (Denmark) and Swiss Diamond (Switzerland) 12-inch woks. Just learning how to use a wok? Check out my "Essential Techniques" section on page 33.

DUTCH OVEN: A 5-quart Dutch oven (the Le Creuset brand calls it a French oven) is worth its weight in gold. It can be used to brown, braise, and simmer dishes with an even heat distribution, and it works like a charm in the oven.

STAINLESS-STEEL SKILLET: I often use a 10- to 14-inch stainless-steel skillet when I don't need the tall sides of a Dutch oven. Stainless-steel skillets work especially well for oven-roasting meats because you can make a gravy directly in the pan with the drippings that accumulate.

CAST-IRON SKILLET: Another essential, a 10- to 12-inch cast-iron skillet is superior for frying and roasting at high temperatures.

SAUCEPAN: A 2-quart saucepan is very handy when making sauces for stir-fries and can fit on a small burner to keep warm while you prepare the rest of the meal.

LARGE STOCKPOT: Perfect for boiling, simmering, and steaming. For the recipes in this book, you'll use a stockpot mostly to make broths and soups.

KITCHEN GADGETS

HIGH-SPEED BLENDER: A blender is important when you want a smooth sauce or paste. While pricey options like Vitamix and Blendtec brand blenders are awesome, the honest truth is that I use my $50 Magic Bullet blender the most often. An immersion blender is also a handy tool when you want to blend a sauce or soup without transferring it to a countertop blender.

FOOD PROCESSOR: Lots of people have food processors, but they are often neglected (but not as much as stand mixers, mind you). You'll get a ton of use out of your food processor when using this book, especially when making the gazillion meatball recipes in here!

OTHER TOOLS

QUICK-READ THERMOMETER: These thermometers are cheap and take the guesswork out of measuring meat and oil temperatures.

CHEESECLOTH: Essential when squeezing liquid out of ingredients (see my Tzatziki Sauce recipe on page 284 for an example) or filtering out solids from liquid (as in my Faster Pho recipe on page 180). Nut milk bags also work well for these purposes.

SHARP KNIFE: A sharp knife seriously lessens the drudgery of cutting. I prefer a 10-inch Santoku or chef's knife. Be sure to get an appropriate sharpener to keep your knife in good condition.

LADLE: A ladle serves as the primary cooking utensil in many Asian kitchens; it allows you to scoop and flatten foods easily and works especially well in a rounded wok. Get a nice metal ladle that feels comfortable in your hand.

OUTDOOR GRILL: Many dishes in this book call for grilling, and I've written instructions for both charcoal and gas grills. The best thing about grilling—no dirty dishes! See page 34 for more info on grilling techniques.

GRILL PAN: Consider buying a grill pan, which rests on your outdoor grill and prevents food from falling through the grates; it's perfect when making Bulgogi (page 142) or fajita vegetables (page 248). Heavy-duty aluminum foil can be used in a pinch.

SPIRAL SLICER: This handy gadget transforms hardy vegetables like zucchini, squash, and sweet potatoes into a series of spirals that take on the form of noodles. My favorite is the Paderno World Cuisine brand Spiral Vegetable Slicer.

ESSENTIAL INGREDIENTS

HERE YOU'LL FIND MANY OF THE INGREDIENTS YOU'LL NEED TO COOK YOUR WAY THROUGH *PALEO TAKEOUT*. MANY OF THESE INGREDIENTS CAN BE FOUND AT YOUR LOCAL ASIAN OR INTERNATIONAL MARKET OR ONLINE. I'VE SET UP A HANDY AMAZON SHOPPING LIST FOR YOU, WHICH INCLUDES EACH INGREDIENT PLUS A LISTING OF THE DISHES THAT USE IT, WHICH YOU CAN FIND AT **http://tdman.us/PTOshopping**. BE SURE TO CONSULT MY SUBSTITUTION GUIDE ON PAGES 304-305 FOR WORKAROUNDS WHEN YOU'RE IN A PINCH.

BASICS

SALTS: Sea salt is harvested from evaporated seawater and contains trace minerals. I used fine sea salt in developing these recipes, which has a saltiness and texture equal to table salt. I also used Diamond Crystal brand kosher salt. If you use Morton's, the other leading brand of kosher salt, reduce the amount called for by one-third (it's much saltier than Diamond Crystal).

WHITE AND BLACK PEPPER: White pepper has a more pungent, direct flavor than black pepper. It is made from the same fruit, but with its dark outer skin removed. You'll want to have both ground white pepper and whole white peppercorns; the latter are used to make Thai curries (pages 170–175), while the former is used in most of the other recipes in this book. Same goes for ground black pepper and peppercorns—or, better yet, you could just keep whole peppercorns on hand and grind them yourself.

STARCHES AND FLOURS: I use a variety of starches in this book. Tapioca starch, made from dried and ground yuca, is stretchy and versatile. Arrowroot starch is an excellent thickener for sauces and mimics cornstarch the best. Potato starch is an excellent starch for coating meat before frying (the other two starches work well also). All three work equally well in making a thin batter for frying. Rice flour thickens like wheat flour when heated and makes an excellent roux (such as for Mashed Potatoes and Gravy, page 292, and Japanese Curry, page 120) or binder for crepes (Bánh Xèo, page 186) and pancakes (Okonomiyaki, page 130, and Korean Seafood Scallion Pancake, page 138).

SWEETENERS: While I mainly use honey to sweeten dishes or to offset the bitterness of tamari, there are a few other sweeteners I use. Dark maple syrup (formerly known as Grade B) is less refined than Golden or Amber maple syrup (formerly known simply as Grade A), and I sometimes use it when I want a distinct maple flavor. Coconut palm sugar is made from the sap of coconut palm flower buds and is often sold in granulated form; I use it when I want to sweeten a dish without adding liquid honey to it (you can find granulated honey, but it's expensive). Blackstrap molasses is a byproduct of making cane sugar and contains a lot of vitamins and minerals. For fermentation, I use organic cane sugar, since most of it is fermented out and other sweeteners, like honey, inhibit the fermentation process. I also use blended fruit (like applesauce) to flavor some dishes. In the end, sugar is sugar, so use it sparingly or omit it if you are avoiding sugar altogether.

LIQUID INGREDIENTS

TAMARI: Tamari is the original soy sauce introduced to Japan from China, and it is made without wheat (unlike most soy sauces today). While most forms of soy are best avoided, I think that fermented soy (tamari and miso especially) is okay for occasional use; the fermentation process drastically reduces the toxic effects of soy (more info on page 18). Tamari and miso go hand in hand, as tamari is the liquid that is left over when making miso. My favorite tamari is from Eden Foods, made with organic ingredients. If you cannot tolerate tamari, coconut aminos (see below) and my Umami Sauce (page 266) are both excellent alternatives.

COCONUT AMINOS: Coconut aminos is a fair substitute for tamari in all my recipes. Because it does not have as bold a flavor as tamari and is a little sweeter, I suggest adding about 25 percent more when substituting coconut aminos for tamari and reducing the amount of honey, fruit, or other sweetener in the recipe by 25 percent. When using a small quantity of coconut aminos, the difference is negligible, so don't sweat it too much. This stuff is pretty expensive, so consider making some Umami Sauce (page 266) instead.

CHINESE COOKING WINE: There are two main varieties of Chinese cooking wine, both made from fermented rice: plain cooking wine (which is clear) and Shaoxing wine (which is amber). Shaoxing wine is slightly fruitier and more complex than plain Chinese cooking wine, but manufacturers often add wheat to Shaoxing wine to give it its signature color. Look for Chinese cooking wine that contains just water, rice, and salt (it is sometimes labeled simply as rice wine). If you don't have access to either wine, dry sherry will work just fine.

MIRIN AND SAKE: Mirin is a wine made from sweet rice. Look for high-quality wines that are free of corn syrup. Eden Foods makes an excellent mirin with organic ingredients and no added sugar. Like mirin, sake is a rice wine, but it is not quite as sweet and has a higher alcohol content.

RICE VINEGAR: Sometimes labeled rice wine vinegar, this is a rice wine that has been fermented for a longer period and has a sharper taste than mirin or sake.

CANE VINEGAR: Used in Filipino cooking, this mild vinegar is made from fermented cane sugar and is slightly sweet. Datu Puti is the easiest brand to find, and my favorite.

APPLE CIDER VINEGAR: Apple cider vinegar, sometimes labeled cider vinegar, is made from fermented apples. It's fruitier than rice vinegar and cane vinegar. I use Bragg's brand.

FISH SAUCE: Fish sauce is an easy way to add tastiness to dishes and condiments. It is usually made from fermented anchovies. Don't let the initial fishiness of the sauce fool you—adding it to a dish often creates a very unfishlike flavor. Look for brands without added sugar, like Red Boat Fish Sauce.

> * **Good to know:** *Many Asian ingredients (tamari, Chinese cooking wine, miso, mirin, and sake) are made by fermenting foods in a fungus called koji (Aspergillus oryzae); if you see that ingredient listed on a package, it's a good thing!*

FATS AND OILS

BUTTER AND GHEE: I'm sure you know what butter is, but let's talk about ghee. It is a clarified butter that is heated so that its milk solids separate and toast and are then discarded. The result is a rich, shelf-stable butterfat that is lactose-free and can be heated to high temperatures without burning. Most folks consider ghee to be Paleo-friendly (it is Whole30-approved), while butter is up to individual tolerance. Pure Indian Farms and Tin Star Foods are my favorite brands of ghee; both are made using dairy from grass-fed cows. Similarly, look for butter made using milk from grass-fed cows (Kerrygold is my favorite), which contains more vitamin K2 than butter from grain-fed cows. I used unsalted butter in developing the recipes in this book.

LARD: Lard is rendered pork fat and is an excellent frying fat. Look for varieties that require refrigeration; shelf-stable lard has been partially hydrogenated (which creates trans fats). Regular lard comes from the pig's back fat; leaf lard is made from the fat surrounding the pig's kidneys and has a more neutral taste. My favorite brand is Tendergrass Farms; they sell both lard and leaf lard.

AVOCADO OIL: Avocado oil is a neutral-tasting oil that makes an excellent Mayo (page 276) and works great in Chili Oil (page 268).

COCONUT OIL: There are two types of coconut oil: virgin and expeller-pressed (also known as refined). Virgin coconut oil has a mild coconut flavor, while expeller-pressed coconut oil has a neutral flavor and can be heated to higher temperatures without burning. I use virgin coconut oil for dishes that fare well with a coconut flavor (Thai curries, for example) and expeller-pressed coconut oil for sautéing when I don't want a coconut flavor.

OLIVE OIL: Extra virgin olive oil is generally my favorite oil for roasting vegetables and using in salads. New studies have proven that extra virgin olive oil does not become carcinogenic when used for frying foods. Kasandrinos brand olive oil is of excellent quality and has a fruity, lightly spicy taste. Olive oil doesn't taste great when used for frying, though, so I don't recommend it.

TOASTED SESAME OIL: Sesame oil is added to many Asian dishes at the end for extra flavor, and sometimes is used in marinades. You could theoretically buy untoasted sesame oil and toast it yourself, but that's a lot of work; the toasted version (which is dark in color) is easier to find and is preferred.

PEPPERS

THAI (BIRD'S-EYE) CHILES: Easily the hottest pepper in this book, both fresh and dried varieties of Thai chiles are used sparingly when making curries or sauces. Fresh chiles can be hard to find, so buy a bag of dried chiles online and keep them handy. Wear gloves when handling, and use the seeds only if you're feeling especially brave!

DRIED CHINESE (SICHUAN) CHILES: Chinese chiles are dark red, about 2 inches long, and only moderately spicy once dried. They are added to many spicy Chinese-American dishes, like General Tso's Chicken (page 72) and Kung Pao Pork (page 92). Crushed red pepper can be used in a pinch.

JALAPEÑOS: My go-to fresh chile pepper, since it is easy to find in the U.S. and isn't frustratingly spicy. I like to use jalapeños in making Thai Green Curry (page 170) and Butter Chicken (page 194). They are also great as garnishes in a variety of Vietnamese, Thai, and Mexican-American dishes.

DRIED MEXICAN CHILES: There are many different types of dried large, mild red chiles, including Anaheim, ancho, guajillo, and New Mexico; they have varying levels of heat and richness. Mostly they are used to impart a chile pepper taste without adding much heat. I used mild guajillo peppers in developing these recipes, but you may use whatever is available to you.

KASHMIRI RED CHILI POWDER: This Indian pepper powder, which is less spicy than cayenne pepper, gives dishes like Tandoori Chicken (page 190) and Chicken Tikka Masala (page 192) their signature red color.

KOREAN RED PEPPER POWDER (고춧가루) Sometimes labeled gochugaru, Korean red pepper powder is an important ingredient when making Kimchi (page 148) and other Korean dishes.

TOGARASHI POWDER: This Japanese pepper powder is used as a condiment in foods like Ramen (page 112) and Japanese Curry (page 120). There are two main varieties: shichimi togarashi, which is a mixture of chili pepper, orange peel, sesame seeds, white pepper, ginger, hemp seed, and seaweed, and nanami togarashi, which doesn't contain hemp seed and has a stronger citrus flavor. Either will work fine for the recipes in this book.

THAI RED CURRY, PAGE 172

THAI (BIRD'S-EYE) CHILES

DRIED MEXICAN CHILES

OTHER INGREDIENTS

GALANGAL: This root is similar to ginger root but has an earthier taste. It is used in Southeast Asian cooking; ginger will work in a pinch. If you happen to find some at your local Asian market, buy a bunch, peel it, and slice it into 1-inch pieces, then freeze it for easy access.

SHRIMP PASTE: Shrimp paste, made from fermented shrimp, is a common flavor enhancer in Southeast Asia. It is similar to fish sauce but is often more pungent. I prefer the terasi (Indonesian) and belacan (Malaysian) versions, which are sold in blocks and are easy to find online. Shrimp sauce, a Chinese invention, is a saltier version of shrimp paste and is available in many Asian markets. Adjust the salt levels in your recipes accordingly if using shrimp sauce.

DRIED SHRIMP: Dried shrimp are exactly what you'd expect. They come in various sizes and can last almost indefinitely in the fridge. They're excellent for adding to soups (like Ramen, page 112) and are an essential ingredient in Green Papaya Salad (page 164). They can be found online for a fair price.

LEMONGRASS: A type of grass common in warm climates, lemongrass is a popular herb in Southeast Asian cuisine. It imparts a subtle but distinct citrus flavor. If you can't find fresh lemongrass locally, check your local Asian market's freezer section, or buy preserved or dried lemongrass online.

CHINESE CABBAGE: The four most common types of Chinese cabbage are sometimes confusing, so let's run through them.

- Won bok (also known as napa cabbage) is a large, dense cabbage not unlike head cabbage. It is most commonly used in Kimchi (page 148).

- Bok choy is both bulbous and leafy and can have a white or green stem. Immature cabbages are often sold as baby bok choy.

- Choy sum is a slender version of bok choy with a thick, cylindrical stem; it is sometimes called flowering Chinese cabbage.

- Kai lan, also known as Chinese broccoli, has a thick stem like choy sum but a flavor similar to broccoli. It has small, edible flower heads.

DRIED MUSHROOMS: Dried mushrooms are relatively inexpensive and pack a ton of flavor. Simply reconstitute them in warm water until soft, about 20 to 30 minutes, then use as you would fresh mushrooms. Buy them online or at your local Asian market. My favorites are shiitake, oyster, maitake, and wood ear mushrooms.

SEAWEED: I use a variety of seaweed at home, including wakame, nori, kombu, and arame. They can be added directly to soups or used to make Dashi (Japanese Soup Stock, page 108). You can get them at your local Asian market or online; my favorite brands are Eden Foods and Emerald Cove. Another favorite is furikake, a rice seasoning made from nori, sesame seeds, and bonito flakes; Urashima brand makes a tasty furikake without additives.

KATSUOBUSHI: These flakes are made from dried, fermented, smoked, and shaved skipjack tuna and are essential when making Dashi (page 108) and Okonomiyaki (page 130). They can be bought online if you can't find them locally.

GELATIN POWDER: Gelatin gives a velvety texture to ground meats, similar to what you'd expect when eating veal. It works especially well in Spaghetti and Meatballs (page 240). Great Lakes Gelatin is my favorite.

HARD-TO-FIND SPICES: There are some uncommon spices used in this book. Consider buying cardamom pods (green and black), fenugreek leaves, mace (the dried leaves that surround nutmeg), star anise, and turmeric online so that you have them on hand when the inclination hits.

HERBS: Fresh herbs are used liberally in this book for a variety of reasons: They are nutrient dense (second only to organ meats when compared by weight), add freshness to dishes, and are easy to cultivate. If you have the space, I suggest starting a small garden of perennial herbs like rosemary, mint, oregano, and thyme, which will return every year. Step up your garden with annual herbs like cilantro, Thai basil, and sweet basil, and you've basically covered every herb called for in this book; the only holdout is parsley, which is a biennial herb (it grows every two years) and is easier to get from your local grocer.

ESSENTIAL TECHNIQUES

STIR-FRYING

Stir-frying is a frequently used cooking technique in Asian cuisine (and in this book). It involves quickly frying food in a wok or skillet with a little fat, which preserves the flavor and texture of the food. Fats with a high smoke point (ghee, expeller-pressed coconut oil, and lard) are ideal for stir-frying.

To stir-fry, heat the fat in a wok over medium-high or high heat until it shimmers (it will appear thinner than water). Typically, you then add fragrant ingredients like onion, garlic, or ginger and stir-fry them briefly (tossing constantly with a spatula or shallow ladle to prevent scorching), then add the remaining ingredients in the order of those that take the longest to cook (meat) to those that take the shortest time to cook (scallions or herbs), again tossing almost constantly to prevent scorching.

Stir-frying raw meat can be somewhat challenging (and a little messy, as the fat splatters during cooking). An alternative to stir-frying meat is a technique called velveting, which I explain on page 44.

It is vital to chop and measure all your ingredients before stir-frying, because you won't have the opportunity to focus on anything else once you heat up the wok. Most of the instructions in this book call for stir-frying over medium-high heat, and that's in order to give you a little wiggle room so that the ingredients don't burn. As you become more comfortable with stir-frying, feel free to increase the heat to high, which will cut down your cooking time a bit.

THICKENING WITH A STARCH SLURRY

Most of the sauces that you find in Asian takeout dishes have been thickened with a cornstarch slurry. I have found that arrowroot starch best mimics the thickening properties of cornstarch. To thicken a sauce with starch, you combine the starch with some cold water in a small bowl to create a liquid slurry. (If you added the starch directly to the sauce, the powder would form clumps.)

Right before adding a slurry to a sauce, it's best to stir the slurry around to make sure that no starch is stuck to the bottom of your small bowl. I recommend adding only half of your slurry initially, since sometimes that is enough to thicken the sauce; you can always add the rest of the slurry if it doesn't thicken enough.

GRILLING

There are two main types of outdoor grills: charcoal and gas grills. Charcoal imparts a smokier flavor to food, but gas is more convenient. Either type of grill will work fine for the recipes in this book.

The easiest way to start a charcoal fire is to employ a chimney starter, which usually uses a little newspaper to start the fire in lieu of lighter fluid.

The thermometers found on the lids of grills are generally inaccurate. An easy way to gauge grill temperature is to see how long you can comfortably hold your hand above the fire, about 5 inches from the cooking grates:

- hot = 2 seconds

- medium-hot = 3 to 4 seconds

- medium = 5 to 6 seconds

- medium-low = 7 seconds

Direct grilling is a technique that cooks food directly over the heat, creating a delicious crust. With a gas grill, this is done by igniting all the burners; with a charcoal grill, it's done by centering the coals. Direct grilling is the easiest cooking method but can burn the outside of the food before it is done on the inside. It is best combined with indirect grilling for foods that require extended cooking times.

Indirect grilling limits the heat to one side of the grill, keeping the other side cool; you place your food on the cool side of the grill. With a charcoal grill, this is done by banking the coals on one side, often with a large aluminum pan under the cool side to catch drippings and prevent the coals from sliding under the meat. With a gas grill, it's done by turning off some of the burners; you'll need to experiment with your gas grill to find out how many burners to turn off in order to get the temperatures you want. Indirect grilling enables you to cook foods on the grill without burning them or causing flare-ups from dripping fat. It is often combined with short periods of direct grilling to create a delicious crust and a fully cooked inside.

NOODLES 101

WHEN FIRST CONCEIVING THIS BOOK, I SPENT SEVERAL DAYS WORKING ON A HOMEMADE NOODLE RECIPE. I TRIED A COMBINATION OF FLOURS, TOOLS, AND TECHNIQUES, AND I WAS GETTING PRETTY CLOSE TO THE REAL DEAL. BUT AFTER A WHILE, I TOOK A STEP BACK AND LOOKED AT WHAT I WAS DOING. AS MUCH FUN AS IT IS TO TACKLE A DIFFICULT RECIPE, IT DIDN'T FIT WITH THE PURPOSE AND SCOPE OF *PALEO TAKEOUT*. I REALIZED THAT HARDLY ANYONE WOULD CONSIDER MAKING HOMEMADE NOODLES THEIR IDEA OF A GOOD TIME, ESPECIALLY IN THE CONTEXT OF RE-CREATING TAKEOUT MEALS WITHOUT SPENDING HOURS IN THE KITCHEN. SO INSTEAD, I DECIDED TO FOCUS ON WHAT'S IMPORTANT—GETTING NOODLES INTO YOUR MOUTH AS QUICKLY AND EASILY AS POSSIBLE. HERE'S WHAT I CAME UP WITH.

SPIRAL-SLICED VEGETABLES

Running vegetables through a special tool called a spiral slicer turns them into noodles. By far, my favorite is the Paderno World Cuisine spiral slicer, which makes two different sizes of noodles and is easy to clean. Zucchini and yellow squash noodles are popular and cook very quickly—they can be added directly to a stir-fry or dropped into soup. Spiral-sliced sweet potatoes have a firmer texture but require a little more preparation.

To prepare spiral-sliced zucchini or yellow squash, simply run the squash through the spiral slicer—no need to peel beforehand. These vegetables lose their texture quickly, so cook for no more than 2 or 3 minutes. If adding to a stir-fry or soup, nothing else is required; if using in place of pasta (like for Spaghetti and Meatballs, page 240), you'll want to parboil them in salted water until they just start to become limp, about 20 to 30 seconds; rinse and drain, and then squeeze out about half of their water before serving.

To prepare spiral-sliced sweet potato, peel the sweet potato, then run it through the spiral slicer. If adding to a soup, simply drop into your prepared broth and cook until softened, about 5 minutes. If using for a stir-fry, steam them a bit beforehand: Heat a wok over medium heat, then add 1 tablespoon of coconut oil. Add the noodles, toss with the oil, and cook for 2 minutes. Add 2 tablespoons of water, cover, and steam for another 2 minutes. Check them for doneness, and if necessary, add another 2 tablespoons of water, cover, and steam until easily pierced with a fork and slightly translucent.

KOREAN SWEET POTATO NOODLES

Not to be confused with spiral-sliced sweet potatoes, Korean sweet potato noodles (sometimes called glass noodles or dangmyeon) are dried noodles that are made using sweet potato starch and water. They have a slightly gray color and are transparent. Their texture is firm but slick. To prepare them, drop them in boiling salted water and simmer until soft, about 6 minutes, stirring often. Drain and rinse with cold water (the noodles will harden back up, and that's fine), then use in stir-fries or soups.

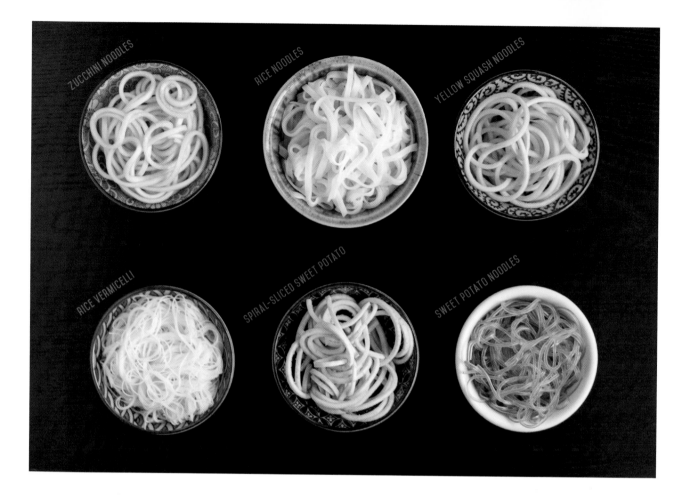

RICE NOODLES

Rice noodles, made using white rice flour and water, are the noodles you typically find in dishes such as Pho (page 180) and Pad Thai (page 166). To prepare them, soak them in warm water for 30 minutes, then drain. Bring a pot of water to a boil and add the noodles; blanch until soft, about 1 minute, then drain and rinse with cold water until cool to the touch.

Rice vermicelli are similar to rice noodles but are thinner and require slightly less preparation (no soaking required). They are traditionally found inside Spring Rolls (page 54) and in Singapore Rice Noodles (page 60) and Pancit (page 206). To prepare them, drop them in boiling water until soft, about 30 seconds, then drain and rinse with cold water until cool to the touch.

OTHER STARCH-BASED NOODLES

Some companies from Vietnam and Thailand make tapioca starch and arrowroot starch noodles, which are similar in taste and texture to rice vermicelli, but sometimes are thicker and more akin to rice noodles. Either way, use the rice noodle cooking instructions at left to prepare them; it's super easy. Look for these varieties online if you can't find them at your local Asian market.

KELP NOODLES

Kelp noodles are made from, ahem, kelp. They are usually made with just kelp and water and are low in calories and carbs. You can find them cheap at most health food stores or online. These noodles don't require cooking; just throw them into your favorite soup or stir-fry.

BREADING 101

BREADED MEAT IS A STAPLE OF MANY FAST FOOD AND TAKEOUT RESTAURANTS; IN FACT, OFTEN IT'S HARD TO FIND SOMETHING THAT'S *NOT* BREADED AND FRIED. I USE A VARIETY OF TECHNIQUES TO REPLICATE THESE DISHES. THESE ARE MY THREE FAVORITES, WHICH CAN BE APPLIED TO ALL SORTS OF RECIPES.

HEAVY BREADING

SERVES: 4 | PREP TIME: 10 MINS | COOK TIME: 25 MINS (WHEN COOKED IN 3 BATCHES)

Heavy breading works best with whole cutlets. I use pork rinds for the outer breading to give a crispy texture without a gazillion carbs (see Tonkatsu, page 118). It's easiest to place the pork rinds in a resealable plastic bag and crush them with a rolling pin.

1/4 cup tapioca, arrowroot, or potato starch

2 tsp sea salt

2 large eggs, beaten

2 cups crushed pork rinds (about 3 oz)

1 tsp black or white pepper

2 lbs chicken breasts or thighs, cube steak, or pork cutlets, sliced or pounded to 1/4-inch thickness

1/4 cup lard or expeller-pressed coconut oil

1. Place the breading ingredients in 3 separate shallow bowls: the starch and salt in one bowl, the eggs in the second bowl, and the pork rinds and pepper in the third bowl.

2. Pat the cutlets dry with paper towels. Heat the lard (you want enough to reach halfway up the cutlets; 1/4 cup is a good standard) in a skillet to 350°F. Dip a cutlet in the starch mixture, shaking off the excess. Dip the cutlet in the egg, again shaking off the excess. Finally, evenly coat the cutlet with the pork rind mixture. Fry in batches until cooked through, about 8 minutes total, turning the cutlets halfway through cooking. Place in a warm (170°F) oven while you cook your other batches.

EGG BREADING

SERVES: 4 | PREP TIME: 10 MINS | COOK TIME: 25 MINS (WHEN COOKED IN 3 BATCHES)

Egg breading uses egg for the outer texture and produces a spongy texture like you'd find in Chicken Nuggets (page 234) or breaded Chinese-American dishes. This simple recipe is mildly flavored to be compatible with many dishes; depending on the context, you could add other spices to the starch, such as garlic powder, onion powder, paprika, or chipotle chili powder, in 1/2-teaspoon portions.

1/4 cup tapioca, arrowroot, or potato starch

2 tsp sea salt

1 tsp white pepper

4 large eggs

2 lbs chicken breasts or thighs or pork loin, cut into chunks, or raw shrimp

1/4 cup lard or expeller-pressed coconut oil

1. In a mixing bowl, combine the starch, salt, and pepper. In a separate bowl, beat the eggs.

2. Pat the protein chunks dry with paper towels. Heat the lard in a skillet to 325°F. Lightly dust a chunk in the starch, then dip in the egg, shaking off the excess, and then add to the oil. Repeat with more chunks until you fill your skillet without crowding. Fry until golden and cooked through, about 8 minutes total, turning halfway through cooking. Keep the cooked chunks in a warm (170°F) oven while you cook your other batches.

BATTER

SERVES: 4 | PREP TIME: 10 MINS | COOK TIME: UP TO 25 MINS (WHEN COOKED IN 3 BATCHES)

Battered dishes have a light breading like you'd expect from Tempura (page 116) or Onion Rings (page 230). Adding a bit of vodka to the batter helps make the breading crispier. Potato vodka is preferred, although research suggests that the distillation process removes toxins from grain-derived vodka (and vodka is usually distilled four to six times).

1/2 cup tapioca, arrowroot, or potato starch, divided

2 tsp sea salt

1/2 tsp white pepper

1/2 tsp baking soda

2 lbs chicken breasts or thighs or pork loin, cut into chunks, or raw shrimp, chicken wings or drumettes, or vegetables

3 tbsp water

1 tsp vodka (optional)

1/2 cup lard or expeller-pressed coconut oil

1. In a mixing bowl, combine 1/4 cup of the starch with the salt, pepper, and baking soda, then toss with the protein or veggies to coat. If you have time, place on a baking sheet lined with a wire rack and refrigerate uncovered for 1 hour (skip this step for veggies). Heat the lard in a skillet to 350°F. Combine the remaining 1/4 cup of starch with the water and vodka, if using—the consistency should be like very thin pancake batter (closer to water than gravy).

2. Dip a protein or veggie chunk into the batter, then allow to drip for a few seconds, and then place in the skillet. Fry in batches until light brown and crispy, flipping and jostling every couple of minutes, about 3 minutes for shrimp and veggies, 6 minutes for boneless meat, or 8 minutes for bone-in meat. Keep the cooked chunks in a warm (170°F) oven while you cook your other batches.

HOW TO MAKE ASIAN MEATBALLS

Asian meatballs are my favorite—they're slightly dense but surprisingly spongy and bouncy. If you've ever had fish cake or even a hot dog, this texture should be familiar to you. The process of making these meatballs is the same in many cultures, so for convenience I've broken down four of the most common types.

These meatballs can be used in a number of contexts, from soups (such as Ramen, page 112, and Bakso, page 188) to stir-fries; actually, just about any of the recipes in the Chinese Kitchen section can be made using meatballs. Vietnamese Pork Meatballs are so tasty that I gave them a recipe of their own (page 182). Feel free to play around with the ingredients; combinations of beef and pork are especially tasty.

ASIAN MEATBALLS

SERVES: 4 | PREP TIME: 15 MINS | COOK TIME: 15 MINS

BEEF MEATBALLS:

1 tbsp fish sauce

1 tsp tamari

1/2 tsp gelatin powder

2 lbs ground beef

1/4 cup tapioca starch

1/2 tsp sea salt

1/2 tsp white pepper

1/2 tsp baking soda

1/4 tsp ground ginger

PORK MEATBALLS:

2 lbs ground pork

1/4 cup tapioca starch

2 tbsp fish sauce

2 tsp tamari

2 tsp coconut palm sugar

1 tsp white pepper

1/2 tsp baking soda

CHICKEN MEATBALLS:

2 lbs ground chicken

1/4 cup tapioca starch

1 tbsp fish sauce

1 tsp tamari

1 tsp coconut palm sugar

1/2 tsp white pepper

1/2 tsp sea salt

1/2 tsp baking soda

1/4 tsp ground ginger

FISH BALLS:

1 lb white, somewhat oily fish meat (such as pollock, bream, milkfish, whiting, mullet, mackerel, or hake), cut into chunks

1 lb raw shrimp, peeled and cut into chunks

2 tbsp tapioca starch

1 tsp sea salt

1/2 tsp white pepper

1. For beef meatballs, combine the fish sauce and tamari with the gelatin and let it sit for 5 minutes before mixing into the rest of the ingredients. This extra step gives the beef meatballs a smoother texture and a richer taste.

2. Combine all the ingredients in a mixing bowl with your hands, then transfer to a food processor and pulse until it turns into a tacky paste called surimi. It is better to overprocess the meat than to underprocess it, so give it a good minute or two in the processor.

3. Forming the meatballs is a little tricky, since the tackiness of the meat mixture makes it a challenge to roll it into balls. Putting the meat in the fridge for a few hours makes it easier to handle, but it's not completely necessary. A common trick is to wet your hand, take a large handful of the surimi, squeeze it through the round hole made by your thumb and index finger, and then scoop it into a ball using a wet spoon in your other hand. The balls will expand when cooking thanks to the tapioca starch, so make them fairly small, a little less than 1 inch in diameter. They don't need to be perfect spheres—no one's going to judge you once they take a bite of the deliciousness within! Two pounds of surimi yields about 40 to 50 small meatballs (about 10 to 12 per person for 4 servings).

4. The easiest way to cook surimi meatballs is to boil them. Simply drop one in boiling water and wait until it floats for 2 minutes, then remove and break it open to test for doneness. If it's cooked all the way through, throw in more meatballs and cook in a similar manner until done. You can then use the meatballs immediately or cool them in an ice water bath and freeze them for quick meals down the road.

5. The meatballs can also be pan-fried, which give them a crispier outer texture and a more rounded shape. Warm 1 tablespoon of coconut oil, ghee, or lard in a large skillet over medium heat, then add some raw meatballs; fry in batches, turning often, until cooked through, about 6 minutes per batch. After cooking the meatballs for a couple of minutes, I like to swirl my skillet for a while so that the meatballs form a nice round shape.

6. Grilling these meatballs isn't out of the question, either. You can skewer them (a bit messy) or flatten them a bit so they don't fall through the grill grates. Grill over direct medium-high heat until cooked through, about 6 minutes, turning halfway through cooking.

*   Consider adding small (1/4-pound) amounts of offal to the food processor in step 2 to increase the nutritional profile with no degradation in taste: liver, kidney, tendon, and tripe all work well. But not in fish balls! Yikes!

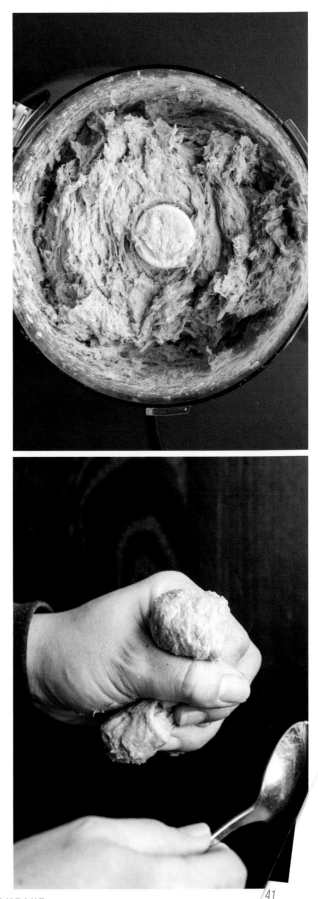

Chinese Kitchen

NOTES ON MEAT

Just like at your favorite Chinese-American restaurant, the proteins called for in this chapter can be used interchangeably. Want to make Sweet and Sour Pork instead of Sweet and Sour Chicken? Easy—make it with pork! Because the sauce is prepared independently of the protein in most of these dishes, every recipe has a plug-and-play approach to it. Asian meatballs (page 40) can be used in any of these recipes as well.

Let's go over some techniques for cooking each protein. First things first: Never overcrowd your wok or skillet with meat, which will cause the meat to steam (yuck) instead of sauté (yum). It's better to cook the meat in two or more batches than to try to knock it out in one fell swoop.

In general, stir-fry your meats at just below high heat (what I refer to as "medium-high") until you are comfortable with stir-frying; then up the heat to high to save yourself a few minutes (more info on page 33). When first adding a protein, quickly toss it in the cooking fat, then let it sit for a minute or two before touching it. This will allow a crust to form and keep the juices from escaping.

A less messy alternative to stir-frying meat is a technique called velveting. Lean meats are thinly sliced and then marinated in a mixture of egg white, starch (usually cornstarch, but we'll use arrowroot), Chinese cooking wine, and salt, then blanched in boiling water and drained. The meat remains deliciously tender and can easily be added to stir-fries (and sticks really well to the sauce!). Here's a quick tutorial:

2 egg whites

3 tbsp arrowroot starch

2 tsp mirin

1/2 tsp salt

2 lbs lean meat (chicken breasts, pork loin or chops, or lean beef like round steak), thinly sliced

1 tbsp expeller-pressed coconut oil

Mix together the egg whites, arrowroot starch, mirin, and salt until smooth. Combine the meat with the marinade ingredients and marinate for 30 minutes. Bring a pot of water to a boil, add the coconut oil, and then stir in the meat, breaking the pieces apart. Blanch until opaque, about 40 seconds, then remove from the water and drain. Set aside and add to stir-fries about 3 minutes before finishing the dish (when you'd normally add vegetables).

For dishes with a robust flavor, it's good to marinate your meat before cooking it (see Kung Pao Pork, page 92), but it's not necessary for most of my recipes (unless you're using the velveting technique above). Truthfully, I love the contrast of unadulterated meat thrown into a flavorful sauce.

CHICKEN

It's remarkably easy to turn lean chicken breast, the unofficial favorite meat of dieticians and picky children alike, into dry, powdery slabs. One culprit is cooking wet chicken at a low temperature; be sure to pat chicken breasts dry before adding them to your wok, and fully preheat the wok beforehand. When grilling chicken breasts, it's helpful to toss them in olive oil before placing them on the grill. One easy way to ensure that chicken breasts don't dry out is to use the velveting technique above. Finally, don't overcook breasts; pull them off the heat right as they reach an internal temperature of 155°F, as they'll continue to cook off the heat.

Chicken thighs are cheaper, more nutritious, and easier to cook with than chicken breasts. Be sure to pat them dry and add them to a hot wok. The rest of the cooking kind of takes care of itself (especially when compared to finicky breasts).

BEEF

In this chapter, you'll be using mostly sliced steak and ground beef. Sliced steak should be cooked quickly at a high temperature, just as you would cook a whole steak. The type of steak is your call, but well-marbled steak (rib eye, strip, or sirloin) is my favorite for stir-fries.

PORK

Aside from fatty, delicious ground pork, pork loin (or loin chops) is the easiest cut of pork to work with in Chinese cuisine, since it is fairly tender and well marbled. Slice and cook pork loin or chops as you would chicken breast, but pull the pork off the heat when it reaches an internal temperature of 145°F.

SHRIMP

Shrimp cooks incredibly fast. When preparing shrimp in a stir-fry, I typically cook it twice; first I cook it at medium-high heat until curling, then I let it rest and cool for 5 to 10 minutes (usually while I'm preparing veggies), and then I return it to high heat to crisp at the end. Like meats, it's important to pat shrimp dry with paper towels before cooking them.

蛋花湯

EGG DROP SOUP

SERVES: 4 | PREP TIME: 2 MINS | COOK TIME: 5 MINS

Egg Drop Soup is a dish that needs no introduction—it exists on nearly every Chinese-American takeout menu. This dish is also served in China, but usually thinner and with add-ins such as green onions and tofu.

Egg Drop Soup is essentially eggs and chicken broth, but adding a bit of white pepper and ginger really expands the flavor. Consider adding thinly sliced vegetables (cabbage, carrots, etc.) and/or precooked meat (Char Siu, page 88, or Asian meatballs, page 40) to the soup when adding the slurry.

SLURRY:

3 tbsp arrowroot starch

2 tbsp cold water

SOUP:

3 cups Chicken Broth (page 264)

1 cup water

1/4 tsp sea salt

1/4 tsp white pepper

1/4 tsp ground ginger

2 large eggs plus 1 large egg yolk, combined and beaten

1 green onion, chopped, to garnish (optional)

1. Stir together the arrowroot starch and cold water to create a slurry, then set aside.

2. In a stockpot, combine the broth, water, salt, pepper, and ginger and bring to a boil over high heat. Once the soup is boiling, stir in half of the arrowroot starch slurry. Continue to stir until thickened, about 1 minute, adding the rest of the slurry if needed. Taste the soup and add more seasonings if needed.

3. Reduce the heat to low and slowly pour the eggs through a fork into the soup. Once the eggs have been added, whisk gently with a fork to prevent clumping, then allow to cook through, 1 more minute.

4. Serve immediately, garnished with green onion if desired.

HOT AND SOUR SOUP

SERVES: 4 | PREP TIME: 20 MINS | COOK TIME: 15 MINS

. . . .

Hot and Sour Soup is nearly as popular as its distant cousin, Egg Drop Soup (page 46). There are many variations of this dish in the United States and China, but its overall taste is based on a combination of sour and spicy flavors. In China, this soup is often served with meat and usually is not thickened with a starch slurry.

Getting the right sour notes requires two readily available ingredients: apple cider vinegar and lime juice.

. . . .

SOUP BASE:

2 cloves garlic, minced

1 inch ginger, peeled and minced, or 1/2 tsp ground ginger

2 dried Chinese (Sichuan) red chile peppers, chopped (see note)

4 cups Chicken Broth (page 264)

1/2 cup apple cider vinegar

2 tbsp Chinese cooking wine

1 tbsp honey

1 tbsp tomato paste

1 tbsp tamari

1/2 tsp sea salt

1/2 tsp white pepper

1/2 tsp crushed red pepper

4 shiitake or wood ear mushrooms, thinly sliced (see note)

1 (8 oz) can sliced bamboo shoots, drained

1 tsp lime juice

1/4 cup arrowroot starch

3 tbsp cold water

1 large egg, beaten

1 green onion, sliced, to garnish

1. In a saucepan, combine the soup base ingredients. Bring to a simmer over medium heat, then simmer for 5 minutes to allow the flavors to marry.

2. Add the mushrooms and bamboo shoots and simmer for another 3 minutes. Add the lime juice and taste, adding more salt and pepper for body, more crushed red pepper for heat, or more lime juice for sourness.

3. In a small bowl, stir together the arrowroot starch and cold water to create a slurry. Add half of the slurry to the soup and stir until thickened, adding more slurry as needed to get your desired consistency. Remove from the heat and slowly pour in the egg, stirring the soup constantly as you pour. Once the egg is incorporated, serve the soup garnished with green onion.

* If you don't have dried Chinese chiles to work with, simply use an additional 1/2 teaspoon crushed red pepper (1 teaspoon total).

* If using shiitake mushrooms, remove the stems before cooking—they are too tough to eat. Dried shiitake or wood ear mushrooms can be used in this dish; just soak them in warm water for 30 minutes before slicing.

* Consider adding some leftover Char Siu (page 88) or cooked ground pork to the soup when adding the mushrooms and bamboo shoots; I suggest using the same ingredients and method found in my Chinese Spring Rolls recipe (page 54, minus the vegetables) to precook the ground pork.

FRIED RICE

SERVES: 4 | PREP TIME: 10 MINS. PLUS TIME TO COOK AND COOL RICE | COOK TIME: 10 MINS

• •

Fried Rice is the best way ever to get rid of leftovers. Honestly, I look forward to Sunday mornings, when our fridge is full of small portions of a bunch of random foods, because I can throw them all into Fried Rice, and it always turns out fine.

This is a basic Chinese Fried Rice recipe; see the notes below for some of my favorite variations. In terms of leftover meat to use in this dish, you can't beat Char Siu (page 88) or Vietnamese Pork Meatballs (page 182).

• •

SAUCE:

1 1/2 tbsp tamari

1 tsp coconut palm sugar or honey

1 tsp fish sauce

1/2 tsp Chinese cooking wine or mirin

1/2 tsp white pepper

3 tbsp expeller-pressed coconut oil, divided (see note)

3 large eggs, beaten

1/2 medium onion, finely chopped

2 cloves garlic, minced

2 cups cold cooked white rice

1/2 lb leftover cooked meat, cut into bite-sized pieces

2 medium carrots, diced

2 cups Chinese cabbage (bok choy, choy sum, or won bok), chopped

1 cup frozen peas, rinsed in cool water and drained

sea salt

1/2 tsp toasted sesame oil

* For added richness, substitute 1 tablespoon ghee for 1 tablespoon of the coconut oil.

* There's also a Thai fried rice dish called "American fried rice" that is made with hot dogs and seasoned with ketchup. Don't knock it until you've tried it!

1. Combine the sauce ingredients and set aside.

2. In a wok or skillet, heat 1 tablespoon of the coconut oil over medium-high heat until shimmering, about 1 minute. Add the eggs and fry until scrambled and mostly dry, about 2 minutes, then remove from the wok and set aside.

3. Add the remaining 2 tablespoons of oil to the wok and warm until shimmering. Add the onion and stir-fry until softened and golden, about 2 minutes. Add the garlic and sauté until aromatic, about 20 seconds, then add the rice. Toss to combine, then toss every 30 seconds; once the rice has brown spots on it, add the meat.

4. Sauté until the meat is warm, about 1 minute, then add the carrots; stir-fry until the carrots are soft around the edges, about 1 minute.

5. Add the cabbage, peas, and sauce, tossing to combine. Stir-fry until the cabbage has wilted, about 2 minutes. Finally, add the eggs back in. Taste and add salt if needed, then toss with the sesame oil, remove from the heat, and serve.

VARIATIONS

* SEAFOOD FRIED RICE: Use cut-up raw shrimp, scallops, and/or squid instead of meat.

* BREAKFAST FRIED RICE: Use cooked bacon, sausage, and/or ham.

* KIMCHI FRIED RICE: Use leftover Kalbi (page 144) or Bulgogi (page 142) and add some chopped Kimchi (page 148) at the end.

* VIETNAMESE FRIED RICE: Use shallots instead of the onion, leftover steamed jasmine rice (page 286), and Vietnamese Pork Meatballs (page 182).

* THAI FRIED RICE: Use shallots instead of the onion, and add 1 tablespoon full-fat coconut milk and 1 teaspoon curry paste.

炒花椰菜飯

CAULIFLOWER FRIED RICE

SERVES: 4 | PREP TIME: 10 MINS, PLUS TIME TO MAKE CAULIFLOWER RICE | COOK TIME: 10 MINS

Cauliflower Fried Rice is like regular Fried Rice (page 50)…but made with cauliflower. No surprises there! The main differences with this dish are the timing (when you add the cauliflower) and the heat; you'll want to increase the heat to high at the very end to make sure the cauliflower doesn't start steaming on you.

SAUCE:

1 1/2 tbsp tamari

1 tsp coconut palm sugar or honey

1 tsp fish sauce

1/2 tsp Chinese cooking wine or mirin

1/4 tsp white pepper

2 tbsp expeller-pressed coconut oil, divided

3 large eggs, beaten

1/2 medium onion, finely chopped

2 cloves garlic, minced

1/2 lb leftover cooked meat, cut into bite-sized pieces

2 medium carrots, diced

2 cups Chinese cabbage (bok choy, choy sum, or won bok), chopped

1 cup frozen peas, rinsed in cool water and drained

1 batch Cauliflower Rice (page 288)

sea salt

1/2 tsp toasted sesame oil

1. Combine the sauce ingredients and set aside.

2. In a wok, heat 1 tablespoon of the oil over medium-high heat until shimmering, about 1 minute. Add the eggs and fry until scrambled and mostly dry, about 2 minutes, then remove from the wok and set aside.

3. Add the remaining 1 tablespoon of oil to the wok and warm until shimmering. Add the onion and stir-fry until softened and golden, about 2 minutes. Add the garlic and sauté until aromatic, about 20 seconds, then add the meat.

4. Sauté until the meat is warm, about 1 minute, then add the carrots and stir-fry until the carrots are soft around the edges, about 1 minute.

5. Increase the heat to high and add the cabbage, peas, cauliflower rice, and sauce, tossing to combine. Stir-fry until the cabbage has wilted, about 2 minutes. Finally, add the eggs back in. Taste and add salt if needed, then toss with the sesame oil, remove from the heat, and serve.

* For added richness, substitute 1 tablespoon ghee for 1 tablespoon of the coconut oil.

* Be sure to consult the regular Fried Rice recipe (page 50) for a list of variations on this dish.

SPRING ROLLS

SERVES: 6 | PREP TIME: 30 MINS | COOK TIME: 30 MINS

Spring Rolls are associated with several different Asian restaurants, so I've included three variations to fit whatever mood you're in. If you're looking for their funky fresh cousins, Summer Rolls, they're on page 178.

I played around with all sorts of solutions for making Spring Rolls, including a wrapper from scratch; they just weren't worth the effort. Rice or tapioca paper wrappers work just fine and are available online or at your local Asian market for cheap. Rice and tapioca/rice papers are easier to find than papers made with only tapioca; the latter can be found at some Asian markets.

Note that these rolls will stick together when uncooked, so be very careful with them. Also, you want a very tight roll with no air bubbles to ensure that the hot fat doesn't seep into the roll and cause its contents to spill out. It takes a bit of practice, but you'll pick it up quickly.

CHINESE SPRING ROLLS (春卷)

1 tbsp expeller-pressed coconut oil

1 lb ground chicken or pork

1 tbsp tamari

1 tsp Chinese cooking wine

1/2 tsp sea salt

1/2 tsp white pepper

1/2 head green cabbage, shredded (about 2 cups)

2 medium carrots, cut into matchsticks

4 cloves garlic, minced

1/2 small white onion, finely chopped

25 tapioca or rice wrappers

2 to 3 cups lard, for frying

VIETNAMESE SPRING ROLLS

1/2 oz dried wood ear mushrooms

1 oz sweet potato noodles or rice vermicelli

1 tbsp expeller-pressed coconut oil

1 lb ground pork

2 tsp tamari

1 tsp fish sauce

1/2 tsp sea salt

1/2 tsp white pepper

4 raw shrimp, peeled and coarsely chopped

2 medium carrots, cut into matchsticks

1/2 cup grated taro, daikon, or jicama

4 cloves garlic, minced

1/2 small white onion, finely chopped

25 tapioca or rice wrappers

2 to 3 cups lard, for frying

FILIPINO SPRING ROLLS (LUMPIA)

1 oz sweet potato noodles or rice vermicelli

1 tbsp expeller-pressed coconut oil

1 lb ground pork

2 tsp tamari

1 tsp fish sauce

1/2 tsp sea salt

1/2 tsp black pepper

2 medium carrots, cut into matchsticks

1/2 head green cabbage, shredded (about 2 cups)

1/2 small white onion, finely chopped

1 green onion, minced

25 tapioca or rice wrappers

2 to 3 cups lard, for frying

1. The process for all three variations is similar. The main difference is that for the Vietnamese Spring Rolls you need to soak the mushrooms in warm water for 20 minutes before slicing, and for the Vietnamese and Filipino Spring Rolls you need to soften the noodles. If using sweet potato noodles, boil them until soft, about 6 minutes, then drain and rinse. If using rice vermicelli, place them in a bowl of very warm (nearly hot) water for 10 minutes to soften, then drain. Cut the noodles into 1 1/2-inch lengths.

2. Heat the oil in a wok or skillet over medium-high heat until shimmering, about 1 minute. Add the ground meat and stir-fry, tossing often to prevent large chunks from forming, until mostly cooked through, about 3 minutes. Add the liquid ingredients and seasonings and stir to combine; continue to stir-fry until the meat is cooked through and the liquid has evaporated, about 3 more minutes.

3. Add the vegetables (and shrimp for Vietnamese Spring Rolls) and toss to combine; sauté until slightly softened, about 1 minute. Transfer to and spread over a baking sheet to cool, about 15 minutes. If making Vietnamese Spring Rolls, drain and add the mushrooms and noodles to the filling after it has cooled. If making Filipino Spring Rolls, add the noodles to the filling after it has cooled.

4. Wrap your Spring Rolls. Dip a wrapper in a shallow bowl of cool water, then let the excess water drip off. Add about 1 1/2 tablespoons of filling, then roll the wrap as indicated in the illustration; place the filling about 1 1/2 inches from the edge of the wrap, tightly tuck in the sides, and then fold the short flap over the filling. Evenly and tightly roll the wrap into a cylinder (no air bubbles!) and repeat until you run out of filling, about 25 Spring Rolls total. For best results, refrigerate the rolls, uncovered, for 30 minutes before frying. This will help them dry out and make them less likely to burst when cooking.

5. In a saucepan, heat the lard to 300°F to 325°F. Fry the rolls until crispy, about 6 minutes per batch. For best results, fry only a few at a time and keep them from touching one another; if they touch before getting crispy, they will stick together and likely tear when you try to separate them.

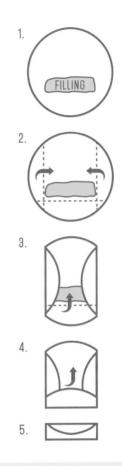

★ Double-wrapping the rolls will ensure that they don't burst while cooking and will create a crispier texture (but will double the carb content, if you're paying attention to that sort of thing).

★ These rolls can be frozen and cooked at a later date. After completing step 4, place the rolls on a baking sheet lined with parchment paper, making sure they don't touch one another. Freeze overnight, then transfer to a resealable plastic freezer bag. They can be fried from their frozen state; just be sure to fry them long enough for the insides to warm through, about 12 minutes. They can also be baked from frozen: Brush them with coconut oil, then put them in a 400°F oven until heated through, about 20 to 25 minutes, turning once at the 10-minute mark.

炒麵

CHOW MEIN

SERVES: 4 | PREP TIME: 10 MINS | COOK TIME: 20 MINS

....

"Chow Mein" is an English corruption of the word *chau-mèing* in Taishanese (a close relative to Cantonese), which literally translates to "fried noodles." There is a lot of confusion about and variance to this dish, especially in the United States. On the East Coast, Chow Mein is served both "crispy" (deep-fried) and steamed (stir-fried), and even served over rice. In other areas, it is often confused with Chop Suey, a dish of stir-fried vegetables.

To replicate the thick, round wheat noodles typically used in Chow Mein, I've found that spiral-sliced sweet potatoes (see page 35) work best. Sweet potato noodles and rice-based spaghetti are a close second. This dish tastes best when stir-fried in two batches; putting all the ingredients in one wok would end up overcrowding the pan, and you'd end up with mush.

....

SAUCE:

1 clove garlic, minced

2 tbsp tamari

1 tbsp mirin

1 tsp coconut palm sugar

1/2 tsp white pepper

sea salt to taste

NOODLES:

2 large sweet potatoes

1 tbsp expeller-pressed coconut oil

2 tbsp water

4 tbsp expeller-pressed coconut oil, divided

1 lb raw shrimp, peeled, or leftover cooked meat, like Char Siu (page 88) or Vietnamese Pork Meatballs (page 182), divided

4 handfuls of mung bean sprouts, divided

4 handfuls of chopped Chinese cabbage (won bok, bok choy, or choy sum), divided

2 medium carrots, julienned, divided

4 splashes of toasted sesame oil, divided

1. Combine the sauce ingredients and set aside.

2. Make the noodles: Peel the sweet potatoes, then run them through a spiral slicer on its largest setting. Heat a wok or skillet over medium heat, then add the coconut oil. Add the noodles, toss with the oil, and sauté for 2 minutes. Add the water, cover, and steam for another 2 minutes or until almost soft; set aside.

3. Increase the heat to high, then add 2 tablespoons of the coconut oil and heat until shimmering, about 30 seconds. Add half of the noodles and stir-fry until slightly crisp, about 2 minutes. Add half of the shrimp or meat and stir-fry until starting to brown at the edges, about 2 minutes, then stir in half of the sauce and toss with the noodles. Add half of the bean sprouts, Chinese cabbage, and carrots; stir-fry until softened, about 1 minute. Add 2 splashes of sesame oil, then serve.

4. Repeat step 3 with the remaining half of the ingredients.

> * To use sweet potato noodles instead of spiral-sliced sweet potatoes, drop 6 ounces of noodles (about three-quarters of a box) in boiling salted water and simmer until soft, about 6 minutes, stirring often. Drain and rinse with cold water (the noodles will harden up again, and that's fine). Proceed to step 3.
>
> * To use rice-based spaghetti, prepare a box of spaghetti as directed on the package, then drain and rinse with cold water. Proceed to step 3.

SINGAPORE RICE NOODLES

SERVES: 4 | PREP TIME: 10 MINS | COOK TIME: 10 MINS

· ·

While this dish is popular in Hong Kong and Western restaurants, it isn't well known in its namesake city-state of Singapore. It's often served as a vegetarian or seafood dish; this version is made with shrimp.

· ·

NOODLES:

6 oz (about 3/4 package) rice vermicelli or

4 zucchini or yellow squash (about 2 lbs total), spiral-sliced (see note)

CURRY POWDER:

1 tbsp mild curry powder (see note)

1/2 tsp white pepper

1/2 tsp sea salt

1/2 tsp ground ginger

2 tbsp expeller-pressed coconut oil, divided

1 lb raw shrimp, peeled

2 cloves garlic, minced

1/2 medium white onion, sliced

1/2 green bell pepper, sliced

1/2 red bell pepper, sliced

1/4 cup Chicken Broth (page 264)

1 medium carrot, julienned

4 green onions, cut into 2-inch lengths

1. Bring a pot of water to boil, then drop in the rice vermicelli. Simmer until softened, about 30 seconds, then drain and rinse with cool water until cool to the touch.

2. While the water is coming to a boil, combine the curry powder ingredients and set aside.

3. In a wok or skillet, warm 1 tablespoon of the coconut oil over medium-high heat until shimmering, about 1 minute. Add the shrimp and stir-fry until opaque and curling, about 3 minutes; set aside.

4. Add the remaining 1 tablespoon of coconut oil to the wok, then add the garlic and sauté until aromatic, about 20 seconds. Add the white onion and sauté until softened, about 2 minutes. Add the bell peppers and sauté until softened, about 1 minute.

5. Add the noodles, broth, and curry powder, tossing to combine. Stir-fry until the broth evaporates, about 1 minute. Add the carrot, green onions, and shrimp; toss until the green onions are bright in color, about 1 minute. Taste and add salt if needed. Remove from the heat and serve.

* If using spiral-sliced zucchini or yellow squash, add it in step 5 when you would add the rice noodles to the wok—no need to parboil.

* To make your own mild curry powder, see page 304.

芙蓉蛋

EGG FOO YOUNG

SERVES: 4 | PREP TIME: 10 MINS | COOK TIME: 20 MINS

• •

Egg Foo Young looks a teeny tiny bit like pancakes and maple syrup, but it couldn't be further from that lumber-jack staple food in terms of taste. This dish is often referred to as a pancake but has a taste and texture that is more akin to an omelet. Who knows how it all fell out, but my guess is that Egg Foo Young served as inspiration for other East Asian pancakes like Okonomiyaki (page 130) and Korean Seafood Scallion Pancake (page 138).

• •

PORK FILLING:

1/2 lb ground pork

1 tsp tamari

1 tsp tapioca starch

1/2 tsp rice vinegar

1/2 tsp sea salt

1/4 tsp white pepper

GRAVY:

1 cup Beef Broth (page 264)

1 tbsp tamari

1/2 tsp fish sauce

1/4 tsp toasted sesame oil

1/4 tsp white pepper

2 tbsp arrowroot starch

1 tbsp cold water

6 large eggs, beaten

1 tbsp tapioca starch

1/2 tsp sea salt

1/4 tsp white pepper

1/4 tsp toasted sesame oil

1 small (5 oz) can water chestnuts, sliced

large handful of mung bean sprouts

6 green onions, thinly sliced

4 oz raw shrimp, peeled and chopped

4 tbsp expeller-pressed coconut oil, divided

2 green onions, thinly sliced

1. Combine the filling ingredients in a skillet and sauté over medium heat until cooked through and slightly dry, about 8 minutes, breaking up chunks as it cooks. Set aside.

2. Make the gravy: Combine the broth, tamari, fish sauce, sesame oil, and pepper in a small saucepan and bring to a simmer over medium heat. Stir together the arrowroot starch and cold water to create a slurry. Stir half of the slurry into the sauce and simmer until thickened; add the rest of the slurry and continue to simmer until the sauce thickens into a gravy. Reduce the heat to low and keep warm while you make the Egg Foo Young.

3. In a large mixing bowl, combine the eggs, tapioca starch, salt, pepper, and sesame oil. Gently stir in the pork filling, water chestnuts, bean sprouts, green onions, and shrimp. It'll look like there's not enough batter to make a pancake, but don't worry, it'll turn out great.

4. Warm 1 tablespoon of the coconut oil in a skillet over medium-high heat until shimmering, about 1 minute. Scoop one-quarter of the egg mixture into the skillet, pressing down with a spoon or ladle to an even thickness. Pan-fry until golden, about 3 minutes, then flip and continue to pan-fry until cooked through, about 2 more minutes.

5. Repeat step 4 to make 3 more portions, distributing the Egg Foo Young onto 4 plates. Ladle on the gravy, garnish with green onions, and serve.

* *Instead of the pork filling, you can use 1/2 batch leftover Vietnamese Pork Meatballs (page 182), minced to the size of ground pork.*

* *To serve this dish family style, stack the 4 pancakes on a plate, ladle on all the gravy at once, and serve.*

CHINESE KITCHEN

酸甜雞

SWEET AND SOUR CHICKEN

SERVES: 4 | PREP TIME: 10 MINS | COOK TIME: 30 MINS

· ·

It is probably not surprising to read that while this dish is served in Chinese restaurants in many Western countries, it doesn't really exist in China. There are several sauces served in China that incorporate both sweet and sour tastes, the most common being from the Hunan province, but they're a far cry from what you can get at your local Chinese-American restaurant. The reality is that this is more of an American dish than a Chinese one.

On the flip side, the Chinese have their own interpretation of Western tastes—like flying fish roe and salmon cream cheese stuffed-crust pizza (at the Hong Kong Pizza Hut). I think it's a fair trade.

· ·

SAUCE:

1 cup Chicken Broth (page 264)

1/4 cup apple cider vinegar

3 tbsp honey

2 tbsp tomato paste

1 tbsp tamari

1/2 tsp sea salt

1/4 tsp garlic powder

1/4 tsp ground ginger

1/4 tsp white pepper

NUGGETS:

2 tbsp expeller-pressed coconut oil

1/4 cup tapioca or arrowroot starch

1 tsp sea salt

1 tsp white pepper

2 lbs boneless, skinless chicken breasts, cut into bite-sized chunks

2 large eggs, beaten

SLURRY:

1 tbsp arrowroot starch

1 tbsp cold water

1/2 tsp sesame seeds, to garnish

2 green onions, sliced, to garnish

1. In a saucepan, combine the sauce ingredients. Bring to a simmer over medium-low heat, then reduce the heat to low to gently simmer as you prepare the rest of the meal; stir occasionally.

2. Preheat your oven to 250°F. In a wok or skillet, warm the coconut oil over medium heat. Combine the tapioca starch, salt, and pepper, then toss the chicken pieces with the starch mixture. With your fingers, dip a starchy chicken piece in the beaten eggs, shake off the excess egg, and then add to the oil. Repeat until you have filled your skillet, being careful not to overcrowd the chicken pieces. Fry the chicken until cooked through, flipping every 2 minutes, about 6 to 8 minutes per batch. As you finish each batch, place the cooked pieces on a plate lined with paper towels; put them in the oven to stay warm. You should be able to cook the chicken pieces in 3 or 4 batches, depending on the size of your skillet.

3. Once the chicken is cooked through, finish the sauce. Taste the sauce and add more salt or pepper if needed. If the sauce is too dark and strong tasting, add a little chicken broth to thin it out. At this point, the sauce should be about as thick as tomato soup and should have a sharp but not overwhelming flavor.

4. In a small bowl, stir together the arrowroot starch and cold water to create a slurry. Raise the sauce temperature to medium; once bubbling, add half of the slurry and stir until thickened, adding more slurry if needed. Remove from the heat.

5. Toss the chicken pieces with the sauce, then garnish with sesame seeds and green onions. Serve over Basic Steamed Rice (page 286) or Cauliflower Rice (page 288).

* Consider adding chunks of onion, bell pepper, or even pineapple to enhance the flavor of this dish. These ingredients should be added with the starch slurry in step 4.

* This dish is equally delicious made with sliced pork loin or shrimp.

ORANGE CHICKEN

SERVES: 4 | PREP TIME: 10 MINS | COOK TIME: 30 MINS

Orange Chicken is a dish that was popularized in the United States, but came from China's Hunan province. The Chinese word for this dish literally translates to "old peel chicken" because traditional preparations use dried citrus peel. In the U.S., fresh orange zest is commonly used, as in this recipe.

SAUCE:

1 cup Chicken Broth (page 264)

1 cup orange juice

2 tbsp honey

1 tsp rice vinegar

1/2 tsp sea salt

1/4 tsp white pepper

1/4 tsp ground ginger

1/4 tsp garlic powder

splash of tamari

pinch of crushed red pepper

grated zest of 1 large orange, divided

NUGGETS:

2 tbsp expeller-pressed coconut oil

1/4 cup tapioca or arrowroot starch

1 tsp sea salt

1 tsp white pepper

2 lbs boneless, skinless chicken breasts, cut into bite-sized chunks

2 large eggs, beaten

SLURRY:

1 tbsp arrowroot starch

1 tbsp cold water

2 green onions, sliced, to garnish

1/2 tsp sesame seeds, to garnish (optional)

1. In a saucepan, combine the sauce ingredients, but use only half of the orange zest. Bring to a simmer over medium-low heat, then simmer to reduce the volume by one-quarter; stir occasionally. Reduce the heat to low and allow to simmer as you prepare the chicken.

2. Preheat your oven to 250°F. In a wok or skillet, warm the coconut oil over medium heat. Combine the tapioca starch, salt, and pepper and toss the chicken pieces with the starch mixture. With your fingers, dip a starchy chicken piece in the beaten eggs, shake off the excess egg, and then add to the oil. Repeat until you have filled your skillet, being careful not to overcrowd the chicken pieces. Fry the chicken until cooked through, flipping every 2 minutes, about 6 to 8 minutes per batch. As you finish each batch, place the cooked pieces on a plate lined with paper towels; put them in the oven to stay warm. You should be able to cook the chicken pieces in 3 or 4 batches, depending on the size of your skillet.

3. Once the chicken is cooked through, finish the sauce. Taste the sauce and add more salt or white pepper if needed. If the sauce is too dark and strong tasting, add a little more chicken broth to thin it out. Stir in the remaining orange zest.

4. In a small bowl, stir together the arrowroot starch and cold water to create a slurry. Raise the sauce temperature to medium; once bubbling, add half of the slurry and stir until thickened, adding more slurry if needed. Remove from the heat.

5. Toss the chicken pieces with the sauce, then garnish with green onions and sesame seeds (if using) and serve.

腰果雞丁

CASHEW CHICKEN

SERVES: 4 | PREP TIME: 10 MINS | COOK TIME: 15 MINS

Cashew Chicken evokes two sentiments. In most Chinese-American restaurants, it's a stir-fried chicken dish with fresh vegetables. But in Springfield, Missouri, a local chef started deep-frying chicken chunks and serving them with a bit of sauce and cashews on top; it was an instant hit, and now there are dozens of local restaurants that prepare Cashew Chicken the same way. This version is the regular (and less exciting) version.

SAUCE:

2 cloves garlic, minced

1/2 inch ginger, peeled and minced, or 1/4 tsp ground ginger

1 cup Chicken Broth (page 264)

2 tbsp Chinese cooking wine

1 tbsp honey

1 tbsp tamari

1/2 tsp sea salt

1/2 tsp white pepper

SLURRY:

1 tbsp arrowroot starch

1 tbsp cold water

2 tbsp expeller-pressed coconut oil, divided

2 lbs chicken thighs, cut into bite-sized chunks

2 cups snow peas

1/2 red bell pepper, cut into chunks

1/2 medium onion, cut into chunks

1 cup unsalted roasted cashews

1. In a saucepan, combine the sauce ingredients. Bring to a simmer over medium-low heat, then reduce the heat to low to gently simmer as you prepare the rest of the meal; stir occasionally. In a small bowl, stir together the arrowroot starch and cold water to create a slurry, then set aside.

2. Preheat your oven to 200°F. Heat 1 tablespoon of the coconut oil in a wok or skillet over medium-high heat until shimmering, about 1 minute. Add half of the chicken and stir-fry until cooked through and slightly crispy, about 4 minutes, then transfer to the oven to keep warm. Repeat this process with the remaining 1 tablespoon of oil and the remaining chicken.

3. Once the chicken is cooked through, add the sauce to the wok (along with the chicken that is in the oven) and bring to a simmer. Add the snow peas, bell pepper, and onion and simmer until brightly colored, about 30 seconds.

4. Add the cashews and pour in half of the arrowroot starch slurry; stir until thickened, adding more slurry if needed. Remove from the heat, taste and add more salt if needed, and serve.

蜜汁芝麻雞

HONEY SESAME CHICKEN

SERVES: 4 | PREP TIME: 10 MINS | COOK TIME: 30 MINS

Honey Sesame Chicken is a Chinese-American favorite sold in a variety of forms, from breaded and fried to char-grilled. Many home recipes call for the addition of ingredients like ketchup or white sugar to make a sweet and tasty sauce, but the combination of broth, honey, and Chinese cooking wine makes for a perfect takeout flavor.

SAUCE:

1 cup Chicken Broth (page 264)

1/4 cup honey

1 tbsp Chinese cooking wine

1 tsp tamari

1/2 tsp sea salt

1/4 tsp white pepper

dash of black pepper

CHICKEN MEATBALLS:

2 lbs ground chicken

1/4 cup tapioca starch

1 tbsp fish sauce

1 tsp tamari

1 tsp coconut palm sugar

1/2 tsp white pepper

1/2 tsp sea salt

1/2 tsp baking soda

1/4 tsp ground ginger

SLURRY:

1 tbsp arrowroot starch

1 tbsp cold water

2 tsp sesame seeds, divided

1. In a saucepan, combine the sauce ingredients and bring to a simmer over medium heat. Reduce the heat to low and simmer gently to allow the flavors to marry while you prepare the chicken.

2. In a mixing bowl, combine the chicken meatball ingredients with your hands, then transfer to a food processor and pulse until the mixture turns into a tacky paste. With wet hands, form 40 balls.

3. You can either pan-fry the chicken meatballs in batches over medium heat or grill them over direct medium-high heat. If pan-frying, put the cooked chicken in a warm (200°F) oven while you make the other batches.

4. Once the chicken meatballs are cooked, stir together the arrow-root starch and cold water to create a slurry, then stir half of the slurry into the sauce. Increase the heat to medium, bring to a simmer, and cook until thickened, about 2 minutes, adding more slurry if needed. Taste and add salt if needed, then stir in half of the sesame seeds.

5. In a mixing bowl, toss the chicken meatballs with the sauce, then transfer to a serving dish. Sprinkle the remaining sesame seeds over the chicken and serve.

> ⋆ *This recipe can also be made with egg-battered chicken breast pieces. Follow the instructions in my Sweet and Sour Chicken recipe (page 64), but use this sauce. Or you can use velveted chicken breasts (see page 44). Finally, consider pan-frying some cut-up chicken thighs and tossing them in the sauce. Easy!*

GENERAL TSO'S CHICKEN

SERVES: 4 | PREP TIME: 10 MINS | COOK TIME: 30 MINS

• •

So, there was an actual General Tso (Zuo Zongtang), who lived in the mid-1800s, but there's no connection between him and this dish. I'm sure that if he were here today, he'd say, "Tso what? This dish is delicious." (Sorry, dad joke.) And this dish is, in fact, tasty. I like to think of it as a darker, spicier cousin of Sweet and Sour Chicken (page 64), thanks to its use of Chinese chiles and a bit of beef broth.

A big shout-out to my friends Bill Staley and Hayley Mason of the blog *Primal Palate;* the General Tso's recipe found in their elegant cookbook *Gather* first got me thinking about making a book based on takeout cuisine.

• •

SAUCE:

1/2 cup Chicken Broth (page 264)

1/2 cup Beef Broth (page 264)

1 inch ginger, peeled and minced, or 1/2 tsp ground ginger

1 clove garlic, minced

4 to 6 dried Chinese (Sichuan) red chile peppers (depending on your heat tolerance)

2 tbsp tamari

1 tbsp Chinese cooking wine

1 tbsp honey

1/4 tsp sea salt

1/4 tsp white pepper

SLURRY:

1 tbsp arrowroot starch

1 tbsp cold water

NUGGETS:

2 tbsp expeller-pressed coconut oil

1/4 cup tapioca or arrowroot starch

1 tsp sea salt

1 tsp white pepper

2 lbs boneless, skinless chicken breasts, cut into bite-sized chunks

2 large eggs, beaten

2 green onions, sliced, to garnish

1. In a saucepan, combine the sauce ingredients. Bring to a simmer over medium-low heat, then reduce the heat to low to gently simmer as you prepare the rest of the meal; stir occasionally. In a small bowl, stir together the arrowroot starch and cold water to create a slurry, then set aside.

2. Preheat your oven to 250°F. In a wok or skillet, warm the coconut oil over medium heat. Combine the tapioca starch, salt, and pepper, then toss the chicken pieces with the starch mixture. With your fingers, dip a starchy chicken piece in the beaten eggs, shake off the excess egg, then add to the oil. Repeat until you have filled your skillet, being careful not to overcrowd the chicken pieces. Fry the chicken until cooked through, flipping every 2 minutes, about 6 to 8 minutes per batch. As you finish each batch, place the cooked pieces on a plate lined with paper towels; put them in the oven to stay warm. You should be able to cook the chicken pieces in 3 or 4 batches, depending on the size of your skillet.

3. Once the chicken is cooked, finish the sauce. Taste the sauce and add more salt or white pepper if needed. If the sauce is too dark and strong tasting, add a little more chicken broth to thin it out. Raise the sauce temperature to medium; once bubbling, pour in half of the arrowroot starch slurry and stir until thickened, adding more slurry if needed. Remove from the heat.

4. Toss the chicken pieces with the sauce, then garnish with green onions.

> ⋆ *Consider adding chunks of onion, bell pepper, or even pineapple to enhance the flavor of this dish. These items should be added with the starch slurry in step 3.*
>
> ⋆ *Steamed broccoli is a perfect pairing for this dish. Make 2 cups of broccoli for 4 servings of chicken.*

的雞与蘑菇

CHICKEN AND MUSHROOMS

SERVES: 4 | PREP TIME: 10 MINS | COOK TIME: 25 MINS

Chicken and Mushrooms, though a staple of shopping mall food courts throughout the United States, is not well known in other countries. It's a shame, too, because authenticity aside, it's a light, mild-flavored dish that is enjoyed by children and adults alike. While button (white) mushrooms are typically used in Chinese-American restaurants, feel free to step it up with cremini, shiitake, or even wood ear mushrooms.

SAUCE:

2 cloves garlic, minced

1/2 inch ginger, peeled and minced, or 1/4 tsp ground ginger

1 cup Chicken Broth (page 264)

1 tbsp Chinese cooking wine

1 tbsp tamari

1/2 tbsp honey

1/2 tsp white pepper

1/2 tsp sea salt, or more to taste

SLURRY:

1 tbsp arrowroot starch

1 tbsp cold water

1 tbsp expeller-pressed coconut oil

2 lbs chicken thighs, cut into bite-sized chunks

sea salt and white pepper

splash of tamari

10 oz button mushrooms or halved large white mushrooms

2 medium zucchini, sliced into thick half-moons

1. Combine the sauce ingredients in a small saucepan over medium-low heat. Once simmering, reduce the heat to low to keep warm while you prepare the rest of the dish. In a small bowl, stir together the arrowroot starch and cold water to create a slurry, then set aside.

2. Preheat your oven to 200°F. In a wok or skillet, warm the coconut oil over medium-high heat until shimmering, about 1 minute. Add half of the chicken chunks and stir-fry until mostly cooked through, about 6 minutes. Add a bit of salt, pepper, and tamari; sauté to caramelize the chicken pieces, about 1 minute, then transfer to a heatproof bowl and keep warm in the oven. Repeat with the other half of the chicken, adding it to the bowl in the oven once cooked.

3. Add the mushrooms and zucchini to the wok, adding a bit more oil if needed. Sauté until the vegetables have softened, about 4 minutes, stirring constantly to prevent scorching.

4. Return the chicken to the wok, then stir to combine. Pour in the sauce and bring to a simmer; pour in half of the arrowroot starch slurry and stir until thickened, adding more slurry if needed. Taste and add salt if needed, then remove from the heat and serve.

蘑菇雞片

MOO GOO GAI PAN

SERVES: 4 | PREP TIME: 10 MINS | COOK TIME: 15 MINS

• •

Moo Goo Gai Pan is an Americanized version of a Cantonese stir-fried chicken and mushroom dish, which translates literally ("Moo Goo" = button mushrooms, "Gai" = chicken, and "Pan" = slices). I like this recipe because it's a cinch to put together and has a light, refreshing body to it. Feel free to experiment with adding more vegetables. How about a bit of cabbage or some bamboo shoots? Sounds good to me!

• •

SAUCE:

2 cloves garlic, minced

1/2 inch ginger, peeled and minced, or 1/4 tsp ground ginger

1 cup Chicken Broth (page 264)

1 tbsp Chinese cooking wine

2 tsp tamari

1 tsp fish sauce

1/2 tsp sea salt

1/2 tsp white pepper

SLURRY:

1 tbsp arrowroot starch

1 tbsp cold water

1 tbsp expeller-pressed coconut oil

2 lbs boneless, skinless chicken breasts, cut into bite-sized chunks

splash of tamari

2 medium carrots, sliced

1 cup snow peas

5 oz white mushrooms, quartered

1 small (5 oz) can water chestnuts, drained and cut in half

1. Combine the sauce ingredients in a small saucepan over medium-low heat. Once simmering, reduce the heat to low to keep warm while you prepare the rest of the dish. In a small bowl, combine the arrowroot starch and cold water to create a slurry, then set aside.

2. In a wok or skillet, warm the coconut oil over medium-high heat until shimmering, about 1 minute. Add the half of the chicken chunks and sauté until mostly cooked through, stirring often, about 6 minutes. Add a bit of salt, white pepper, and tamari; sauté to caramelize the chicken pieces, about 1 minute, then transfer to a bowl. Repeat with the rest of the chicken and add to the bowl.

3. Add the carrots, snow peas, mushrooms, and water chestnuts to the wok, adding more oil if needed. Sauté until softened, about 3 to 4 minutes, stirring constantly to prevent scorching.

4. Return the chicken and any accumulated juices to the wok, then stir to combine. Pour in the sauce and bring to a simmer; pour in half of the arrowroot starch slurry and stir until thickened, adding more slurry if needed. Taste and add salt if needed, then remove from the heat and serve.

生菜包雞

CHICKEN LETTUCE WRAPS

SERVES: 4 AS AN APPETIZER | PREP TIME: 10 MINS | COOK TIME: 15 MINS

A couple of years ago my wife and I met up with our friends Matt McCarry and Stacy Toth, the Paleo Parents, for dinner at a popular Asian-themed chain restaurant. It was our first time visiting the restaurant, and Stacy strongly recommended (demanded?) that I try to re-create the Chicken Lettuce Wraps. Never one to turn down a challenge, I accepted.

For my version I made a few minor adjustments. I used honey instead of what I assume is gobs of sugar (we taste-tested the original dish a few times, and I was surprised by how sweet it is), and I made fried noodle sticks using sweet potato noodles instead of rice or mung bean noodles, which I assume is what they use in the restaurant recipe.

SAUCE:

2 tbsp honey

1 tbsp Chinese cooking wine

1 tbsp tamari

1 tsp rice vinegar

1 tsp toasted sesame oil

1/2 tsp crushed red pepper

1/2 inch ginger, peeled and grated or minced, or 1/4 tsp ground ginger

1/2 tsp sea salt

1/2 tsp white pepper

CRISPY SWEET POTATO NOODLES:

2 tbsp expeller-pressed coconut oil

10 sweet potato noodles, cut into 4-inch pieces

FILLING:

2 tbsp expeller-pressed coconut oil

2 cloves garlic, minced

1 lb ground chicken

1 small (5 oz) can water chestnuts, drained and chopped

2 shiitake mushrooms, stems removed, chopped (see note)

3 green onions, chopped

1/2 head iceberg lettuce, leaves separated

1. Combine the sauce ingredients and set aside.

2. Making the Crispy Sweet Potato Noodles is super easy. Heat 2 tablespoons of the coconut oil in a wok or skillet over medium-high heat until shimmering, about 1 minute. Add a few uncooked noodles; after they've initially puffed up, tilt the pan so the oil bunches up on one side, then submerge the noodles for a couple of seconds to make sure that every part of the noodle gets puffy (sure beats wasting a bunch of oil to deep-fry the noodles!). Set them aside to cool on paper towels.

3. Heat the remaining 2 tablespoons of the oil in the wok over medium-high heat until shimmering, about 1 minute, then add the garlic. Stir-fry until aromatic, about 20 seconds, then add the chicken. Stir-fry until almost fully cooked (a little pink), about 3 minutes, tossing often. Be sure to break up the larger chunks.

4. Stir in the water chestnuts and mushrooms and stir-fry until the mushrooms start to soften, about 1 minute. Increase the heat to high and add the sauce and green onions. Toss and stir-fry for another minute or two, until the liquid has mostly evaporated and the chicken is starting to crisp. Taste and add salt if needed.

5. Serve with the Crispy Sweet Potato Noodles and lettuce leaves for wrapping.

> * *Dried mushrooms can be used in this dish; just soak them in warm water for 30 minutes before using.*

牛肉和西蘭花

BEEF AND BROCCOLI

SERVES: 4 | PREP TIME: 10 MINS | COOK TIME: 15 MINS

Beef and Broccoli is the quintessential representation of Chinese-American chefs creating a dish to satisfy the Western palate. Broccoli may seem old hat to most modern families, but it didn't become popular until after the 1920s, when Italian immigrants brought it into vogue. The classic dish that we know today is a pairing of this new, "cool" vegetable and a typical Chinese-American brown sauce.

SAUCE:

1/4 cup Beef Broth (page 264)

1/4 cup tamari

2 tbsp Chinese cooking wine

2 tbsp arrowroot starch

1 inch ginger, peeled and grated, or 1/2 tsp ground ginger

4 cloves garlic, minced

1 tsp honey

1/2 tsp white pepper

pinch of crushed red pepper

2 lbs steak (rib eye, strip, or sirloin), sliced against the grain

1 cup Beef Broth (page 264)

2 tbsp expeller-pressed coconut oil, divided

1 bunch broccoli, cut into small chunks

1. Combine the sauce ingredients, then divide in half. Combine half of the sauce with the steak and set aside. Combine the other half of the sauce with the beef broth in a saucepan over medium-low heat; once simmering, reduce the heat to low to keep warm while you stir-fry the steak.

2. In a wok or skillet, warm 1 tablespoon of the coconut oil over high heat until shimmering, about 30 seconds. Add half of the steak and stir-fry until browned, about 2 minutes, then set aside. Repeat with the other half of the steak, then set it aside with the first batch.

3. Reduce the heat to medium-high and add the broccoli and sauce to the wok. Simmer until the broccoli is bright green, about 1 minute, then add the steak and its accumulated juices. Stir-fry until the sauce has thickened, about 1 minute, then serve.

> * *This dish is equally delicious made with thinly sliced chicken breast in place of the beef. It also lends especially itself well to the velveting technique described on page 44.*

MONGOLIAN BEEF

SERVES: 4 | PREP TIME: 10 MINS | COOK TIME: 25 MIN

· ·

Mongolian Beef is made with a rich and dark sauce paired with green onions and crispy noodles. Tip of the hat to Matt McCarry and Stacy Toth, the Paleo Parents, whose idea to incorporate molasses into this dish is pure genius. You can find their version of Mongolian Beef in their latest cookbook, *Real Life Paleo*.

· ·

SAUCE:

1/2 inch ginger, peeled and grated, or 1/4 tsp ground ginger

2 cloves garlic, minced

1/4 cup tamari

1/4 cup Beef Broth (page 264)

2 tbsp Chinese cooking wine

1 1/2 tbsp honey

1 tbsp blackstrap molasses or honey

splash of toasted sesame oil

1/4 tsp sea salt

1/4 tsp white pepper

2 tbsp arrowroot or tapioca starch

1/2 tsp sea salt

1/4 tsp white pepper

2 lbs steak (rib eye, strip, or sirloin), cut into bite-sized chunks

CRISPY SWEET POTATO NOODLES:

2 tbsp expeller-pressed coconut oil

10 sweet potato noodles, cut into 4-inch pieces

SLURRY:

2 tbsp arrowroot starch

1 tbsp cold water

2 tbsp expeller-pressed coconut oil, divided

4 green onions, cut into 2-inch lengths

1. Combine the sauce ingredients in a small saucepan and bring to a simmer over medium heat. Reduce the heat to medium-low and gently simmer for 10 minutes to allow the flavors to marry while you prepare the beef.

2. Combine the starch, salt, and pepper in a mixing bowl. Add the steak pieces and toss to coat with the starch mixture. Shake off any excess starch from the steak, then set aside.

3. Make the Crispy Sweet Potato Noodles: Heat the coconut oil in a wok or skillet over medium-high heat until shimmering, about 1 minute. Add a few uncooked noodles; after they've initially puffed up, tilt the pan so the oil bunches up on one side, then submerge the noodles for a couple of seconds to make sure that every part of the noodle gets puffy (sure beats wasting a bunch of oil to deep-fry the noodles!). Set aside to cool on paper towels.

4. Raise the sauce heat to medium. In a small bowl, stir together the starch and cold water to create a slurry. Pour half of the slurry into the sauce and stir until thickened, adding more slurry if needed, then reduce the heat to low to keep warm while you cook the beef.

5. In the wok or skillet, warm 1 tablespoon of the coconut oil over medium-high heat until shimmering, about 1 minute. Add half of the steak and stir-fry until browned and slightly crispy, about 4 minutes, stirring occasionally. Remove the steak and set on paper towels to drain. Add the remaining 1 tablespoon of oil to the wok and wait for it to come to temperature, about 30 seconds. Add the rest of the steak and cook in the same manner, then remove and set on paper towels to drain. Reduce the heat to medium and pour off and discard all but about 1/2 tablespoon of the oil.

6. Return the steak to the wok and add the green onions. Stir-fry until the onions have softened slightly, about 15 seconds, then pour in the thickened sauce and toss to combine. Serve over the Crispy Sweet Potato Noodles.

* Some restaurants like to include large slices of white onion in this dish. Simply add them at the end of step 5, before turning the heat down and pouring off most of the oil. Sauté until the onion shows brown spots, then reduce the heat to medium, pour off the oil, and proceed to step 6.

四川牛肉

SZECHUAN BEEF

SERVES: 4 | PREP TIME: 10 MINS | COOK TIME: 15 MINS

· ·

Szechuan Beef is influenced by the bold, pungent, and spicy cuisine of the Sichuan province in northern China. (See also Kung Pao Pork on page 92.) This recipe calls for steak, but the dish is equally delicious made with chicken thighs. Simply cut the chicken thighs into bite-sized pieces and follow the recipe as directed.

· ·

SAUCE:

2 cloves garlic, minced

1/2 inch ginger, peeled and minced, or 1/4 tsp ground ginger

6 dried Chinese (Sichuan) red chile peppers, chopped, or more to taste

2 cups Chicken Broth (page 264)

2 tbsp apple cider vinegar

2 tbsp tamari

1 tbsp honey

1 tsp tomato paste

1/2 tsp shrimp or anchovy paste

1/2 tsp sea salt

1/4 tsp white pepper

SLURRY:

1 tbsp arrowroot starch

1 tbsp cold water

2 tbsp expeller-pressed coconut oil, divided

2 lbs steak (rib eye, strip, or sirloin), sliced against the grain

2 cups chopped broccoli or Chinese cabbage (bok choy, choy sum, or kai lan)

2 medium carrots, julienned

2 green onions, sliced

1. In a saucepan, combine the sauce ingredients. Bring to a simmer over medium-low heat, then reduce the heat to low to gently simmer as you prepare the rest of the meal; stir occasionally. In a small bowl, stir together the arrowroot starch and cold water to create a slurry, then set aside.

2. In a wok or skillet, warm 1 tablespoon of the coconut oil over medium-high heat until shimmering, about 1 minute. Add half of the steak and stir-fry until browned and slightly crispy, about 4 minutes, stirring occasionally. Remove the steak and set on paper towels to drain. Add the remaining 1 tablespoon of oil and wait for it to come to temperature, about 30 seconds. Add the rest of the steak and cook in the same manner, then remove and set on paper towels to drain. Pour off and discard all but about 1/2 tablespoon of the oil.

3. Add the broccoli to the wok and stir-fry until bright green, about 1 minute. Add the sauce and reduce the heat to medium. Once simmering, add the steak, carrots, green onions, and half of the slurry; stir until thickened, adding more slurry if needed. Remove from the heat and serve.

* *To enhance the flavor of this dish, consider adding chunks of onion or bell pepper along with the carrots in step 3.*

青椒牛

PEPPER STEAK

SERVES: 4 | PREP TIME: 10 MINS | COOK TIME: 15 MINS

· ·

Pepper Steak is a Chinese-American dish that borrows heavily from a similar recipe made with pork from the Fujian province. My version is not unlike Beef and Broccoli (page 80), the most notable differences being that it uses a milder sauce and doesn't include any broccoli!

· ·

SAUCE:

1 cup Chicken Broth (page 264)

2 tbsp tamari

2 tbsp Chinese cooking wine

1 tbsp honey

1/2 inch ginger, peeled and minced, or 1/4 tsp ground ginger

2 cloves garlic, minced

1/2 tsp black pepper

1/4 tsp sea salt

SLURRY:

2 tbsp arrowroot starch

1 tbsp cold water

2 tbsp expeller-pressed coconut oil, divided

2 lbs steak (rib eye, strip, or sirloin), sliced into strips

1 medium onion, cut into chunks

1 green bell pepper, cut into chunks

1 red bell pepper, cut into chunks

1. Combine the sauce ingredients in a small saucepan and bring to a simmer over medium heat; reduce the heat to low. Stir together the arrowroot starch and cold water to create a slurry.

2. Return the heat to medium, then stir half of the slurry into the sauce. Stir until thickened, adding more slurry if needed, then reduce the heat to low again to keep warm while you cook the steak.

3. In a wok or skillet, warm half of the coconut oil over medium-high heat until shimmering, about 1 minute. Add half of the steak and stir-fry until browned and slightly crispy, about 4 minutes, stirring occasionally. Remove the steak and set on paper towels to drain; add the remaining oil and wait for it to come to temperature, about 30 seconds. Add the rest of the steak and cook in the same manner; then remove the steak and set on paper towels to drain. Pour off and discard all but about 1/2 tablespoon of the oil.

4. Add the onion and sauté until just softened, about 2 minutes, then add the bell peppers and sauté until just starting to soften, about 1 minute. Return the steak to the wok, pour in the sauce, and toss to combine. Simmer until thickened, about 1 minute, then serve.

CHAR SIU

SERVES: 4 | PREP TIME: 25 MINS. PLUS AT LEAST 30 MINS TO MARINATE | COOK TIME: 35 MINS

Char Siu (literally "fork burn/roast") is one of the most well-known Chinese roasted meat dishes. Today this dish is often made with maltose, which is a malt sugar made from barley. Honey is a suitable substitute and is still used by some chefs. Many restaurants also use red dye to simulate that signature roasted look, but we're going for the real deal in this recipe, adding a bit of paprika to the sauce to help it along. If you really want that red color, your best bet is to add beet powder (a natural food dye), which you can purchase online.

Char Siu not only is served on its own, but is commonly used as a component in other dishes as well. I like to make a double batch and use the leftovers for Fried Rice (page 50), Chow Mein (page 58), or Ramen (page 112).

SAUCE:

4 cloves garlic, minced

1 inch ginger, peeled and grated, or 1/2 tsp ground ginger

1/4 cup honey or 3 tbsp coconut palm sugar

2 tbsp tamari

1 tbsp Chinese cooking wine

1 tbsp apple cider vinegar

1 tsp Chinese five-spice powder

1 tsp toasted sesame oil

1 tsp beet powder (optional)

1/2 tsp paprika

1/2 tsp sea salt

1/2 tsp white pepper

2 lbs pork loin or boneless chops, cut into 2-inch pieces

CHINESE MUSTARD:

1/4 cup dry mustard (I like Coleman's)

pinch of white pepper

3 tbsp cold water

sesame seeds, to garnish (optional)

1. In a saucepan, combine the sauce ingredients. Bring to a simmer over medium-low heat, then simmer for 5 minutes. Remove from the heat and allow to cool, about 20 minutes.

2. Combine the pork pieces and half of the sauce in a resealable plastic bag; refrigerate for at least 30 minutes, overnight preferred. The longer you let it marinate, the more the flavor and color will penetrate the meat. Transfer the other half of the sauce to a small container, cover, and refrigerate.

3. Prepare your grill for indirect grilling by igniting the burners on only one side (gas grill) or by banking the coals to one side (charcoal grill). Skewer the pork pieces and place them on the cool side of the grill for 15 minutes. As they roast, prepare the Chinese mustard by combining the ingredients in a small bowl; set aside.

4. Transfer the skewers to the hot side of the grill and baste with the remaining sauce. Grill over direct high heat, basting and turning every 2 minutes, until caramelized, about 10 minutes total.

5. Allow the pork to rest for 10 minutes before slicing and serving with the Chinese mustard. Garnish with sesame seeds if desired.

> * I'm a big fan of metal skewers because they are reusable. If using bamboo skewers, be sure to soak them in water for at least 30 minutes before grilling to prevent burning.

木須肉

MOO SHU PORK

SERVES: 4 | PREP TIME: 10 MINS | COOK TIME: 20 MINS

· ·

Moo Shu Pork is a northern Chinese dish that first started appearing in the United States in the 1960s, particularly on the East Coast. Today, it is served in most Chinese-American restaurants, often with thin pancakes and Hoisin Sauce (page 270). My Flatbread (page 298) is an excellent substitute for the pancakes.

· ·

SAUCE:

2 cloves garlic, minced

1/2 inch ginger, peeled and minced, or 1/4 tsp ground ginger

1 cup Chicken Broth (page 264)

1 tsp Chinese cooking wine

1 tsp apple cider vinegar

1 tsp honey

1/2 tsp fish sauce

1/2 tsp sea salt

1/2 tsp white pepper

SLURRY:

1 tbsp arrowroot starch

1 tbsp cold water

2 tbsp expeller-pressed coconut oil, divided

2 large eggs, beaten

2 lbs pork tenderloin or boneless chops, cut into thin strips, or 2 lbs ground pork

splash of tamari

2 medium carrots, julienned

2 cups won bok (napa) cabbage, shredded

1/2 cup wood ear or shiitake mushrooms, cut into strips (see note)

1 small (5 oz) can sliced bamboo shoots, drained

1. Combine the sauce ingredients in a small saucepan and bring to a simmer over medium-low heat. Once simmering, reduce the heat to low to keep the sauce warm while you prepare the rest of the dish.

2. In a small bowl, stir together the arrowroot starch and cold water to create a slurry, then set aside.

3. In a wok or skillet, warm 1 tablespoon of the coconut oil over medium-high heat until shimmering, about 1 minute. Add the eggs and scramble until cooked through, then remove and set aside.

4. Warm the remaining 1 tablespoon of oil in the wok until shimmering, then add the pork and sauté until mostly cooked through, stirring often, about 4 minutes. Add a bit of salt, white pepper, and tamari; sauté to caramelize the pork, about 1 minute, then transfer to a bowl.

5. Add the carrots, cabbage, mushrooms, and bamboo shoots to the wok, adding more oil if needed. Sauté until softened, about 2 minutes, stirring constantly to prevent scorching.

6. Return the pork and any accumulated juices to the wok, then stir to combine. Add the sauce and bring to a simmer; pour in half of the arrowroot starch slurry and stir until thickened, adding more slurry if needed. Taste and add salt if needed, then remove from the heat and serve.

* If using shiitake mushrooms, remove the stems before cooking—they are too tough to eat. Dried mushrooms can be used in this dish; just soak them in warm water for 30 minutes before using.

* Some folks like to add bean sprouts to this dish. Go for it!

KUNG PAO PORK

SERVES: 4 | PREP TIME: 25 MINS | COOK TIME: 20 MINS

Kung Pao Pork is the less popular little brother of the enormously famous Kung Pao Chicken, but truth be told, I had too many chicken dishes in this book, so this one was an easy transfer to the pork side. This dish is a product of spicy and flavorful Szechuan cuisine. If you're a Kung Pao Chicken purist, never fear; just make it with chicken thighs instead.

MARINADE:

2 tbsp tamari

2 tbsp Chinese cooking wine

2 tbsp arrowroot starch

1 tbsp Chicken Broth (page 264)

1 tbsp apple cider vinegar

1 tbsp fish sauce

1 tsp sea salt

1/2 tsp garlic powder

1/2 tsp ground ginger

1/2 tsp white pepper

2 lbs pork loin or boneless chops, cut into bite-sized chunks

2 tbsp Chicken Broth (page 264)

3 tbsp expeller-pressed coconut oil, divided

1/4 cup unsalted roasted cashews, cut in half crosswise

6 dried Chinese (Sichuan) red chile peppers

2 stalks celery, sliced

1 red bell pepper, cut into chunks

1. Stir together the marinade ingredients, then divide the mixture in half. Combine half of the marinade with the pork, then set aside to marinate for 20 minutes. Combine the other half of the marinade with the broth and set aside.

2. In a wok or skillet, heat 1 tablespoon of the coconut oil over medium-high heat until shimmering, about 1 minute. Add the cashews and dried chiles and stir-fry until toasted but not burned, about 1 minute. Add the celery and bell pepper; stir-fry until the vegetables are soft and starting to form charred spots, about 1 minute. Transfer to a bowl.

3. Add 1 tablespoon of the oil and half of the marinated pork to the wok and stir-fry until cooked through and slightly crispy, about 4 minutes, then remove and set aside. Add the remaining 1 tablespoon of oil to the wok and cook the other half of the pork in the same manner.

4. Return the first half of the pork to the wok and add the marinade/broth mixture. Simmer until thickened, about 1 minute, then add the vegetables, toss to combine, and serve.

蝦龍糊

SHRIMP WITH LOBSTER SAUCE

SERVES: 4 | PREP TIME: 10 MINS | COOK TIME: 10 MINS

To be honest, I had never heard of this dish until my family moved to the East Coast in 2008. I first ordered it out of curiosity; what the heck is lobster sauce, and why are they selling it for so cheap? I found the answer soon enough, since "lobster" sauce should be more appropriately named "lobster-free sauce." Turns out that lobster is a Cantonese-inspired dish made with broth and eggs, similar to other sauces that are poured over lobster dishes (there's the connection!).

In the end, I fell in love with lobster sauce; it's like a thick version of Egg Drop Soup (page 46) and is super tasty when served over rice. This dish is commonly made with just egg whites, but you can definitely use whole eggs for a bit more nutrients.

SLURRY:

3 tbsp arrowroot starch

2 tbsp cold water

SAUCE:

3 cups Chicken Broth (page 264)

1/4 cup Chinese cooking wine

2 tsp tamari

1 tsp sea salt

1 tsp white pepper

1/2 tsp ground ginger

2 lbs raw shrimp, peeled and cut in half

1/2 cup chopped carrots

1/2 cup frozen peas, rinsed in cool water and drained

3 shiitake mushrooms, stems removed, thinly sliced (see note)

2 large eggs, beaten

2 green onions, sliced

1. Stir together the arrowroot starch and cold water to create a slurry, then set aside.

2. In a stockpot, combine the sauce ingredients and bring to a simmer over medium heat. Once the sauce is simmering, add half of the arrowroot starch slurry and stir until thickened, about 1 minute, adding more slurry if needed. Add the shrimp, carrots, peas, and mushrooms, return to a simmer, and simmer until the shrimp are just pink, about 1 minute.

3. Slowly pour the eggs through a fork into the sauce. Whisk gently with a fork to prevent the eggs from clumping, then allow to cook through, about 30 seconds. Stir in the green onions and serve.

> * Dried shiitake mushrooms can be used in this dish; just soak them in warm water for 30 minutes before slicing.

核桃蝦

HONEY WALNUT SHRIMP

SERVES: 4 | PREP TIME: 30 MINS | COOK TIME: 10 MINS

I have a long and storied history with Honey Walnut Shrimp. It's wildly popular in Hawaii, and I was obsessed with it while I lived there. In fact, after our Vegas wedding in 2007, my wife and I had another reception in Hawaii for friends and family who couldn't travel to Nevada for the wedding; we held the reception at a Chinese restaurant, mostly because I wanted everyone to try this dish.

I first made Honey Walnut Shrimp on my blog in 2011, only to find that the wonderful, entertaining Michelle Tam of the blog *Nom Nom Paleo* later developed her own (better) recipe, which is featured in her bestselling cookbook, *Nom Nom Paleo: Food for Humans*. Not one to leave a challenge sitting on the table, I redeveloped and perfected my original recipe for this cookbook. Ball's in your court now, Michelle! (Actually, at this point our recipes are nearly identical, so that's a good sign.)

CANDIED WALNUTS:

1 cup raw walnuts

2 tbsp honey or maple syrup

1 tbsp expeller-pressed coconut oil or ghee

pinch of sea salt

SAUCE:

3 tbsp Mayo (page 276)

1 tbsp honey

1/2 tbsp full-fat coconut milk

1 tbsp lemon juice

1/4 tsp white pepper

pinch of sea salt

BATTERED SHRIMP:

1/4 cup lard, ghee, or expeller-pressed coconut oil

1 large egg white

1/4 cup potato or tapioca starch

1 tsp sea salt

2 lbs raw shrimp, peeled

1. Prepare the candied walnuts: Preheat your oven to 350°F. Combine the walnuts, honey, coconut oil, and salt, then spread in a single layer on a rimmed baking sheet lined with parchment paper. Bake until they appear shiny and candy-coated, about 15 minutes; watch closely so they don't burn. Set aside to cool while you build the rest of the dish.

2. Combine the sauce ingredients in a small bowl, then set aside.

3. In a wok or skillet, heat the lard over medium-high heat until shimmering, about 5 minutes. As it warms, whip the egg white until frothy, then add the starch and salt and stir to combine into a batter. Toss the shrimp in the batter to coat.

4. Add the coated shrimp to the wok in batches and fry until golden brown, about 5 minutes per batch, then place on paper towels to drain.

5. Toss the shrimp with the sauce, then add the candied walnuts and serve.

BAM BAM SHRIMP

SERVES: 4 | PREP TIME: 10 MINS | COOK TIME: 10 MINS

This dish is very similar to Honey Walnut Shrimp (page 96) but has a tangier, spicier sauce. It is popular in many chain restaurants, and for good reason: tangy, spicy, sweet, and seafood flavors all at once? Consider me sold.

SAUCE:

3 tbsp Mayo (page 276)

1 tbsp honey

1 tbsp lemon juice

1 tsp Frank's RedHot Sauce, or more to taste

1 tsp chipotle chili powder

1/4 tsp sea salt

1/4 tsp white pepper

BATTERED SHRIMP:

1/4 cup lard, ghee, or expeller-pressed coconut oil

1 large egg white

1/4 cup potato or tapioca starch

1 tsp sea salt

2 lbs raw shrimp, peeled

2 green onions, sliced

sesame seeds, to garnish

1. Combine the sauce ingredients in a small bowl and set aside.

2. In a wok or skillet, heat the lard over medium-high heat until shimmering, about 5 minutes. As it warms, whip the egg white until frothy, then add the starch and salt and stir to combine into a batter. Toss the shrimp in the batter to coat.

3. Add the coated shrimp to the wok in batches and fry until golden brown, about 5 minutes per batch, then place on paper towels to drain.

4. Toss the shrimp with the sauce and green onions, then garnish with sesame seeds and serve.

奶油椰子蝦

CREAMY COCONUT SHRIMP

SERVES: 4 | PREP TIME: 10 MINS | COOK TIME: 10 MINS

This dish isn't often offered in Chinese takeout restaurants; rather, it's a staple in your everyday Chinese buffet (along with crazy random foods like Texas Toast and fried plantains!). Essentially, these shrimp swim in a creamy sauce until a hungry patron comes to scoop some up. I've replicated the experience for you, without the added difficulty of having to walk past the dessert buffet. (Someone please explain to me why Chinese-American buffets often serve Nilla Wafer pies!)

SAUCE:

1 (14 oz) can full-fat coconut milk

1 tbsp honey

1 tbsp Chinese cooking wine

1/2 tsp sea salt, or more to taste

1/2 tsp white pepper, or more to taste

BATTERED SHRIMP:

1/4 cup lard, ghee, or expeller-pressed coconut oil

1 large egg white

1/4 cup potato or tapioca starch

1 tsp sea salt

2 lbs raw shrimp, peeled

SLURRY:

2 tbsp arrowroot starch

2 tbsp cold water

1. Combine the sauce ingredients in a saucepan. Bring to a simmer over medium heat, then reduce the heat to low to gently simmer as you prepare the shrimp.

2. In a wok or skillet, heat the lard over medium-high heat until shimmering, about 5 minutes. As it warms, whip the egg white until frothy, then add the starch and salt and stir to combine into a batter. Toss the shrimp in the batter to coat.

3. Add the coated shrimp to the wok in batches and fry until golden brown, about 5 minutes per batch, then place on paper towels to drain.

4. Stir together the arrowroot starch and water to create a slurry. Stir half of the slurry into the sauce until thickened, adding more slurry if needed.

5. Return the cooked shrimp to the wok, stir in the sauce, and serve.

VEGETABLES IN WHITE SAUCE

SERVES: 4 | PREP TIME: 10 MINS | COOK TIME: 5 MINS

Nearly every Chinese takeout restaurant offers a generic "Steamed Vegetables in White Sauce" dish to help off-set the meat- and breading-heavy dishes that prevail on the rest of the menu. This recipe is intended to act as a template for a myriad of vegetable side dishes to accompany the other meat-centered dishes found in this chapter.

The listed vegetables are just a suggestion. Consider using any vegetables you have in your fridge, and maybe some canned veggies, too (I'm looking at you, bamboo shoots and water chestnuts).

SLURRY:

1 tbsp arrowroot starch

1 tbsp cold water

SAUCE:

1/2 cup Chicken Broth (page 264)

1 tbsp mirin

1/2 tsp fish sauce

1/4 tsp white pepper

1/4 tsp ground ginger

1 tbsp expeller-pressed coconut oil

2 cloves garlic, minced

2 medium carrots, peeled and sliced

4 oz white or cremini mushrooms, quartered

8 oz broccoli, coarsely chopped

8 oz snow peas

8 oz Chinese cabbage (won bok, bok choy, or choy sum), coarsely chopped

1. Stir together the arrowroot starch and cold water to create a slurry, then set aside. Similarly, stir together the sauce ingredients and set aside.

2. Heat the coconut oil in a wok or skillet over medium-high heat until shimmering, about 1 minute. Add the garlic and sauté until aromatic, about 30 seconds. Add the carrots and sauté for 1 minute, then add the mushrooms and sauté until slightly softened, about 1 minute.

3. Add the sauce, broccoli, and snow peas to the wok, stirring to combine. Once simmering, add the cabbage; sauté until wilted, about 1 minute.

4. Stir in half of the arrowroot starch slurry, then continue to stir until thickened, about 1 minute, adding more slurry if needed. Remove from the heat and serve.

乾煸四季豆

STIR-FRIED GREEN BEANS

SERVES: 4 | PREP TIME: 10 MINS | COOK TIME: 5 MINS

Like Creamy Coconut Shrimp (page 100), Stir-Fried Green Beans are commonly found on Chinese buffet lines. What's cool about this dish is that it is fairly common in China, too—finally, a dish that we can agree on! I love to whip it up because it's easy to put together; you'll spend more time trimming the green beans than you will cooking them.

1 tbsp lard or expeller-pressed coconut oil

1 lb green beans, trimmed

1/2 tsp tamari

1/2 tsp Chinese cooking wine

1/4 tsp sea salt

dash of white pepper

6 cloves garlic, sliced

1. In a wok or skillet, heat the lard over medium-high heat until shimmering, about 1 minute. Add the green beans and stir-fry until bright green, about 1 minute.

2. Add the remaining ingredients and toss to combine. Stir-fry until the garlic is golden and aromatic, about 30 seconds, then serve.

JAPANESE AND KOREAN FAVORITES

DASHI (JAPANESE SOUP STOCK)

Dashi is a basic soup stock and a fundamental part of Japanese cuisine; in fact, research on a basic dashi stock led to the identification of the "umami" taste sensation in 1908. My Deluxe Dashi recipe is a combination of a few different methods. To the Basic Dashi foundation, I incorporated flavors from shiitake dashi (which is basically just the water you soak mushrooms in) and iriko dashi (made with anchovies). It's super good, but if you don't have those ingredients on hand, Basic Dashi will do just fine.

The kombu (dried seaweed) and katsuobushi (bonito fish flakes) can be used once more to make a second batch of dashi (called niban dashi). I like to rinse off and slice the kombu and add it directly to my soups. Additionally, when making the Deluxe Dashi, be sure to reserve the mushrooms for use in other dishes! Think of it like you're just borrowing them for a bit.

BASIC DASHI

YIELD: 2 QUARTS | PREP TIME: 35 MINS | COOK TIME: 15 MINS

1 quart Chicken Broth (page 264)

1 quart water

24 square inches kombu (about 1 oz)

1 cup loosely packed katsuobushi

sea salt

1. Combine the broth, water, and kombu in a large saucepan and let the kombu soak for 30 minutes. Bring to a boil over medium-high heat, then add the katsuobushi and reduce the heat to medium-low. Gently simmer for 5 minutes, then remove from the heat and allow to steep for 10 more minutes.

2. Strain the liquid through a cheesecloth or coffee filter, reserving the kombu and katsuobushi. Season with salt to taste.

> ✴ *Dashi freezes well in jars. Consider making a double batch so that you can prepare quick soups when the inclination hits.*

DELUXE DASHI

YIELD: 2 QUARTS | PREP TIME: 35 MINS | COOK TIME: 25 MINS

1 quart Chicken Broth (page 264)

1 quart water

24 square inches kombu (about 1 oz)

1/2 cup dried shiitake mushrooms

1/2 cup dried anchovies or baby sardines

1 cup loosely packed katsuobushi

pinch of white pepper

sea salt

1. Combine the broth, water, kombu, and mushrooms in a large saucepan and let the kombu and mushrooms soak for 30 minutes. Bring to a boil over medium-high heat; once boiling, add the dried anchovies or sardines and reduce the heat to medium-low. Gently simmer for 10 minutes.

2. Turn off the heat, add the katsuobushi, and allow to steep for 10 minutes. Strain the liquid through a cheesecloth or coffee filter, reserving the kombu and katsuobushi. Season with white pepper and salt to taste.

MISO SOUP

SERVES: 4 AS A SIDE | PREP TIME: 5 MINS, PLUS TIME TO MAKE DASHI | COOK TIME: 10 MINS

Miso Soup is an essential Japanese dish, served before many meals. It's simple to put together; all you really need is some Dashi (page 108), miso paste, and complementary add-ins like seaweed and green onions.

Miso paste is made by fermenting soybeans in *Aspergillus oryzae,* a fungus known as koji in Japan. It is high in protein, vitamins, and minerals, and many of the toxins found in soy are removed during the fermentation process. Be careful when buying miso paste, as some manufacturers add wheat or barley to the process. I like Miso Master brand organic red miso paste, which is made with just soybeans, koji, sea salt, and water.

1 quart Dashi (page 108)

2 tbsp miso paste

2 tbsp dried wakame seaweed

2 green onions, sliced, to garnish

1. Bring the dashi to a boil over medium-high heat, then reduce the heat to medium-low to gently simmer.

2. Add the miso paste and wakame, stirring to combine. Allow the seaweed to soften, about 5 minutes, then ladle into 4 bowls. Garnish with green onions and serve.

RAMEN

SERVES: 4 | PREP TIME: UP TO 35 MINS, PLUS TIME TO MAKE DASHI AND GARNISHES | COOK TIME: 10 MINS

• •

Not to be confused with Top Ramen, a company I helped keep in business during my teenage years, Japanese Ramen is a simple soup that can be deceptively complex depending on the regional variation. Heck, there is even a ramen museum in Yokohama, highlighting the history and diversity of this soup. I've provided some of my favorite variations on the opposite page.

• •

NOODLES:

12 oz rice noodles or sweet potato noodles or

2 large sweet potatoes (about 2 lbs total) or

4 zucchini or yellow squash (about 2 lbs total)

2 quarts Dashi (page 108)

GARNISHES:

1/2 batch Fish Balls (page 40)

1/2 batch Char Siu (page 88), sliced

10 shiitake mushrooms (about 6 oz), stems removed, sliced

1/2 head won bok (napa) cabbage, thinly sliced

4 green onions, sliced

2 large eggs, medium-boiled (see note)

Japanese Chili Oil (page 268)

1. Prepare the noodles. If making rice noodles, soak them for 30 minutes in warm water, then add to a pot of boiling salted water and parboil until soft, about 1 minute. Drain and rinse in cold water until cool to the touch. If making sweet potato noodles, boil until tender, about 6 minutes, then drain and rinse in cold water until cool to the touch. If using sweet potatoes, run them through a spiral slicer on its largest setting and parboil until just tender, about 2 minutes, then drain and gently rinse in cold water until cool to the touch. Finally, if using zucchini or yellow squash, simply spiral-slice them to your desired thickness and set aside.

2. Bring the dashi to a boil over medium-high heat, then reduce the heat to medium-low and gently simmer while you prepare your ramen bowls.

3. Distribute the noodles among 4 bowls, then add the garnishes over the noodles. If using Fish Balls, add them to the dashi to simmer until floating. Ladle the dashi into the bowls and serve.

---

* *The easiest way to make medium-boiled eggs: Carefully add the eggs to a pot of boiling, salted water. Gently boil for 6 1/2 minutes, then spoon the eggs into a bowl of ice water. Allow to cool, about 5 minutes; then peel.*

* *Other garnish ideas: Carnitas (page 250), Gyoza Bites (page 114), partially cooked bacon slices, shrimp, clams, crab, spinach, mushrooms (all kinds), bean sprouts, Kimchi (page 148), and seaweed (all kinds).*

* *Some seasoning ideas: togarashi powder, black pepper, white pepper, sesame seeds, curry powder, a dash of apple cider vinegar, or even some Tabasco.*

VARIATIONS

A basic dashi broth is known as a shio ("salt") ramen. Here are some other broth and regional variations:

BASIC MISO RAMEN: Add 2 tablespoons miso paste to the dashi.

BASIC SHOYU RAMEN: Add 1 tablespoon tamari to the dashi.

TONKATSU RAMEN: Boil 1 pound pork neck bones in water for 5 minutes, then drain and thoroughly rinse in cool water. Add the bones to the dashi and simmer for 1 hour.

ASAHIKAWA RAMEN: Make your dashi using 1 quart chicken broth and 1 quart pork broth, and spoon 1 teaspoon melted lard into each ramen bowl before serving.

SAPPORO RAMEN: Add 2 tablespoons miso paste, 2 cloves minced garlic, and 1/2 inch grated ginger to the dashi, and add 1 teaspoon melted butter to each ramen bowl before serving.

KYOTO RAMEN: Make your dashi using 1 quart chicken broth and 1 quart pork broth, add 1 tablespoon tamari, and season with white pepper to taste.

TOKUSHIMA RAMEN: Make Tonkatsu Ramen and add a raw egg to each ramen bowl after ladling in the hot broth.

Looking for another favorite noodle soup, Udon? Simply use thicker noodles and adjust the cooking time accordingly!

GYOZA BITES

SERVES: 4 AS AN APPETIZER | PREP TIME: 10 MINS | COOK TIME: 15 MINS

• •

Gyoza are Japanese dumplings based on the Chinese dumplings jiaozi, which are characterized by their crimped edges. They are most often steamed and pan-fried at the same time, resulting in a dish that is soft on one side and crispy on the other.

Replicating the thin wrapper dough of traditional gyoza turned out to be too much of a challenge for the weeknight home cook, so I developed this Gyoza Bites recipe instead, which can be made quickly and tastes just as great.

• •

DIPPING SAUCE:

2 tbsp tamari

1 tbsp mirin

1 tsp rice vinegar

1/2 tsp togarashi powder

SURIMI (MEAT PASTE):

1 lb ground pork

1/2 inch ginger, peeled and grated, or 1/4 tsp ground ginger

2 cloves garlic, minced

2 tbsp tapioca starch

1 tbsp mirin

1 tsp tamari

1 tsp sea salt

1/2 tsp white pepper

1 cup finely chopped green cabbage

1 green onion, finely chopped

2 tbsp expeller-pressed coconut oil, divided

1. Combine the dipping sauce ingredients in a small bowl and set aside.

2. Combine the surimi ingredients in a food processor and pulse until tacky and well mixed. Transfer to a mixing bowl and mix together with the cabbage and green onion using your hands. Form into 20 to 25 small balls using wet hands.

3. Heat 1 tablespoon of the coconut oil in a skillet over medium-high heat until shimmering, about 1 minute. Add half of the balls and pan-fry until cooked through, rotating often, about 5 minutes. Transfer to a plate. Add the remaining 1 tablespoon of oil and the remaining balls and pan-fry until cooked through, then serve with the dipping sauce.

TEMPURA

SERVES: 4 | PREP TIME: 20 MINS, PLUS TIME TO MAKE DASHI | COOK TIME: 20 MINS

· ·

Tempura, a dish of battered and fried seafood and vegetables, is one of the most recognizable Japanese dishes worldwide. This technique was first introduced to Japan by Portuguese Jesuit missionaries in Nagasaki in the 1500s. It's speculated that the original Portuguese dish, *Peixinhos da horta,* was first introduced to Portuguese cuisine by colonists in Goa (West India)—quite a trip this little fried dish has taken!

· ·

DIPPING SAUCE:

1/2 cup Dashi (page 108)

1/2 cup water

2 tbsp mirin

1 tbsp tamari

BATTER:

1/4 cup tapioca starch

1/4 cup potato or arrowroot starch (or a combination)

2 large eggs, beaten

1 tsp sea salt

1/2 tsp white pepper

1/2 lb raw shrimp, peeled and deveined

1 cup lard

VEGETABLES AS DESIRED:

broccoli, cut into bite-sized chunks

carrots, thinly sliced

eggplant, thinly sliced

green beans, trimmed

sweet potatoes, thinly sliced

zucchini, thinly sliced

1. Combine the dipping sauce ingredients in a saucepan and bring to a boil over medium heat. Reduce the heat to low and simmer for 5 minutes. Remove from the heat and allow to cool.

2. Combine the batter ingredients in a bowl, then add enough cold water until it reaches a thin batterlike consistency (runnier than pancake batter but thicker than water). Set aside.

3. Prepare the shrimp by making 4 or 5 shallow perpendicular cuts along the length of each shrimp's belly, being careful not to slice through the shrimp. Rotate the shrimp, back side up, then pinch and press on the shrimp to straighten and lengthen it.

4. Heat the lard in a skillet over medium-high heat to 360°F. Rapidly stir the batter, then quickly and carefully dip in a shrimp or vegetable. Pull from the batter and allow the excess to run off, then quickly place in the lard to fry. Add more pieces, but do not overcrowd the skillet.

5. Fry until golden, 2 to 3 minutes, then let cool on a baking sheet lined with a wire rack. Repeat until all the shrimp and vegetables are cooked, then serve.

とんかつ チキンカツ

TONKATSU AND CHICKEN KATSU

SERVES: 4 | PREP TIME: 10 MINS, PLUS TIME TO MAKE TONKATSU SAUCE | COOK TIME: 30 MINS

Tonkatsu is a fried pork cutlet dish, first developed in Tokyo in the 1800s as a type of yōshoku (Japanese versions of foreign food, like Japanese Curry, page 120). Today you can find it in many contexts, like in Katsudon (page 122).

Chicken Katsu (sometimes referred to as Torikatsu) is prepared in the same manner as Tonkatsu, but with chicken thighs. It is not common in Japan but is a staple of Hawaiian plate lunches, which is where I first learned about this dish.

4 boneless pork chops (about 2 lbs total) or 2 lbs chicken thighs

1/4 cup lard or expeller-pressed coconut oil

INITIAL BREADING:

1/4 cup potato starch

1 tsp sea salt

EGG WASH:

2 large eggs, beaten

OUTER BREADING:

2 cups crushed pork rinds (about 3 oz; see note)

1/2 tsp black or white pepper

1 batch Tonkatsu Sauce (page 270)

1/2 head green cabbage, shredded

1. Pound the pork or chicken to 1/4-inch thickness, then sprinkle with a bit of salt and pepper and set aside. Combine the initial breading ingredients and transfer to a wide, shallow bowl. Similarly, place the egg wash in a wide, shallow bowl. Finally, combine the outer breading ingredients and transfer to a wide, shallow bowl. Place these 3 bowls alongside one another so that you can bread the cutlets with minimal mess.

2. Preheat your oven to 170°F and warm the lard in a skillet over medium heat. You want a temperature of around 325°F; adjust the heat as needed to maintain that temperature.

3. Bread 2 cutlets: Dust them with the potato starch mixture, dip them in the eggs (shake off the excess), then coat with the outer breading mixture. Fry in the lard until golden brown and cooked through, 6 to 8 minutes per cutlet, turning every few minutes. Set the cooked cutlets on a plate lined with paper towels and place in the oven to keep warm while you bread and cook the second batch.

4. Once finished, slice the cutlets into large strips and serve with Tonkatsu Sauce over a bed of shredded cabbage.

> ∗ *The easiest way to crush the pork rinds to an even size is to place them in a resealable plastic bag and crush them with a rolling pin.*

JAPANESE CURRY

SERVES: 6 | PREP TIME: 10 MINS | COOK TIME: 20 MINS

Curry is a relatively new dish to Japan, and it has a rich and interesting history. In the 19th century, sailors in the Japanese Navy often suffered from beriberi, a disease caused by a lack of vitamin B1 (thiamine), mostly due to the fact that their diet consisted almost exclusively of white rice. To solve this problem, the Navy tried to introduce bread, but it didn't catch on. In the early 20th century, the Japanese Navy observed that the British Navy served curry to its sailors and decided to follow suit, adding a wheat flour roux to the curry to increase its vitamin B1 content. The resulting starchy, sticky curry was an instant hit in the Navy and spread to the rest of the country from there. Today, curry houses are among the most prominent restaurants in Japan, and curry is a common meal; estimates show that the average Japanese person eats curry at least once a week.

Serve this curry over rice with Tonkatsu (page 118) or Gyudon (page 124), or on its own. In Hawaii, curry houses serve Kimchi (page 148) with their curry, and it's awesome.

1 tbsp expeller-pressed coconut oil

1/2 medium onion, coarsely chopped

1 quart water

3 russet potatoes (about 2 lbs total), peeled and cut into 1 1/2-inch chunks

3 medium carrots, cut into large chunks

3 tbsp butter

3 1/2 tbsp rice flour or coconut flour

1/4 cup S&B Oriental Curry Powder

2 tbsp honey

1/2 cup unsweetened applesauce or 1 apple, peeled and grated

2 tsp sea salt

1. In a stockpot, warm the coconut oil on medium heat until shimmering, about 2 minutes. Add the onion and sauté until softened, about 4 minutes.

2. Add the water and bring to a simmer. Stir in the potatoes and carrots, adding more water if needed to cover everything, then reduce the heat to medium-low and simmer, uncovered, until the potatoes start to soften around the edges, about 10 minutes.

3. While the potatoes and carrots are simmering, prepare your rice flour roux. In a small saucepan, melt the butter on medium-low heat for 1 minute, then stir in the rice flour. Toast until slightly golden, about 3 minutes, then remove from the heat and set aside.

4. Once the potatoes are ready, gently stir in the roux, curry powder, honey, applesauce, and salt, being careful not to break up the potatoes. Simmer until thickened, about 2 minutes, stirring occasionally. Add more salt and honey to taste and serve over Basic Steamed Rice (page 286) or Cauliflower Rice (page 288).

* This curry is fairly spicy, but if you want to make it spicier, add cayenne pepper or togarashi powder to taste.

* Want to tackle making your own Japanese curry powder? Refer to page 305.

KATSUDON

SERVES: 4 | PREP TIME: 10 MINS, PLUS TIME TO MAKE TONKATSU AND DASHI | COOK TIME: 15 MINS

Katsudon gets its name from the words *tonkatsu* ("fried pork cutlet," page 118) and *donburi* ("rice bowl dish"). It's a common ritual for students to eat Katsudon on the eve of a big test, since the word *katsu* can also mean "to be victorious." Personally, I eat it because it tastes good—the onion and dashi sauce in which the egg is basted is simple but elegant.

1 batch Tonkatsu or Chicken Katsu (page 118)

1 cup Dashi (page 108)

2 tbsp tamari

1 tbsp ghee or expeller-pressed coconut oil

1 medium red onion, sliced

4 large eggs, beaten

2 green onions, sliced

4 cups Basic Steamed Rice (page 286) or 1 batch Cauliflower Rice (page 288), for serving

nori strips, to garnish (optional)

1. Prepare the Tonkatsu or Chicken Katsu. Slice and set aside.

2. In a small saucepan, warm the dashi and tamari over medium-low heat until simmering; reduce the heat to low and keep warm.

3. In a skillet, warm the ghee over medium heat, then add the red onion. Sauté until softened and translucent, about 6 minutes, then transfer to a plate. Keep the skillet on the heat.

4. Katsudon is best made in individual batches. Add one-quarter of the sautéed red onion to the skillet, along with one-quarter of the dashi. Bring to a simmer, then place one of the sliced Tonkatsu cutlets over the onion. Pour one beaten egg and one-quarter of the green onions over the cutlet, cover, and simmer for 1 minute.

5. Uncover and transfer the Katsudon to a bowl of rice, then add the nori strips to garnish, if desired. Repeat step 4 with the remaining ingredients and serve.

牛丼

GYUDON

• •

Gyudon, a donburi (rice bowl) dish, first became popular in the 1800s as Japan westernized and started eating more beef. Today, this dish is associated with quick meals. Nearly every Gyudon shop in Japan serves this dish with complimentary Miso Soup (page 110).

• •

1 tbsp ghee or expeller-pressed coconut oil

1 medium onion, thinly sliced

1/2 cup Dashi (page 108) or Chicken Broth (page 264)

2 tbsp tamari

2 tbsp sake or mirin

1 tbsp honey

2 cloves garlic, minced

1/2 inch ginger, peeled and grated, or 1/4 tsp ground ginger

1/2 tsp sea salt

1/4 tsp white pepper

2 lbs thinly sliced marbled beef (sirloin, tenderloin, or rib eye; see note)

4 cups Basic Steamed Rice (page 286) or 1 batch Cauliflower Rice (page 288), for serving

4 large egg yolks, divided, for serving

sesame seeds, to garnish

2 green onions, sliced, to garnish

1. In a wok or skillet, warm the ghee over high heat until shimmering, about 30 seconds. Add the onion and sauté until softened and showing brown spots, about 4 minutes. Add the dashi, tamari, sake, honey, garlic, ginger, salt, and pepper; bring to a boil, reduce the heat to medium-high, and simmer until the liquid has reduced by half, about 4 minutes. Add the beef and simmer until the liquid has mostly evaporated and caramelized into a thick sauce, another 4 minutes.

2. Divide the rice among 4 bowls, then transfer the Gyudon to the bowls of rice. Top each bowl with an egg yolk and serve garnished with sesame seeds and green onions.

★ *In Japan, many people like to eat this dish with extra broth; if you're up for it, try doubling the broth ingredients and see how you like it.*

★ *Before slicing the beef, it's easiest to freeze it for 10 minutes so that it will stay firm when slicing.*

★ *Garnish this dish with your favorite pickled vegetable or togarashi powder.*

鳥照り焼き

CHICKEN TERIYAKI

SERVES: 4 | PREP TIME: 20 MINS, PLUS AT LEAST 30 MINS TO MARINATE | COOK TIME: 20 MINS

Teriyaki sauce can be traced back to the Edo period in Japan (starting in the early 17th century). An increase in urbanization and exposure to outside cultures resulted in an influx of new ingredients, which converged to make this tangy, sweet sauce that is perfect for grilling.

Japanese restaurants gained prominence in the United States in the 1960s, and teriyaki sauce became the household name that it is today.

1/2 batch (1 cup) Teriyaki Sauce (page 272), divided

2 lbs boneless, skinless chicken thighs

sesame seeds, for serving

1. Prepare the Teriyaki Sauce and let cool. Reserve half of the sauce and place in the fridge. Marinate the chicken thighs in the remaining sauce for at least 30 minutes or up to 4 hours.

2. Prepare your grill for indirect grilling by igniting the burners on only one side (gas grill) or by banking the coals to one side (charcoal grill). Place the chicken over direct high heat, brush with the marinade, and grill until browned, about 5 minutes. Flip the chicken and brush again, grilling for another 5 minutes or until the other side has browned.

3. If needed, move the chicken to the cool side of the grill and roast until it has reached an internal temperature of 160°F, about 5 minutes. Brush with the reserved sauce before serving with sesame seeds sprinkled on top.

鮭の照り焼き

SALMON TERIYAKI

SERVES: 4 | PREP TIME: 20 MINS, PLUS 10 MINS TO MARINATE | COOK TIME: 10 MINS

Salmon Teriyaki is a close cousin to Chicken Teriyaki (page 126) in terms of popularity in Japanese-American restaurants; you'll rarely see one on a menu without the other. Something about the sweet, tangy flavor of teriyaki really complements the fatty richness that's often associated with salmon.

1/2 batch (1 cup) Teriyaki Sauce (page 272), divided

4 (6 oz) salmon fillets, skin-on preferred

1 tbsp expeller-pressed coconut oil or ghee, melted

sliced green onions, for serving

1. Prepare the Teriyaki Sauce and let cool; reserve half for another use. Set aside 1/4 cup of the remaining sauce and place in the fridge. Marinate the salmon fillets in the remaining 1/4 cup of sauce for 10 minutes.

2. Grilling is the preferred cooking method. Prepare your grill for direct grilling by igniting all the burners (gas grill) or centering the coals (charcoal grill). Place 2 sheets of heavy-duty aluminum foil over the grill grates, then brush with the coconut oil. Place the salmon fillets on top of the foil, skin side down, and grill until the skin is crispy, about 4 minutes, then turn and grill until just flaking, another 3 minutes. Brush with more sauce before serving with green onions sprinkled on top.

3. The salmon can also be broiled in the oven. Preheat your oven to 450°F, then turn it to the broil setting. Brush the oil on a baking sheet, then place the salmon fillets on top, skin side down, and broil until just flaking, about 8 minutes. Brush with the remaining sauce after 6 minutes. Serve with green onions sprinkled on top.

4. You can also pan-fry the salmon for a crispier texture. Heat the oil in a skillet over medium-high heat until shimmering, about 1 minute, then add the salmon fillets, skin side down. Pan-fry until the skin is crispy, about 4 minutes, then turn and pan-fry until just flaking, another 3 minutes. Brush with more sauce before serving with green onions sprinkled on top.

OKONOMIYAKI

SERVES: 4 | PREP TIME: 15 MINS. PLUS TIME TO MAKE OKONOMIYAKI SAUCE | COOK TIME: 30 MINS

It sounds funny to say, but I know more people who have lost sleep from dreaming about Okonomiyaki than any other dish. This dish is wildly popular in Japan, especially in the Hiroshima area, and is the favored food of Japanophiles around the world. The fervor exists for a reason; the only people I've met who haven't been thrilled about Okonomiyaki are the folks who haven't tried it yet.

KEWPIE-STYLE MAYO [マヨネーズ]

5 tbsp Mayo (page 276)

1 tbsp lemon juice

1 tsp honey

dash of sea salt

dash of white pepper

6 oz bacon, coarsely chopped

BATTER:

1/2 cup white rice flour (see note)

1/2 cup tapioca starch

2/3 cup Chicken Broth (page 264)

2 large eggs, beaten

1/2 tsp sea salt

1/4 tsp white pepper

1/4 medium white onion, finely chopped

2 cloves garlic, minced

1/2 inch ginger, peeled and grated, or 1/4 tsp ground ginger

FILLING:

1/2 head won bok (napa) cabbage, shredded (about 4 cups)

6 oz raw shrimp, peeled and chopped

2 tbsp katsuobushi

TOPPINGS:

1/2 batch Okonomiyaki Sauce (page 270)

2 large nori sheets, ground (about 1/4 cup; see note)

1/4 cup katsuobushi

1. Prepare the Kewpie-Style Mayo: Combine the mayo ingredients and refrigerate.

2. Cook the bacon in a skillet over medium-low heat until just crispy, about 8 minutes, then remove with a slotted spoon and set aside. Reserve the bacon fat.

3. Combine the batter ingredients and stir until smooth. You want the consistency of a thin batter; add more broth if needed. Add the filling ingredients and the bacon and gently mix together.

4. Warm 1 tablespoon of the bacon fat in the skillet over medium-high heat until shimmering, about 1 minute. Scoop one-quarter of the filling mixture into the skillet, pressing down with a spatula or ladle to an even thickness. Pan-fry until golden, about 3 minutes, pressing down often, then flip and continue to pan-fry until cooked through, about 2 more minutes.

5. Repeat step 4 to make 3 more pancakes. Place each pancake on a plate, drizzle with the Okonomiyaki Sauce and Kewpie-Style Mayo in a crisscross pattern, and then scatter the nori and katsuobushi on top.

* If you are avoiding white rice flour, substitute 1/4 cup tapioca starch and one more egg for the rice flour and use only 1/2 cup of broth initially (add more if needed).

* To grind the seaweed, any high-speed blender should work fine; or grind it in a mortar and pestle. You could even whack it a bunch of times with a knife; I won't tell.

* If you run out of reserved bacon fat, use lard or coconut oil.

QUICK JAPANESE SIDES (TSUKEMONO)

SERVES: 4 | PREP TIME: UP TO 30 MINS | COOK TIME: 5 MINS

Tsukemono is a class of Japanese pickled vegetables. There is an entire culture (pun not intended) to these vegetables, with hundreds of different varieties and regional specialties. Tsukemono is served with nearly every traditional Japanese meal and has many uses, including as a garnish, relish, condiment, palate cleanser, or digestive. The vegetables are usually served in various stages of pickling and can be made several months ahead or just a few minutes before serving.

The ideas presented here are just a sample of what's out there. For this recipe in particular, I opted for dishes that can be made and served immediately. Feel free to experiment with various vegetables and flavor combinations; the underlying theme is to add salt and something acidic, like vinegar, wine, or miso.

MISOZUKE (味噌漬け)

1 tbsp miso paste

1 tsp water

2 cups won bok (napa) cabbage, chopped

Misozuke are miso-flavored pickled vegetables, simply seasoned with miso paste and a bit of water. To make Misozuke, combine the miso paste and water in a large mixing bowl, then mix together with the cabbage using your hands. Taste and add more miso paste if needed. Misozuke can be served immediately or left out to ferment for a few hours. Other vegetables to consider: carrots, rhubarb, radishes, turnips, daikon, and rutabaga.

SHIOZUKE (塩漬け)

1/2 cup water

1 tbsp sea salt

1 oz kombu

1 tbsp rice vinegar

1/2 inch ginger, peeled and grated, or 1/4 tsp ground ginger

1 medium cucumber, sliced

Shiozuke are salt-pickled vegetables. Adding other ingredients like kombu, rice vinegar, and/or ginger creates a more complex taste dynamic. To make Shiozuke, bring the water to a boil, then add the salt, kombu, and vinegar, stirring together to dissolve the salt. Allow the water to cool, about 20 minutes, then slice the kombu and add the ginger and cucumber, mixing thoroughly. Shiozuke can be served immediately or left out to ferment for up to 3 hours. Other vegetables to consider: carrots, daikon, and cabbage.

KYURI ASAZUKE [きゅうりの浅漬け] ————————

1 tsp sea salt, or more to taste
1 medium cucumber, cut into chunks
1 tsp apple cider vinegar
togarashi powder, to garnish

Kyuri Asazuke are salt-brined pickles, often flavored with togarashi powder and vinegar. They are often served whole on a stick by street vendors during festivals. To make Kyuri Asazuke, salt the cucumber, then mix with the vinegar. Garnish with togarashi powder and serve.

NUKAZUKE [糠漬け] ————————————

1 tsp sea salt, or more to taste
dash of white pepper
2 medium carrots, cut into chunks
1 tsp sake or rice vinegar
dried lemon peel, to garnish

Nukazuke is an assortment of vegetables pickled in rice bran and served alongside main dishes (teishoku). This simpler version is seasoned with sake and dried lemon peel (available at most spice shops). To make Nukazuke, salt and pepper the carrots, then toss with the sake. Garnish with lemon peel and serve. Other vegetables to consider: cucumber, eggplant, daikon, radishes, and turnip.

沢庵

TAKUAN

SERVES: 4 | PREP TIME: 30 MINS | FERMENT TIME: 2 TO 3 DAYS

Takuan, a pickled daikon radish dish, is also popular in Korea, where it is called Danmuji (단무지) and is usually a little sweeter than its Japanese counterpart. It is typically made from sun-dried daikon, which gives the dish its signature color but is hard to replicate in the United States; this version is made with the fresh stuff and a bit of turmeric to help with the color.

2 cups water

2 tbsp sea salt

3 tbsp organic cane sugar or honey (see note)

1/4 tsp turmeric

2 tbsp rice vinegar

1 daikon (about 1 lb)

1. In a pot, bring the water to a boil over high heat. Once boiling, add the salt, sugar, and turmeric and stir until dissolved. Remove from the heat and allow to cool, about 20 minutes, then stir in the vinegar.

2. As the water cools, slice the daikon into half-moons and pack it into a quart-sized jar.

3. Once the water has cooled, add it to the jar of daikon (you may have leftover liquid, which is fine). Cover the jar and leave it at room temperature for 2 to 3 days if using sugar. Be sure to burp the lid daily to release excess gas.

4. Place the jar in the fridge and store for up to a month.

> ✶ *If you use honey instead of sugar, the Takuan won't ferment due to the natural antibacterial nature of honey. Instead, you can mix in the honey and let it sit for a few hours before enjoying. It will still keep in the fridge for up to a month, and its flavor will mature over time.*

べつたら漬

BETTARAZUKE

SERVES: 4 | PREP TIME: 30 MINS | FERMENT TIME: 2 TO 3 DAYS

Bettarazuke is a pickled daikon dish that is usually made with unfiltered sake (meaning that it still contains the sticky koji bacteria that ferments rice into wine). Koji is easy to find online and can be added to this dish for an authentic texture, but isn't totally necessary—it'll still be delicious without the koji.

2 cups water

2 tbsp sea salt

3 tbsp organic cane sugar or honey (see note)

1 tbsp rice vinegar

3 tbsp sake

1/2 tsp koji (optional)

1 daikon (about 1 lb)

1. In a pot, bring the water to a boil over high heat. Once boiling, add the salt and sugar and stir until dissolved. Remove from the heat, add the vinegar and sake, and allow to cool, about 20 minutes.

2. As the water cools, slice the daikon into half-moons and pack it into a quart-sized jar.

3. Once the water has cooled, add it to the jar of daikon (you may have leftover liquid, which is fine). Cover the jar and leave it at room temperature for 2 to 3 days if using sugar. Be sure to burp the lid daily to release excess gas.

4. Place the jar in the fridge and store for up to a month.

*   *If you use honey instead of sugar, the Bettarazuke won't ferment due to the natural antibacterial nature of honey. Instead, you can mix in the honey and let it sit for a few hours before enjoying. It will still keep in the fridge for up to a month, and its flavor will mature over time.*

해물파전

KOREAN SEAFOOD SCALLION PANCAKE

SERVES: 4 | PREP TIME: 25 MINS | COOK TIME: 20 MINS

Quick language lesson: *jeon* means "pancake" in Korean. This term is associated with a variety of pancakes, from kimchi to kale pancakes. *Pajeon* means "scallion pancakes" and is a subculture within the Korean pancake world. This dish, Haemul Pajeon, is a seafood scallion pancake and yet another layer in the pancake underground. It is so popular that many Korean markets sell frozen bags of prechopped seafood to make it even easier to prepare.

DIPPING SAUCE:

2 tbsp tamari

2 tsp rice vinegar

1 clove garlic, minced

1/2 tsp toasted sesame oil

1/2 tsp Korean red pepper powder

1/2 tsp honey

1/2 tsp sesame seeds

BATTER:

1/2 cup Chicken Broth (page 264)

1/4 cup white rice flour (see note)

1/4 cup tapioca starch

1 large egg, beaten

1/2 tsp fish sauce

1/2 tsp mirin

1/2 tsp sea salt

1/4 tsp white pepper

FILLING:

12 green onions, cut to 3-inch lengths

1/2 red bell pepper, sliced

1 lb raw seafood (shrimp, scallops, squid), coarsely chopped

1 clove garlic, minced

4 tbsp expeller-pressed coconut oil, divided

1. Prepare the dipping sauce: Combine the sauce ingredients in a small bowl and set aside to allow the flavors to marry.

2. Prepare the batter and filling: Place the batter ingredients in a large mixing bowl and stir to combine. You want the consistency of a thin batter; add more broth if needed. Gently stir in the filling ingredients.

3. Warm 1 tablespoon of the coconut oil in a skillet over medium-high heat until shimmering, about 1 minute. The batter will pool at the bottom of the mixing bowl, so be sure to stir it before scooping each portion into the skillet. Scoop one-quarter of the batter into the skillet, pressing down with a spatula or ladle to an even thickness. Pan-fry until golden, about 3 minutes, then flip and pan-fry until cooked through, about 2 more minutes.

4. Repeat step 3 to make 3 more pancakes. Serve with the dipping sauce.

* *Avoiding rice flour? Simply replace it with an additional 1/4 cup of tapioca starch.*

KOREAN FRIED CHICKEN

SERVES: 4 | PREP TIME: 10 MINS, PLUS 1 HOUR TO REFRIGERATE | COOK TIME: 40 MINS

· ·

Korean Fried Chicken is a relatively new phenomenon, but one that has taken the Korean restaurant world by storm. Today, you can find entire restaurants dedicated to these succulent, lightly battered pieces of gold. Most restaurants fry their chicken twice in order to get it extra-crispy, but tossing the wings in a starch coating and setting them in the fridge works just as well. I adopted this technique from J. Kenji López-Alt, the managing culinary director of *Serious Eats*.

While often tossed in sauce at the end, I prefer to eat these wings plain; either way, sauce instructions are provided below. A common accompaniment to this chicken is Takuan (page 134). Also: lots of alcohol.

· ·

INITIAL COATING:

1/4 cup arrowroot, tapioca, or potato starch

2 tsp kosher salt

1/2 tsp baking soda

2 to 3 lbs chicken wings and drumettes

2 cups lard, tallow, or expeller-pressed coconut oil

BATTER:

1/2 cup arrowroot starch

1/4 cup water

1 tbsp vodka (optional)

SAUCE (OPTIONAL):

1/4 cup water

1/4 cup tamari

1/4 cup honey

1/4 cup mirin

1 tsp toasted sesame oil

1 tsp rice vinegar

1/2 tsp Korean red pepper powder

1/2 inch ginger, peeled and minced or grated, or 1/4 tsp ground ginger

1 tbsp arrowroot starch

1 tbsp cold water

1. Combine the initial coating ingredients, then toss with the chicken. Shake off any excess coating. Place on a baking sheet lined with a wire rack, then refrigerate uncovered for 1 hour.

2. Preheat your oven to 170°F. In a skillet, heat the lard to a stable 350°F (medium-high heat). Combine the batter ingredients—the consistency should be like very thin pancake batter (closer to water than gravy). With your fingers, dip a chicken wing into the batter, allow to drip for a few seconds, and then add to the hot fat. Repeat with more wings; you'll likely need to fry them in several batches depending on the size of your skillet. (I was able to fit about 12 wings at a time in a 12-inch skillet.) Fry the chicken until light brown and crispy, flipping and jostling every couple of minutes, about 10 minutes per batch. Place the cooked wings on a different baking sheet lined with paper towels with a cooling rack set on top, then lightly salt them. Place in the oven to keep warm while you cook the next batch.

3. Repeat this process until all the wings are cooked, then serve and enjoy.

4. To make the sauce, combine all the ingredients except the arrowroot starch and cold water in a small saucepan. Bring to a simmer over medium-low heat, about 5 minutes. Stir together the arrowroot starch and cold water to create a slurry, then add half of the slurry to the simmering sauce. Increase the heat to medium and stir until combined and thickened, about 1 minute, adding the other half of the slurry if the sauce doesn't thicken. Toss with the chicken wings before serving.

BULGOGI

SERVES: 4 | PREP TIME: 10 MINS, PLUS AT LEAST 30 MINS TO MARINATE | COOK TIME: 10 MINS

Bulgogi is one of the first Korean words I learned. I have fond memories of entering a restaurant in South Korea as a young man, looking thoughtfully at the waitress, proudly proclaiming my newfound word, and basically being treated to a magical meal. The word *bulgogi* literally translates to "fire meat," indicating that this marinated beef dish is best prepared over a grill, though I also provide stovetop cooking instructions at the end of the recipe.

MARINADE:

1 pear or apple, cut into chunks, or 1/2 cup unsweetened applesauce

1/2 medium onion, cut into chunks

1 tbsp tamari

2 tbsp honey

4 cloves garlic

1/2 inch ginger, peeled and sliced, or 1/4 tsp ground ginger

1/2 tsp white pepper

2 tsp toasted sesame oil

splash of mirin

2 lbs thinly sliced marbled beef (sirloin, tenderloin, or rib eye)

2 green onions, sliced, to garnish

sesame seeds, to garnish

1. Combine the marinade ingredients in a blender and blend until smooth. Place the marinade and beef in a resealable plastic bag and marinate for at least 30 minutes, overnight preferred.

2. Prepare your grill for direct grilling by igniting all the burners (gas grill) or centering the coals (charcoal grill). Place a grill pan or a couple sheets of heavy-duty aluminum foil on the grill grates, then add the beef. Grill over direct high heat until cooked through and browned, about 5 minutes, then garnish with green onions and sesame seeds and serve.

3. To cook the beef on the stovetop, heat 1 tablespoon coconut oil in a wide skillet over high heat until shimmering, about 30 seconds. Add the beef in batches and stir-fry until cooked through and browned. Garnish with green onions and sesame seeds and serve.

KALBI

SERVES: 4 | PREP TIME: 15 MINS. PLUS TIME TO MARINATE OVERNIGHT | COOK TIME: 10 MINS

· ·

At some point in my life, I woke up one morning and Kalbi had unexpectedly dethroned Bulgogi (page 142) as my favorite Korean meat dish. This recipe in particular, which uses cross-cut short ribs, is a lot of fun to eat; not only do you get to enjoy tender ribs, but you get to gnaw on the connective tissue (which I lovingly refer to as "meat gum") that surrounds each bone. Even better is the fact that I'm the only one in my family who likes the connective tissue; more for me!

Serve with Basic Steamed Rice (page 286), Kimchi (page 148), Quick Korean Sides (pages 152–155), and lettuce leaves to wrap around the meat.

· ·

MARINADE:

1 pear, peeled and grated, or 1/2 cup unsweetened applesauce

6 cloves garlic, minced

1/2 inch ginger, peeled and grated, or 1/4 tsp ground ginger

1/2 cup soda water

1/2 cup tamari

1/4 cup honey

1/4 cup toasted sesame oil

2 tbsp Chinese cooking wine

2 tbsp sesame seeds

juice of 1 lime (2 tbsp)

3 lbs short ribs, cut across the bone (often referred to as flanken, English, or L.A. cut)

1. Combine all the marinade ingredients, then pour over the ribs in a resealable plastic bag and mix thoroughly to coat all the pieces evenly. Marinate in the refrigerator overnight.

2. The next day, prepare your grill for direct grilling by igniting all the burners (gas grill) or centering the coals (charcoal grill). Grill the ribs over direct high heat until cooked through, about 3 minutes per side.

> *Kalbi is often dipped in gireumjang, which is made by combining 2 parts salt and 1 part black pepper and then adding sesame oil until it becomes a thick, grainy sauce.*

MEAT JUN

SERVES: 4 | PREP TIME: 10 MINS, PLUS 1 HOUR TO MARINATE | COOK TIME: 15 MINS

• •

Meat Jun isn't actually a Korean dish, but a dish that is served in Korean restaurants in Hawaii. Much like Chinese-American cuisine, Koreans living in Hawaii wanted to make a dish that appealed to the local clientele, and they started battering and frying thin slices of marinated beef (referred to as "teri beef" in Hawaii). Today, it's one of the most iconic and popular Korean dishes in Hawaii.

• •

2 lbs rib eye or flank steak

SAUCE:

1/4 cup water

2 tbsp tamari

2 tbsp Chinese cooking wine

2 tbsp honey

1 tsp toasted sesame oil

4 cloves garlic, minced

2 tbsp Korean red pepper powder

1/4 cup expeller-pressed coconut oil or lard

2 tbsp white rice flour

2 tbsp tapioca starch

1/2 tsp sea salt

1/4 tsp black pepper

3 large eggs, beaten

1. Prepare the beef. Some butchers will preslice beef upon request; otherwise, freeze the meat for 10 minutes, then thinly slice it into cutlets. If you're up for it, you can also gently pound the beef to tenderize it.

2. Combine the sauce ingredients, then divide in half. Place the beef in a resealable plastic bag with half of the sauce; mix thoroughly. In a blender, combine the remaining half of the sauce with the Korean red pepper powder and blend into a smooth red sauce, called gochujang; add water if it's too thick. Refrigerate the beef and the gochujang sauce for 1 hour.

3. Warm the coconut oil in a large skillet over medium-high heat. Remove the gochujang sauce from the fridge to warm while you cook the beef. Remove the beef from the marinade and gently pat dry. Combine the flour, starch, salt, and pepper. In batches, dredge the beef in the flour mixture, then in the beaten eggs, and then add to the oil. Fry until golden brown, about 1 minute per side, then set on paper towels to drain. Repeat with the remaining slices of beef.

4. Slice and serve with the gochujang sauce.

KIMCHI AND WHITE KIMCHI

YIELD: 2 QUARTS (ABOUT 12 SERVINGS) | PREP TIME: 40 MINS | FERMENT TIME: 3 TO 7 DAYS

Kimchi is an integral part of the Korean identity, well beyond its cuisine; since Korean winters are harsh, fermenting vegetables was the only way that early Koreans were able to eat a balanced diet during the cold months. Moreover, the probiotic content of fermented vegetables allowed the Korean people to better digest their first grains, barley and millet. Essentially, Kimchi contributed to the survival of the people living on the Korean peninsula.

Baek Kimchi (otherwise known as White Kimchi) is made without regular Kimchi's trademark red pepper powder. This version is a great alternative for children and is autoimmune friendly since it contains no nightshades.

1 to 2 lbs won bok (napa) cabbage

2 tbsp sea salt

2 tbsp fish sauce

3 cloves garlic

1/2 small white onion, quartered

1/4 pear or Asian pear

1/2 inch ginger, peeled and chopped, or 1/4 tsp ground ginger

3 tbsp Korean red pepper powder (omit for White Kimchi)

2 tbsp julienned daikon

2 green onions, sliced into 2-inch pieces

1. Peel off and discard any damaged outer layers of the cabbage. Make a slice lengthwise through the center of the bottom third of the cabbage, then pull the halves apart with your hands. This enables you to cut the cabbage in half lengthwise without damaging the leaves. Repeat with each half to cut the cabbage into quarters. Cut these quarters into 1 1/2-inch-wide pieces, discarding the bottom inch (which looks more like a stem than leaves). Don't fret over cutting the cabbage exactly to specification; this is just how it's often cut in Korea.

2. Place a large colander in the sink, then rinse the cabbage. Salt liberally and mix thoroughly with your hands. Let the cabbage sit in the colander for 30 minutes, then rinse and drain and pat dry with paper towels.

3. In a blender, blend the fish sauce, garlic, white onion, pear, and ginger, then mix in the Korean red pepper powder (omit for White Kimchi), daikon, and green onions. Put the cabbage in a large bowl, then mix in the blended sauce.

4. Pack the mixture into two quart-sized jars (leave about 1/2 inch of space at the top of each jar), cover, and ferment at room temperature for at least 3 days or up to a week. Burp the lids at least once a day to prevent pressure buildup; it'll build up faster than you might expect. If you forget to burp for a day or two, be sure to burp it in the sink to catch any pressurized juices. Once the taste is to your liking, transfer the jars to the fridge and store for up to a month.

JAPANESE AND KOREAN FAVORITES

CUCUMBER KIMCHI

YIELD: 2 QUARTS (ABOUT 12 SERVINGS) | PREP TIME: 40 MINS | FERMENT TIME: 2 TO 3 DAYS

Cucumber Kimchi (Oisobagi) is a delicious way to enjoy kimchi in a new way. Even better is the fact that cucumbers take less time to ferment than cabbage, so you can enjoy this dish sooner! Some people like to eat this dish immediately after making it, without fermenting it at all. That's fine, but bear in mind that it won't have those cool probiotic bugs without a proper fermentation.

When selecting cucumbers, try to get them fresh from the farm, or buy organic if from a supermarket; *lactobacillus* bacteria covers the skin of cucumbers, which starts the fermentation process. Non-organic cucumbers often don't have the bacteria, but you can still start the fermentation process by adding 1/2 teaspoon whey (the liquid found at the top of yogurt; see my Tzatziki Sauce recipe, page 284) or some juice from previously pickled Kimchi.

4 medium cucumbers (about 2 lbs total), cut into chunks

1 tbsp sea salt

2 tbsp fish sauce

3 cloves garlic

1/2 medium white onion

1/2 pear or Asian pear

1/2 inch ginger, peeled and chopped, or 1/4 tsp ground ginger

2 tbsp grated daikon

2 tbsp Korean red pepper powder

2 green onions, sliced into 2-inch pieces

1. Place a large colander in the sink, then add the cucumber chunks. Salt liberally and mix thoroughly with your hands. Let the cucumbers sit in the colander for 30 minutes, then rinse and drain and pat dry with paper towels.

2. In a blender, blend the fish sauce, garlic, white onion, pear, and ginger until smooth. In a large mixing bowl, combine the blended sauce, cucumbers, daikon, red pepper powder, and green onions; mix thoroughly with your hands.

3. Pack the mixture into two quart-sized jars (leave about 1/2 inch of space at the top of each jar), cover, and ferment at room temperature for 2 to 3 days. Burp the lids at least once a day to prevent pressure buildup, and start tasting after the first day. Once the taste is to your liking, transfer the jars to the fridge and store for up to a month.

QUICK KOREAN SIDES

Korean side dishes, commonly referred to as banchan, contain a variety of flavors that complement the entire meal. They're super easy to make and can be thrown together in minutes; pair them with Kimchi (shown, page 148) and/or Cucumber Kimchi (page 150) and you're good to go.

KOREAN BEAN SPROUTS (숙주나물)

SERVES: 4 | PREP TIME: 5 MINS | COOK TIME: 8 MINS

1 lb mung bean sprouts

2 cloves garlic, minced

1 tsp tamari

1 tsp toasted sesame oil

1 tsp sesame seeds

1/4 tsp white pepper

sea salt to taste (about 1 tsp)

Bring a pot of salted water to a boil, then add the bean sprouts. Reduce the heat to medium and simmer until softened, about 4 minutes, then drain and rinse with cold water until cool to the touch. Squeeze out any remaining water from the sprouts, then transfer to a mixing bowl. Toss with the remaining ingredients and serve.

KOREAN SPINACH (시금치나물)

SERVES: 4 | PREP TIME: 5 MINS | COOK TIME: 5 MINS

1 lb fresh spinach or baby spinach, washed

2 cloves garlic, minced

1 tbsp tamari

1/2 tbsp sesame seeds

1 tsp toasted sesame oil

1/4 tsp togarashi powder or Korean red pepper powder

Bring a pot of salted water to a boil, then add the spinach. Reduce the heat to medium and parboil until bright green and soft, about 30 seconds, then drain and rinse with cold water until cool to the touch. Squeeze out any remaining water from the spinach, then transfer to a mixing bowl. Toss with the remaining ingredients and serve.

KOREAN CUCUMBERS (오이나물)

SERVES: 4 | PREP TIME: 30 MINS

2 cucumbers or 4 Persian cucumbers

2 tbsp sea salt

1 tsp rice vinegar

1/2 tsp toasted sesame oil

1/4 white pepper

sea salt

Thinly slice the cucumbers, then salt liberally. Allow to sit for 30 minutes to draw their water out. Drain, then wrap in a cloth towel and squeeze out as much water as possible. Combine with the remaining ingredients, season with salt to taste, and serve.

KOREAN SEASONED SEAWEED (돌자반무침)

SERVES: 4 | PREP TIME: 10 MINS

1/2 cup mixed seaweed (wakame, arame, or kombu)

2 cloves garlic, minced

1 tsp sesame seeds

1/2 tsp toasted sesame oil

1/4 tsp white pepper

sea salt

Place the seaweed in a large bowl, then cover with about 2 cups warm water. Allow to sit until soft, about 10 minutes. Squeeze most of the water out of the seaweed, then combine with the remaining ingredients. Season with salt to taste and serve.

BI BIM BAP

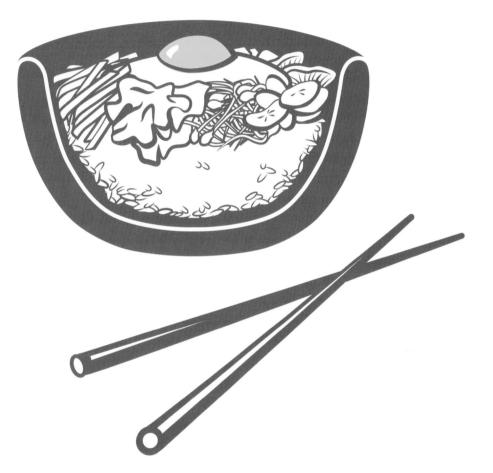

* *Looking for a quick meal? Serve these sides in a rice bowl with Kimchi (page 148), Bulgogi (page 142), and a fried egg; congratulations, you've just made Bi Bim Bap, one of my favorite dishes to say (and eat).*

southeast Asia and Beyond

ต้มข่าไก่

TOM KHA GAI

SERVES: 4 AS A SIDE, 2 AS A MAIN | PREP TIME: 10 MINS, PLUS TIME TO MAKE CHILI OIL | COOK TIME: 25 MINS

Tom Kha Gai is a coconut soup whose name literally translates to "chicken galangal soup." I wasn't familiar with this soup until recently (I always ordered Tom Yum, page 162), but one day I helped my friends Brent Schrader and Heather Gerum make some for their excellent blog, *Virginia is for Hunter-Gatherers,* and I was instantly smitten.

In Laos, this soup is served with fresh dill instead of cilantro. It's delicious that way, too.

SOUP BASE:

4 cups Chicken Broth (page 264)

2 cups water

6 fresh or dried kaffir lime leaves, roughly torn, or grated zest of 1 lime

2 stalks lemongrass, white parts only, thinly sliced

2 inches galangal or ginger, peeled and coarsely chopped

2 boneless, skinless chicken breasts (about 1 lb total), thinly sliced

1 (14 oz) can full-fat coconut milk

6 oz mushrooms (straw, enoki, shiitake, oyster, or white; see note)

1 tbsp fish sauce

juice of 1/2 lime (1 tbsp)

1 tsp coconut palm sugar or honey (optional)

sea salt to taste (about 1 tsp)

TO GARNISH:

large handful of fresh cilantro, stems included, chopped

Thai Chili Oil (page 268)

1. Combine the soup base ingredients in a stockpot and bring to a boil over high heat. Reduce the heat to medium-low and gently simmer for 15 minutes to allow the flavors to marry. Strain and discard the solids, returning the broth to the stockpot.

2. Add the chicken to the broth and bring to a simmer over medium heat, then reduce the heat to medium-low and simmer until just cooked through, about 4 minutes. Stir in the coconut milk and mushrooms and simmer until the mushrooms are tender, about 2 minutes, then add the fish sauce, lime juice, and sugar. Taste and add salt and more fish sauce and lime juice if desired.

3. Serve garnished with cilantro and Thai Chili Oil.

* *If using shiitake mushrooms, remove the stems before cooking—they are too tough to eat.*

* *Optional ingredients to consider when adding the mushrooms: Chinese cabbage, bell pepper, and carrots.*

GANG JUED

SERVES: 4 AS A SIDE, 2 AS A MAIN | PREP TIME: 15 MINS, PLUS TIME TO MAKE MEATBALLS AND CHILI OIL | COOK TIME: 10 MINS

• •

Not quite as popular as Tom Kha Gai (page 158) or Tom Yum Goong (page 162), Gang Jued has a reputation in Thailand for being the ideal soup to eat when you are not feeling well. Its reputation is well deserved; the addition of chicken broth gives it that hearty chicken soup feel, and the generous amount of Chinese cabbage in this dish gives it a refreshing texture. Also, this may be the only time I've added cucumbers to a hot soup, and it's an awesome experience.

• •

FRIED SHALLOTS (MAKES 1/2 CUP):

1/4 cup expeller-pressed coconut oil

3 shallots, thinly sliced

pinch of sea salt

4 cups Chicken Broth (page 264)

2 cups water

1 batch Vietnamese Pork Meatballs (page 182)

1 lb Chinese cabbage, chopped

2 tsp fish sauce

1 tsp lime juice

1 tsp sea salt

1/2 tsp white pepper

2 cucumbers, peeled, seeded, and cut into 1/2-inch-thick half-moons

TO GARNISH (OPTIONAL):

chopped fresh cilantro

sliced green onions

Thai Chili Oil (page 268)

1. Prepare the fried shallots. Warm the coconut oil in a wok or skillet over medium-high heat until shimmering, about 2 minutes. Add the shallots and fry, stirring constantly to avoid burning, until golden brown, about 5 minutes. Transfer the shallots to a plate lined with paper towels to cool and season with the salt. Cover and use within a week. Reserve the oil for other cooking adventures.

2. Combine the broth and water in a stockpot and bring to a simmer over medium heat. Add the meatballs and cabbage and simmer until the cabbage is bright green, about 1 minute. Add the fish sauce, lime juice, salt, and pepper; taste and add more salt if needed.

3. Remove from the heat and stir in the cucumbers. Garnish as desired.

> * This dish can be made by simmering raw meatballs, saving you the step of grilling or pan-frying them separately. To do so, prepare the meatball mixture as directed on page 182, then form it into small balls and drop into the simmering broth. Simmer until the meatballs begin to float, then add the cabbage and finish the recipe as instructed above.

ต้มยำกุ้ง

TOM YUM GOONG

SERVES: 4 | PREP TIME: 10 MINS, PLUS TIME TO MAKE CHILI OIL | COOK TIME: 15 MINS

You might think that the Thai words *Tom Yum* have something to do with someone named Tom really liking this soup, but they don't—they mean "hot" and "sour." This version of the soup is made with shrimp and is probably the most recognizable form of this tasty, refreshing dish. It is one of the most popular soups in Southeast Asia.

SOUP BASE:

2 cups Chicken Broth (page 264)

4 cups water

1 stalk lemongrass, white part only, thinly sliced

1 inch galangal or ginger, peeled and coarsely chopped

4 fresh or dried kaffir lime leaves

1 lb raw shrimp (see note)

10 oz mushrooms (white, straw, oyster, or shiitake), sliced (see note)

1 tbsp fish sauce

1 tsp sea salt

1/2 tsp white pepper

juice of 1 lime (2 tbsp)

TO GARNISH (OPTIONAL):

chopped fresh cilantro

Thai basil leaves

Thai Chili Oil (page 268)

thinly sliced Thai chiles

1. Combine the soup base ingredients in a stockpot and bring to a boil over medium-high heat. Reduce the heat to medium-low and simmer for 10 minutes to allow the flavors to marry. Strain and discard the solids, returning the broth to the stockpot.

2. Increase the heat to medium. Add the shrimp and sliced mushrooms to the stockpot and simmer until the mushrooms have softened and the shrimp are pink and curled, about 3 minutes. Add the fish sauce, salt, and pepper; taste and add more salt if needed.

3. Remove from the heat, add the lime juice, and serve with any desired garnishes.

★ *If desired, peel the shrimp ahead of time so that they're easier to eat.*

★ *If using shiitake mushrooms, remove the stems before cooking—they are too tough to eat.*

ส้มตำ

GREEN PAPAYA SALAD

SERVES: 4 | PREP TIME: 20 MINS, PLUS TIME TO MAKE CHILI OIL

It's not often that you would associate a salad with unripe fruit, dried shrimp, or spiciness, but that's basically what you experience with Green Papaya Salad. The hardest ingredient to find for this dish is the green papaya itself, but if you have a local Asian market nearby, it will likely carry them.

2 tbsp dried shrimp

SAUCE:

2 cloves garlic

juice of 1 1/2 limes (3 tbsp)

2 tbsp fish sauce

1 tbsp coconut palm sugar or honey (optional)

1 tbsp Thai Chili Oil (page 268)

1 tsp crushed red pepper, or more to taste

1/2 tsp sea salt

1 medium green papaya (about 2 lbs)

handful of green beans, trimmed and cut in half crosswise

20 cherry tomatoes, sliced in half

1/4 cup chopped roasted macadamia nuts, divided

1. Submerge the shrimp in hot water for 20 minutes, then drain and set aside.

2. While the shrimp soak, prepare the sauce and papaya. Combine the sauce ingredients in a blender; blend until smooth, then set aside. Cut the papaya in half crosswise, then peel off its skin. Using a julienne peeler or cheese grater, cut the papaya into 3-inch-long strips.

3. Place the green beans in a large mixing bowl, then bruise with a large spoon or ladle to release their juices. Add the papaya, cherry tomatoes, half of the macadamia nuts, soaked shrimp, and sauce and toss until well mixed.

4. Taste and add salt if needed. Serve topped with the remaining macadamia nuts.

★ Reserve the shrimp-flavored water for other shrimp-based cooking adventures, like Tom Yum Goong (page 162).

PAD THAI

SERVES: 4 | PREP TIME: 15 MINS, PLUS UP TO 30 MINS TO MAKE NOODLES | COOK TIME: 30 MINS

It's somewhat surprising, but Pad Thai, despite being one of Thailand's national dishes, actually comes from Vietnam. Originally influenced by Chinese cuisine, the dish was relatively unknown in Thailand until the 20th century. It was part of a Thai government campaign in the 1940s to create a national dish that both reflected the Thai spirit and increased rice noodle production to help propel the Thai economy.

The key to authentic-tasting Pad Thai is tamarind, which can be found at most Asian and Hispanic markets. This dish is made in a hot wok and turns out best when prepared in small batches (in this case, individual servings).

SAUCE:

1 tbsp expeller-pressed coconut oil

30 roasted macadamia nuts, chopped

3 cloves garlic, minced

3 tbsp tamarind paste (see note)

3 tbsp fish sauce

1 1/2 tbsp honey

1 1/2 tsp sea salt

1 1/2 tsp white pepper

1/2 tsp cayenne pepper

NOODLES:

6 zucchini or yellow squash (about 3 lbs total) or

12 oz sweet potato noodles or

12 oz rice noodles

CHICKEN:

1 tbsp expeller-pressed coconut oil

1 lb boneless, skinless chicken thighs, cut into bite-sized pieces

THE REST (DIVIDE INTO FOURTHS):

4 tbsp expeller-pressed coconut oil

1 lb raw shrimp, peeled

2 carrots, julienned

handful of mung bean sprouts

2 large eggs, scrambled

20 roasted macadamia nuts, chopped

handful of chopped fresh cilantro

juice of 1 lime (2 tbsp)

sea salt and white pepper

1. In a small pan, warm 1 tablespoon of coconut oil over medium-low heat. Add the macadamia nuts and garlic and toast until golden and aromatic, about 1 minute. Add the remaining sauce ingredients and simmer until well mixed and slightly thickened, about 4 minutes, then set aside. This sauce can be prepared ahead of time and stored in the fridge for up to a week or in the freezer for up to 3 months.

2. Prepare the noodles. If using zucchini or yellow squash, spiral-slice them, blanch in boiling water for 30 seconds, then rinse in cold water and squeeze out half of the liquid. If using sweet potato noodles, boil until tender, about 6 minutes, then drain and rinse with cold water. If using rice noodles, soak in warm water for 30 minutes, blanch in boiling water until tender, about 1 minute, and then drain and rinse with cold water.

3. Heat 1 tablespoon of coconut oil in a wok or skillet over medium-high heat until shimmering, about 1 minute. Add the chicken and stir-fry until just cooked through, about 4 minutes, then remove from the wok and set aside.

4. Add 1 tablespoon of coconut oil and one-quarter of the shrimp to the wok and stir-fry until the shrimp are pink and curling, about 2 minutes. Add one-quarter of the chicken and sauce and stir-fry until combined, about 1 minute. Add one-quarter of the noodles and stir-fry until softened, 1 to 2 minutes depending on the type of noodle. Add one-quarter of the carrots, bean sprouts, eggs, macadamia nuts, cilantro, and lime juice and stir-fry to combine. Taste and add salt and pepper if needed, then transfer to a serving dish.

5. Repeat step 4 to prepare 3 more servings.

* Some tamarind paste has shell chunks in it. To prepare the paste, place it in a small pot and add enough water to cover it; bring to a boil and strain out the shell chunks, then return the watery tamarind paste to the pot and boil down until thick, about 5 minutes.

* This dish is a great way to have a fun family night where everyone chooses the ingredients they want and the cook makes the Pad Thai to order. Consider adding other ingredients to the mix, like shallots, green onion, daikon, or cabbage.

PAD SEE EW

SERVES: 4 | PREP TIME: 10 MINS, PLUS UP TO 30 MINS TO MAKE NOODLES | COOK TIME: 20 MINS

• •

Pad See Ew (sometimes spelled Phat Si Io) is a Chinese-influenced Thai and Laotian dish made with thick rice noodles. You can see its Chinese influence right in the name; "See Ew" is derived from the same word as the "Siu" found in Char Siu (page 88).

Although it often takes a backseat to its more popular cousin, Pad Thai (page 166), the balanced sweet and savory taste of Pad See Ew cannot be overstated. In addition to chicken, this dish can be made with thin slices of pork loin, steak, or shrimp.

• •

NOODLES:

6 zucchini or yellow squash (about 3 lbs total) or

12 oz sweet potato noodles or

12 oz wide, flat rice noodles

SAUCE:

1/4 cup tamari

1/4 cup coconut palm sugar or honey

2 tbsp fish sauce

2 tsp Chinese cooking wine

2 tsp shrimp paste

1 tsp white pepper

5 tbsp expeller-pressed coconut oil, divided

2 large eggs, beaten

4 cloves garlic, minced, divided

2 lbs boneless, skinless chicken thighs, thinly sliced, divided

1 lb Chinese cabbage (choy sum or kai lan) or broccoli, cut into 2-inch pieces, divided

1 to 3 bird's-eye chiles (depending on your heat tolerance), seeds and ribs removed, sliced

1. Prepare the noodles. If using zucchini or yellow squash, spiral-slice them, blanch in boiling water for 30 seconds, then rinse in cold water and squeeze out half of the liquid. If using sweet potato noodles, boil until tender, about 6 minutes, then drain and rinse with cold water. If using rice noodles, soak for 30 minutes in warm water, blanch in boiling water until tender, about 1 minute, and then drain and rinse with cold water.

2. Combine the sauce ingredients in a small bowl and set aside.

3. In a wok or skillet, warm 1 tablespoon of the coconut oil over medium-high heat until shimmering, about 1 minute, then add the eggs. Cook, stirring occasionally, until cooked through and scrambled, then remove from the wok and set aside.

4. It's best to make this dish in 2 batches to prevent overcrowding. Add 2 tablespoons of the remaining coconut oil to the wok and increase the heat to high. When the oil is shimmering, add half of the garlic and sauté until lightly browned, about 15 to 20 seconds. Add half of the sliced chicken and stir-fry until mostly cooked through, about 5 minutes, adding 1 tablespoon of the sauce during the last minute of cooking. Add half of the cabbage and stir-fry until wilted, about 2 minutes. Add half of the noodles, stir in 1/4 cup of the sauce, and toss until well combined but before the noodles start to melt, about 1 minute. Add half of the scrambled egg, remove from the wok, and set aside.

5. Repeat step 4 with the remaining ingredients, then garnish with the sliced chiles and serve.

THAI GREEN CURRY

SERVES: 4 | PREP TIME: 10 MINS | COOK TIME: 20 MINS

The Thai word for green curry actually translates to "sweet green curry," but that doesn't imply that this dish is sweet. Instead, "sweet green" means "light green" in Thai.

While the idea of making curry from scratch may be daunting initially, nothing could be further from the truth; it's actually pretty fun. My curry paste has quite a few ingredients, but basically all you do is throw them together in a blender; the paste will keep for a month in the fridge or up to 6 months in the freezer. This recipe yields enough paste to make three batches of curry. If you don't have access to the ingredients needed, Mae Ploy and Maesri premade curry pastes are tasty and convenient and have relatively clean ingredient lists (they have a little added sugar).

Making the actual curry dish is even easier—it's a 20-minute meal, if not less. Serve over Basic Steamed Rice (page 286) or Cauliflower Rice (page 288).

PASTE (MAKES 1 1/2 CUPS. ENOUGH FOR 3 CURRIES):

handful of fresh cilantro, stems included

handful of Thai basil leaves

2 jalapeños, seeds and ribs removed, sliced

1 stalk lemongrass, white part only, thinly sliced

1 inch galangal or ginger, peeled

2 large shallots

4 cloves garlic

1 green cardamom pod or 1/4 tsp ground cardamom

1 tsp shrimp paste

1 tsp fish sauce

1 tsp sea salt

1/2 tsp ground coriander

1/2 tsp ground cumin

1/2 tsp white pepper

juice of 1 lime (2 tbsp)

grated zest of 1 lime

2 tbsp virgin coconut oil

1 (14 oz) can full-fat coconut milk, divided

2 lbs chicken thighs, cut into bite-sized chunks

1 tbsp fish sauce

10 Thai basil leaves, plus extra for garnish

sliced Thai chiles, to garnish (optional)

1. In a blender, combine all the curry paste ingredients and blend into a smooth paste. Add water if needed to help the blending process, but the shallots may release enough liquid on their own. The curry paste can be made ahead and stored in the fridge for up to a month or frozen for up to 6 months.

2. In a large skillet, warm the coconut oil on medium heat until shimmering, about 2 minutes. Add 1/2 cup of the curry paste and stir to combine with the oil. Sauté until fragrant and the oil starts to separate from the paste, 2 to 3 minutes.

3. Stir in one-third of the coconut milk. Bring to a simmer, reduce the heat to medium-low, and cook until slightly darkened, about 3 minutes.

4. Stir in the chicken and another third of the coconut milk. Simmer until the chicken is cooked through, about 8 to 10 minutes, stirring occasionally.

5. Stir in the remaining coconut milk, fish sauce, and Thai basil leaves. Return to a simmer, then remove from the heat once the leaves have softened. Serve garnished with more Thai basil leaves and sliced Thai chiles, if desired.

* *Vegetables can be added at the end of step 4. Try eggplant, broccoli, bell pepper, carrots, mushrooms, Chinese cabbage, snow or snap peas, or bamboo shoots.*

* *Any protein can be substituted for the chicken. Try thinly sliced steak or pork loin, firm white fish, or shrimp. Simply adjust step 4 to simmer until the protein is cooked through.*

THAI RED CURRY

SERVES: 4 | PREP TIME: 15 MINS, PLUS 30 MINS TO SOAK CHILES | COOK TIME: 20 MINS

Like Thai Green Curry (page 170), this red curry is spicy and soupy in nature. While it's typically made with spicy red Thai chiles, I've found that using large dried chiles (like Anaheim, guajillo, or New Mexico chiles) imparts a red color and similar taste without making the dish overwhelmingly hot. As written, this recipe is mildly spicy; to kick it up a notch, add more Thai chiles.

PASTE (MAKES 1/2 CUP, ENOUGH FOR 2 CURRIES):

4 large dried red chile peppers, seeds removed

2 Thai chiles or 1 jalapeño, seeds removed (add more for more heat)

10 cloves garlic

1 tsp ground cumin

1 tsp ground coriander

1/2 tsp shrimp paste

1 tbsp white peppercorns

3 shallots

grated zest of 1/2 lime

1 inch galangal or ginger, peeled

1 stalk lemongrass, white part only, thinly sliced

small handful of fresh cilantro stems

2 tbsp virgin coconut oil

2 lbs steak, chicken breasts, chicken thighs, or shrimp, cut into bite-sized chunks

1 (14 oz) can full-fat coconut milk, divided

1 tbsp fish sauce

1 red bell pepper, thinly sliced

juice of 1/2 lime (1 tbsp)

small handful of Thai basil leaves

TO GARNISH:

sliced Thai chiles (optional)

lime wedges

fresh cilantro

1. Soak the dried chiles in warm water for 30 minutes.

2. Place the soaked chiles, 1/4 cup of the water in which you soaked them, and the rest of the curry paste ingredients in a blender. Blend until smooth, adding water if needed to help the blending process, then set aside. The curry paste can be made ahead and stored in the fridge for up to a month or frozen for up to 6 months.

3. Warm the coconut oil in a large skillet over medium-high heat, then add the steak, chicken, or shrimp. Stir-fry until browned and cooked through, in batches if needed, 1 minute for shrimp, 3 minutes for steak, or 6 minutes for chicken. Remove from the skillet and set aside.

4. Reduce the heat to medium and add 1/4 cup of the curry paste to the skillet. Bring to a simmer and sauté until aromatic and darkened, stirring constantly, about 4 minutes.

5. Add half of the coconut milk and stir to incorporate. Simmer until thick and darkened, about 8 minutes, then stir in the steak, chicken, or shrimp and any accumulated juices. Stir in the remaining coconut milk, fish sauce, and bell pepper and cook until the pepper starts to soften, about 1 minute, then add the lime juice and Thai basil leaves. Taste and add salt if needed, then serve, garnished with sliced Thai chiles (if using), lime wedges, and cilantro.

แกงมัสมั่น

MASSAMAN CURRY

SERVES: 4 | PREP TIME: 10 MINS, PLUS TIME TO MAKE CHILI OIL AND 30 MINS TO SOAK CHILE | COOK TIME: 30 MINS

Massaman Curry is not of purely Thai origin; it's an interpretation of a Persian dish. The word *Massaman* is a variation on the word *Mussulman,* a synonym for the word *Muslim.* This dish is wildly popular worldwide; in fact, in 2011, CNNGo ranked this curry as the most delicious food in the world.

CURRY PASTE (MAKES 1/2 CUP, ENOUGH FOR 2 CURRIES):

1 large dried red chile pepper, seeds removed

10 cloves garlic

2 Thai chiles or 1 jalapeño, seeds removed

3 whole cloves

2 shallots, coarsely chopped

2 stalks lemongrass, white parts only, thinly sliced

2 green cardamom pods or 1/2 tsp ground cardamom

small handful of fresh cilantro stems (1/4 bundle)

1 whole star anise

2 tbsp virgin coconut oil, melted

1 tbsp unsalted roasted cashews

1 tbsp unsalted roasted macadamia nuts

1 tsp ground coriander

1 tsp ground cumin

1 tsp ground cinnamon

1 tsp white peppercorns

1/2 tsp shrimp paste

1/2 tsp ground mace

1/2 tsp ground nutmeg

2 tsp fish sauce

1 (14 oz) can full-fat coconut milk

1 medium onion, coarsely chopped

2 lbs russet potatoes, peeled and cut into large chunks

2 lbs chicken thighs or steak, cut into bite-sized pieces

2 tbsp unsalted roasted cashews, chopped

sea salt to taste (about 1 tsp)

1 tbsp Thai Chili Oil (page 268), for serving (optional)

1. Soak the dried chile in warm water for 30 minutes.

2. Place the soaked chile and the rest of the curry paste ingredients in a blender. Blend until smooth, adding water if needed to help the blending process.

3. In a wok or deep skillet, toast the curry paste over medium heat until dark brown and strongly aromatic, about 6 minutes. Transfer half of the paste to a storage container; it will keep for 2 weeks in the fridge or 3 months in the freezer and won't need to be retoasted—you can skip directly to step 4 next time.

4. Add the coconut milk to the wok and stir until blended. Add the onion, potatoes, and chicken or steak. Bring to a simmer, then cover, reduce the heat to medium-low, and gently simmer until the meat is cooked through and the potatoes are fork-tender and rounded at the edges, about 12 minutes. Adjust the heat as needed to maintain a gentle simmer.

5. Stir in the cashews, then season with salt to taste. Serve with Thai Chili Oil, if desired.

LARB

SERVES: 4 | PREP TIME: 20 MINS, PLUS TIME TO MAKE CHILI OIL | COOK TIME: 15 MINS

Not to be confused with Live Action Roleplay, Larb is a warm minced-meat salad made with chicken, beef, duck, pork, or fish. It's popular in Laos and Thailand; the Laotian version is the more commonly available one. There is a version of this dish that is made with raw meat, kidney, fat, and bile; that is not the version we'll be making.

One of the signature mix-ins for this dish is toasted and crushed sticky rice. If you're avoiding rice, simply omit it and you'll still have an excellent meal.

1 tbsp sweet rice (optional)

2 lbs ground beef

2 shallots, thinly sliced

1 1/2 tbsp fish sauce

4 dried Chinese (Sichuan) red chile peppers, crushed, or 1 tbsp Korean red pepper powder

1 tsp Thai Chili Oil (page 268)

1 tsp sea salt

1/2 tsp white pepper

1/2 tsp coconut palm sugar

2 handfuls of Chinese cabbage, thinly sliced

juice of 1 lime (2 tbsp)

2 green onions, sliced

20 Thai basil leaves

10 mint leaves

1. If you wish to serve your Larb with toasted sticky rice, prepare it. Toast the rice in a shallow pan over medium-low heat until just golden, about 6 minutes, swirling the pan often. Transfer to a mortar and pestle and pound until only slightly grainy, about 5 minutes.

2. Heat a wok or skillet over medium-high heat until hot, about 20 seconds. Add the ground beef and sauté until mostly cooked through, about 4 minutes, breaking up chunks as they form.

3. Drain half of the fat from the beef, then remove the beef from the wok and set aside. Add a bit of the beef fat back to the wok, then add the shallots and sauté until fragrant, about 1 minute. Return the beef to the wok. Add the fish sauce, crushed chiles, chili oil, salt, pepper, and sugar and sauté until the shallots have softened, about 2 minutes. Add the Chinese cabbage and sauté until bright green, about 1 minute.

4. Remove from the heat and stir in the lime juice, green onions, Thai basil, mint, and toasted sticky rice. Taste, add salt if needed, and serve.

SUMMER ROLLS

SERVES: 4 (2 ROLLS PER PERSON) | PREP TIME: 15 MINS, PLUS TIME TO MAKE CHILI OIL | COOK TIME: 20 MINS

· ·

Goi Cuon, which literally translates to "salad rolls," are a fitting summer treat; these rolls are light and refreshing and complement other lighter fare like Pho (page 180) or Bún Cha (page 184).

Although these Summer Rolls are commonly served with Hoisin Sauce (page 270) or peanut sauce, this cashew sauce is just perfect, as is Nuoc Cham (page 184). The wrappers are typically made with rice flour or a combination of rice flour and tapioca starch, but wrappers made with just tapioca starch can be found online.

· ·

CASHEW DIPPING SAUCE:

3 tbsp cashew or almond butter

juice of 1/2 lime (1 tbsp)

1 tbsp Thai Chili Oil (page 268)

1 tsp coconut palm sugar

1 tsp fish sauce

1/2 tsp tamari

chopped roasted cashews, to garnish

4 oz rice vermicelli or sweet potato noodles

16 peeled and cooked shrimp, sliced in half lengthwise

8 (9-inch) round rice or tapioca wrappers

1 cup fresh mint leaves or Thai basil leaves (or a combination)

8 leaves green leaf lettuce, chopped

1 cup julienned or shredded carrots

1. Stir together the dipping sauce ingredients, adding a bit of water if it gets too thick, then set aside. When serving this sauce, sprinkle some chopped cashews on top.

2. If using rice vermicelli, place in a bowl of hot water for 10 minutes to soften, then drain and cut into 6-inch lengths. If using sweet potato noodles, boil until soft, about 6 minutes, drain and rinse, and then cut into 6-inch lengths.

3. Cook the shrimp however you like: poach them in simmering water, skewer and grill them, or pan-fry them. Cool and slice lengthwise.

4. Wrap your Summer Rolls: Dip a wrapper in a shallow bowl of warm water until soft but not limp, then let any excess water drip off. Roll the wrap as shown in the illustration on page 55; place the filling about 1 1/2 inches from the edge of the wrapper, in this order: 4 shrimp halves (cut side up), mint or basil leaves, lettuce, noodles, carrots, and more lettuce. Tuck in the sides, then fold the short flap over the filling. Evenly and tightly roll the wrap into a cylinder, gently tugging back on the roll as you roll it. Place on a platter and cover with plastic wrap; repeat with the remaining ingredients.

5. Slice the rolls in half diagonally and serve with the dipping sauce.

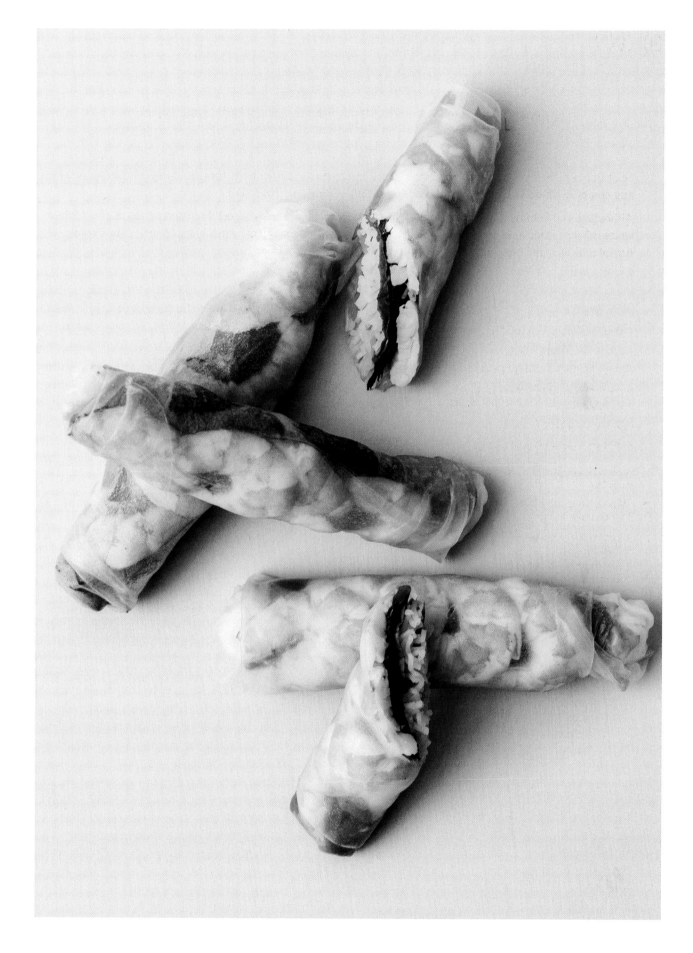

FASTER PHO

SERVES: 4 | PREP TIME: 40 MINS, PLUS TIME TO MAKE HOISIN SAUCE | COOK TIME: 45 MINS

Pho is one of my favorite dishes. It was one of the first meals I ate when I moved to Hawaii in 2001, and I've enjoyed it regularly ever since. To this day, if I'm feeling under the weather, I reach for the nearest pho bowl that's lying around (if only it were that easy!).

I spent years working on a good recipe of my own, which I wrote on my blog in 2012 (confidently declaring it my "definitive recipe"—ha!). I then updated and improved on the recipe for *The Ancestral Table*. I love that cookbook recipe, and I would confidently put it toe-to-toe with your favorite bowl of soup. Unfortunately, it takes over 7 hours to make from start to finish, since the broth is made from scratch. While spending a whole day making one soup is very satisfying (and slightly therapeutic), I wanted to put together a faster version with similar flavors.

1 (1 lb) package rice noodles (see note)

SOUP BASE:

1/2 medium white onion (use other half below)

1 inch ginger, peeled, or 1/2 tsp ground ginger

2 quarts Beef Broth (page 264)

2 quarts water

4 whole star anise

4 green cardamom pods or 1 tsp ground cardamom

1 black cardamom pod

1/2 tsp white peppercorns

1/4 tsp whole cloves

1/4 tsp fennel seeds

1/4 tsp coriander seeds

2 cinnamon sticks

1 parsnip, cut into large chunks

1 tbsp fish sauce

sea salt

1 lb raw eye of round

1/2 lb leftover cooked beef (roast, steak, meatballs, or meat from making broth)

small handful of fresh cilantro, chopped

2 green onions, sliced

1/2 medium white onion, thinly sliced

TO GARNISH (OPTIONAL):

handful of mung bean sprouts

handful of Thai basil leaves

1 lime, cut into wedges

1 jalapeño, sliced into rings

Hoisin Sauce (page 270)

1. Soak the noodles in a large pot of warm water for 30 minutes. As they soak, char the onion and ginger either over a grill or using your oven's broiler setting, about 5 minutes, then set aside.

2. Prepare the soup base. In a large pot, bring the broth and water to a simmer over high heat, then reduce to medium heat to maintain a steady simmer. In a small pan, toast the star anise, cardamom pods, peppercorns, cloves, fennel seeds, and coriander seeds over medium heat until aromatic, about 4 minutes, then transfer to a tea ball or bag (or wrap in cheesecloth). Add the tea ball, cinnamon sticks, parsnip, and charred onion and ginger to the broth and continue to simmer for 25 minutes.

3. As the soup base simmers, prepare the beef. Freeze the eye of round for 10 minutes, then thinly slice it. Take any leftover beef you have on hand and slice or tear it into bite-sized pieces—leftover Asian Beef Meatballs (page 40) are especially good.

4. Bring a separate pot of water to a boil, then add the soaked noodles. Simmer until soft, about 30 seconds, then remove with tongs and distribute directly into 4 large soup bowls. Garnish each bowl with the beef, cilantro, and sliced green onions, then set aside as you finish making the broth.

5. Add the fish sauce to the broth, then taste, adding salt until it is perfectly seasoned. Remove and discard the tea ball, cinnamon sticks, parsnip, onion, and ginger. Ladle the soup into the bowls (the eye of round will cook in the hot broth) and garnish as desired.

* Practice your timing with this recipe; once you have the method down, you can char the onion and garlic and prep the broth as the noodles soak, cutting down on the cooking time significantly. After you get the hang of the steps, you can have the whole thing done in 45 minutes.

* Don't worry if you don't have every single ingredient for the broth. I listed everything, but getting 75 percent of the way there is good enough; I would say that the star anise, cloves, and cinnamon are the most essential.

* If you're avoiding rice, you can use sweet potato noodles instead of rice noodles. Simply parboil them until tender, about 6 minutes, then drain and transfer to bowls.

* Feel free to simmer the broth for longer if you have the time. It tastes great after 30 minutes but even better after an hour. Save any extra broth for even faster pho next time.

VIETNAMESE PORK MEATBALLS

SERVES: 4 | PREP TIME: 10 MINS | COOK TIME: 10 MINS

While I wrote up a whole guide to making Asian meatballs (page 40), I feel that these meatballs deserve their own page; they're used as the basis for many Vietnamese dishes. These grilled meatballs are a tasty addition to any meal but work especially well with Bún Cha (page 184) and Bánh Xèo (page 186); don't discount their tastiness when added to Fried Rice (page 50), too.

1 lb ground pork

2 tbsp tapioca starch

1 tbsp fish sauce

1 tsp tamari

1 tsp coconut palm sugar

1/2 tsp white pepper

1. Combine all the ingredients in a food processor and pulse until smooth and tacky, about 2 minutes.

2. Prepare your grill for direct grilling by igniting all the burners (gas grill) or centering the coals (charcoal grill). Form the meatball mixture into 8 small patties, then grill over direct medium-high heat until cooked through, about 4 minutes per side.

* If you'd like, skewer the meatballs for easier grilling (as demonstrated on page 45).

* These meatballs can also be pan-fried. Warm 1 tablespoon coconut oil in a skillet over medium-high heat until shimmering, about 1 minute. Add the meatballs and pan-fry, in batches if needed, until cooked through, about 4 minutes per side.

* Consider doubling this recipe, since these meatballs work in many dishes and freeze well.

BÚN CHA

SERVES: 4 | PREP TIME: 10 MINS, PLUS TIME TO MAKE MEATBALLS | COOK TIME: 10 MINS

Originally from Hanoi, this cold rice noodle dish is a light, refreshing meal and the perfect lunch. When visiting Vietnamese restaurants, my wife Janey is always torn: order her favorite, the always delicious Bún Cha, or branch out and try a new dish? Nine times out of ten she chooses this dish, and I don't blame her. After all, I almost always order Pho (page 180).

NUOC CHAM (DIPPING SAUCE):

1/4 cup hot water

2 tbsp honey

2 tbsp fish sauce

juice of 1/2 lime (1 tbsp)

2 cloves garlic, minced

pinch of minced hot chile pepper

pinch of julienned carrots

1 batch Vietnamese Pork Meatballs (page 182)

NOODLES:

12 oz rice vermicelli or kelp noodles

or

6 zucchini or yellow squash (about 3 lbs total), spiral-sliced

1 lime, cut into wedges

handful of fresh mint leaves

4 medium carrots, julienned

2 medium cucumbers, julienned

2 heads green leaf lettuce, torn

OPTIONAL:

1/2 cup unsalted roasted cashews, chopped

1 jalapeño, sliced into rings

1.   Make the Nuoc Cham: Combine the hot water and honey; stir to combine, then set aside to cool for 10 minutes. Add the remaining ingredients and stir to combine, then refrigerate as you prepare the rest of your meal.

2.   Prepare the meatballs.

3.   Bring a pot of water to a boil, then drop in the rice vermicelli. Simmer until softened, about 30 seconds, then drain and rinse with cool water until cool to the touch. If making this dish with spiral-sliced zucchini or yellow squash, parboil the squash for 30 seconds, drain and rinse in cold water, then squeeze out half of the liquid. If using kelp noodles, no preparation is necessary.

4.   Arrange the noodles and the remaining ingredients on 4 large bowls or plates, then serve with the Nuoc Cham.

> * *Consider adding Vietnamese Spring Rolls (page 54) to your meal to make Bún Cha Giò, a popular variation on the original dish.*

BÁNH XÈO

SERVES: 4 | PREP TIME: 15 MINS, PLUS TIME TO MAKE MEATBALLS AND NUOC CHAM | COOK TIME: 20 MINS

. . . .

Bánh Xèo is a perfect example of French influence in Vietnam, as its crepelike texture is unmistakable. Its signature yellow color would lead you to believe that there are a ton of eggs in the dish, but it's actually the result of using turmeric as one of the main spices. This particular recipe is the Southern variation of the dish, where coconut milk is added to the crepe batter; it makes for a soft, rich crepe.

. . . .

1/2 batch Vietnamese Pork Meatballs (page 182), cut into bite-sized pieces

CREPES:

1 large egg, beaten

1/2 cup tapioca starch

1/2 cup white rice flour (see note)

1/2 can (about 7 oz) full-fat coconut milk

1 tsp turmeric

1 tsp mild curry powder (see note)

1/2 tsp sea salt

2 tbsp expeller-pressed coconut oil, divided

2 cloves garlic, minced

8 oz raw shrimp, peeled

large handful of mung bean sprouts

1 tsp fish sauce

1/2 tsp tamari

4 medium carrots, julienned, divided

handful of fresh cilantro, chopped

2 heads green leaf lettuce

handful of fresh mint leaves

1 lime, cut into wedges

1 batch Nuoc Cham (page 184), for serving

1. Prepare the meatballs.

2. Combine the crepe ingredients in a pourable container (like a liquid measuring cup), then stir in enough cold water to make a thin batter. Set aside.

3. Make the filling: Heat 1 tablespoon of the coconut oil in a wok or skillet over medium-high heat until shimmering, about 1 minute. Add the garlic and shrimp and sauté until the shrimp are pink and opaque, about 2 minutes. Add the meatball pieces, bean sprouts, fish sauce, tamari, and a small handful of the carrots and sauté until the sprouts have softened slightly, about 1 minute. Stir in the cilantro, remove from the heat, and set aside.

4. Heat a skillet over medium-low heat. Grease the skillet with the remaining coconut oil, then pour off any excess. Add about 2 tablespoons of the crepe batter, then swirl around to evenly coat the skillet. Cook until dry, about 1 minute, then carefully flip and cook until slightly crisp, 1 more minute. Set on a plate and continue this process until you have used all the batter; it should make about 8 crepes.

5. Distribute the remaining ingredients among 4 plates, then stuff the crepes with the filling, add to the plates, and serve with the Nuoc Cham.

> ⋆ If you are avoiding rice flour, substitute 1/4 cup blanched almond flour and 1/4 cup more tapioca starch.
>
> ⋆ To make your own mild curry powder, see page 304.

BAKSO

SERVES: 4 | PREP TIME: 15 MINS | COOK TIME: 40 MINS

• •

Bakso is a popular Indonesian beef ball soup. Bakso vendors can be found on most busy Indonesian city streets. Recently, there has been a health stigma against Bakso vendors, since additives such as borax and MSG are often found in the beef balls or broth. But in its natural form—as found in this recipe—Bakso is delicious and healthy.

• •

BEEF BALLS:

1 lb ground beef

1 lb ground pork or chicken

1/4 cup tapioca starch

1 tbsp fish sauce

1 tsp sea salt

1/2 tsp black pepper

1/2 tsp baking soda

1/2 tsp onion powder

1/2 tsp garlic powder

1/2 inch ginger or galangal, peeled and grated, or 1/4 tsp ground ginger

1/4 cup water

SOUP:

4 cups water

4 cups Beef Broth (page 264)

1 inch ginger or galangal, peeled, or 1/2 tsp ground ginger

1 cinnamon stick

2 black cardamom pods or 1/2 tsp ground cardamom

4 whole cloves

1/2 tbsp fish sauce

juice of 1/2 lime (1 tbsp)

1/2 tsp white pepper

sea salt to taste (about 2 tsp)

1 lb Chinese cabbage (bok choy, choy sum, or won bok), sliced

4 medium carrots, julienned

chopped fresh cilantro, to garnish

1. Mix together the beef ball ingredients using your hands, then transfer to a food processor and pulse until bright pink and tacky, stopping the processor every minute to scrape down the sides with a spatula. Transfer the meat paste to a bowl, cover with plastic wrap, and refrigerate until you're ready to make the beef balls. (You can make the paste up to 4 hours ahead.)

2. In a stockpot, combine the water, broth, ginger, cinnamon stick, cardamom pods, and cloves. (If you like, put the ginger, cinnamon stick, cardamom pods, and cloves in a tea bag or cheesecloth to make it easier pull them out later.) Bring to a boil over medium-high heat; once boiling, reduce the heat to medium-low and gently simmer for 20 minutes.

3. Cook the beef balls directly in the soup for added flavor. With wet hands, grab some of the meat paste in one hand, squeeze it between your thumb and index finger, then scoop away the ball with a spoon and gently drop it into the simmering water. Once the ball starts to float, let it simmer for 2 more minutes, then fish it out and place it in a bowl of ice water. Check your first beef ball or two to make sure they're cooked through. Once all the balls are cooked and in the ice bath, drain and rinse them gently with cold water. At this point, your beef balls are done—enjoy them right away or refrigerate or freeze for later use.

4. Spoon out any fat or chunks from the soup, then fish out and discard the ginger, cinnamon stick, cardamom pods, and cloves. Add the fish sauce, lime juice, pepper, and salt to taste to the soup.

5. Using a handled strainer, dip the Chinese cabbage in the soup and blanch for 30 seconds, then remove and distribute the cabbage among the soup bowls. Do the same with the carrots, but blanch them for only 10 seconds. Add the beef balls to the soup and return to a simmer, then scoop into the soup bowls. Garnish with cilantro and serve.

★ The accompaniments are just a suggestion—you can add all sorts of things, like rice noodles, zucchini noodles, sweet potato noodles, enoki mushrooms, green onions, fried shallots, Thai Chili Oil (page 268), or hard-boiled eggs. The possibilities are endless.

SIMPLE TANDOORI CHICKEN

SERVES: 4 | PREP TIME: 15 MINS. PLUS AT LEAST 30 MINS TO MARINATE | COOK TIME: 45 MINS

Tandoori Chicken gets its name from the clay oven in which it is traditionally cooked, a tandoor, which has been in use for over 5,000 years. Marinated in yogurt and spices, this dish is popular in India and beyond and remains one of the most identifiable Indian dishes today.

I always cook a double batch of this recipe so that I have plenty of leftovers for making Butter Chicken (page 194) or Chicken Tikka Masala (page 192). Kashmiri red chili powder and garam masala can be found at Asian groceries or online; while you're shopping, be sure to grab some fenugreek leaves and mace, which you'll need for Butter Chicken.

4 lbs bone-in chicken thighs, drumsticks, leg quarters, or split breasts, skin and excess fat removed

MARINADE:

1 cup plain full-fat yogurt (coconut yogurt okay)

1 inch ginger, sliced, or 1/2 tsp ground ginger

2 cloves garlic

1 tbsp Kashmiri red chili powder or 2 tsp cayenne pepper

1 tbsp beet powder (optional; see note)

1 tbsp garam masala

1 tsp ground coriander

1 tsp sea salt

2 tbsp ghee, melted

1 lemon, cut into wedges, for serving

1. Slice deep cuts into the chicken to allow the marinade to penetrate the meat. Also slice across the leg joints (if using leg quarters) and sever the tendon connected to each ankle joint (for both leg quarters and drumsticks). Place the marinade ingredients in a blender and blend until smooth, then combine with the chicken pieces in a gallon-sized resealable plastic bag and refrigerate for at least 30 minutes, overnight preferred.

2. Cooking over a charcoal or gas grill is preferred but not required; the chicken can also be roasted in the oven (skip to step 3). Prepare your grill for indirect grilling by igniting the burners on only one side (gas grill) or by banking the coals to one side (charcoal grill). Grill the chicken pieces bone side down (what would be skin side up if the skin was intact) over direct heat (the hot side of the grill) for 10 minutes. Once slightly charred, move to the cool side of the grill and brush with the melted ghee. Continue to grill until the internal temperature of the chicken reaches 160°F, about 30 more minutes.

3. To roast the chicken in the oven, preheat your oven to 450°F. Place the chicken pieces on a wire rack set over a rimmed baking sheet and roast until the chicken is cooked through, about 45 minutes. Brush with the melted ghee about 20 minutes into cooking.

4. Serve with lemon wedges.

> * For a red appearance similar to what you find in Indian restaurants (where they use red dye to get that color), add 1 tablespoon beet powder to the marinade, which you can purchase online.

CHICKEN TIKKA MASALA

SERVES: 4 | PREP TIME: 15 MINS, PLUS AT LEAST 30 MINS TO MARINATE | COOK TIME: 1 HOUR

The origin of Chicken Tikka Masala is disputed. It's commonly believed that it was first whipped up in Indian restaurants in the United Kingdom (Glasgow in particular is often cited), but many people argue that it was influenced by dishes from the Punjab region of India and Pakistan well before it appeared in restaurants in the U.K.

Putting the curry together is actually pretty simple—start to finish in under an hour. It gets a little complicated when the chicken comes into play, since it should be marinated beforehand (overnight preferred). But with a little forethought, this is an excellent weeknight meal. Having some leftover Tandoori Chicken (page 190) on hand will speed up the process immensely; instructions are provided in the notes below.

SPICE BLEND:

1 tbsp turmeric

1 tbsp garam masala

2 tsp ground coriander

2 tsp ground cumin

2 tsp kosher salt

2 tsp Kashmiri red chili powder or 1 tsp cayenne pepper

4 cloves garlic, minced

1/2 inch ginger, peeled and grated, or 1/2 tsp ground ginger

1 cup plain full-fat yogurt (coconut yogurt okay)

2 lbs boneless, skinless chicken breasts or thighs, cut into large chunks

2 tbsp ghee

1 medium onion, chopped

2 cloves garlic, minced

1 (28 oz) can diced tomatoes

3 green cardamom pods or heaping 1/2 tsp ground cardamom

1/2 tsp white pepper

1 cup heavy cream (see note)

sea salt

1/2 cup fresh cilantro, chopped, for serving

1. Combine the spice blend ingredients and divide in half. Combine half of the spice blend with the garlic, ginger, yogurt, and chicken in a resealable plastic bag and refrigerate for at least 30 minutes, overnight preferred.

2. Warm the ghee in a skillet over medium heat. Add the onion and sauté until softened, about 5 minutes. Add the garlic and sauté until aromatic, another minute. Add the tomatoes, cardamom pods, pepper, and the other half of the spice blend. Stir to combine, then reduce the heat to medium-low and gently simmer until dark and thick, about 40 minutes.

3. While the sauce is darkening, prepare the chicken. Skewer the marinated chicken pieces (metal skewers preferred) and grill over direct high heat until cooked through, about 3 minutes per side, flipping once. Alternatively, you can broil the chicken in the oven, about 6 to 8 minutes per side. You'll want to time this step to finish near the end of cooking the sauce so that the chicken doesn't get too cold.

4. Once the sauce is dark, transfer it to a blender and blend until smooth. Return the sauce to the skillet, straining it through a colander to catch the cardamom shells and unblended tomato chunks. Stir in the cream, return to a simmer, and cook until slightly darkened, about 10 minutes. Taste and add salt if needed, and add water if the sauce appears too thick; it should be the consistency of tomato soup.

5. Add the chicken pieces, cover, and simmer until warm, about 2 minutes. Remove from the heat. Serve garnished with chopped cilantro.

* *If using leftover Tandoori Chicken (page 190), make a half portion of the spice blend and proceed to step 2.*

* *To make this dish dairy-free, use 1/2 cup each full-fat coconut milk and Chicken Broth (page 264) instead of the cream.*

BUTTER CHICKEN

SERVES: 4 | PREP TIME: 15 MINS, PLUS AT LEAST 30 MINS TO MARINATE | COOK TIME: 1 HOUR

Butter Chicken, also known as Murgh Makahni, is a classic Indian dish and an unforgettable combination of savory, sweet, and rich tastes. Better yet, this dish is surprisingly easy to put together once you have the ingredients.

Butter Chicken first appeared in 1920 in the famous Moti Mahal restaurant, owned by Kundan Lal Gujral in the present-day Pakistani city of Peshawar. When India was partitioned in 1947, Gujral relocated the restaurant to Delhi. Today, Moti Mahal has more than 100 franchises in India, and Gujral is credited with inventing the modern recipes for both Butter Chicken and Tandoori Chicken.

Having some leftover Tandoori Chicken (page 190) lying around will speed up the cooking process immensely; instructions are provided in the notes that follow the recipe.

SPICE BLEND:

1/2 tbsp turmeric

1/2 tbsp garam masala

1 tsp ground coriander

1 tsp ground cumin

1 tsp kosher salt

1 tsp Kashmiri red chili powder or 1/2 tsp cayenne pepper

4 cloves garlic, minced

1/2 inch ginger, peeled and grated, or 1/2 tsp ground ginger

1 cup plain full-fat yogurt (coconut yogurt okay)

2 lbs boneless, skinless chicken breasts or thighs, cut into large chunks

2 tbsp ghee

3 green cardamom pods or heaping 1/2 tsp ground cardamom

1 jalapeño, serrano, or other hot green chile, seeds and ribs removed, julienned

1 inch ginger, peeled and julienned, or 1/2 tsp ground ginger

3 blades mace or 1 tsp ground mace

2 cloves garlic

1 (28 oz) can diced tomatoes

3 tbsp butter

1 tsp Kashmiri red chili powder or 1/2 tsp cayenne pepper

1/2 tsp ground coriander

1/2 tbsp honey

1 tsp crushed fenugreek leaves (kasuri methi)

sea salt

1/2 cup heavy cream (see note)

lemon wedges, to garnish

chopped fresh cilantro, to garnish

1. Stir together the spice blend ingredients, then combine with the chicken pieces in a resealable plastic bag; refrigerate for at least 30 minutes, overnight preferred.

2. Heat the ghee in a large skillet on medium heat until shimmering, about 1 minute. Add the cardamom pods, chile, ginger, mace, and garlic and sauté until aromatic, about 2 minutes. Add the tomatoes and sauté until they are starting to break apart, about 6 minutes. Pour everything into a blender and blend until smooth, adding water if the sauce gets too thick. You want it to be the consistency of tomato soup.

3. Return the sauce to the skillet, straining it through a colander to catch the cardamom shells and unblended tomato chunks. Stir in the butter, chili powder, and coriander and simmer on medium-low heat until darkened, about 30 minutes.

4. While the sauce is darkening, prepare the chicken. Skewer the marinated chicken pieces (metal skewers preferred) and grill over direct high heat until cooked through, about 4 minutes per side, flipping once. Alternatively, you can broil them in the oven, about 6 to 8 minutes per side. You'll want to time this step to finish near the end of cooking the sauce so that the chicken doesn't get too cold.

5. Once the sauce has darkened, add the honey, fenugreek, and salt to taste, adding more water if the sauce is too thick. Add the chicken, cover, and simmer until warm, about 2 minutes. Remove from the heat and stir in the cream before serving. Serve garnished with lemon wedges and cilantro.

* If using leftover Tandoori Chicken, proceed directly to step 2.

* To make this dish dairy-free, use 1/4 cup each full-fat coconut milk and Chicken Broth (page 264) instead of the cream.

LAMB VINDALOO

SERVES: 4 | PREP TIME: 10 MINS, PLUS AT LEAST 30 MINS TO MARINATE | COOK TIME: 1 HOUR (PRESSURE COOKER), 2 HOURS (STOVETOP)

Vindaloo is the Indian interpretation of the Portuguese dish carne de vinha d'alhos ("meat with wine and garlic"), borrowed from the Portuguese colony in Goa (West India). The original dish is seasoned with vinegar, and that slightly sour taste remains in most Indian interpretations today.

As with the original Portuguese dish, many vindaloo curries contain potatoes. The Indian interpretation of this dish does stray from its source in that carne de vinha d'alhos is usually made with pork, and the vindaloos you'll find in Indian restaurants are most often made with lamb. Likewise, the Indian dish is moderately spicy, unlike its Portuguese counterpart. For this recipe, I kept the heat fairly mild; to spice it up, simply add more chili powder.

Lamb shoulder requires an extended cooking time on the stovetop in order to tenderize the meat; if you have a pressure cooker, that cooking time is drastically reduced. Instructions for both methods are provided.

MARINADE:

1/2 tsp cumin seeds

1/2 tsp black or yellow mustard seeds

1/2 medium onion, cut into quarters

4 cloves garlic

1 inch ginger, peeled and sliced, or 1/2 tsp ground ginger

2 tbsp apple cider vinegar

1 tbsp olive oil

1/2 tsp ground cinnamon

1/2 tsp sea salt

1/4 tsp ground cloves

3 lbs lamb shoulder, cut into 1-inch chunks

CURRY SAUCE:

2 cups Chicken Broth (page 264)

2 bay leaves

1 green cardamom pod or 1/4 tsp ground cardamom

1 tsp paprika

1 tsp Kashmiri red chili powder or 1/2 tsp cayenne pepper

1 tsp ground coriander

1/2 tsp turmeric

1/2 tsp white pepper

2 tbsp ghee

1 lb waxy potatoes (such as red or Yukon Gold), quartered

handful of fresh cilantro, chopped

1. In a small pan over medium heat, toast the cumin and mustard seeds until aromatic, about 2 minutes. In a blender, combine the seeds with the remaining marinade ingredients and blend until smooth. Place the lamb and marinade in a resealable plastic bag and marinate for at least 30 minutes, overnight preferred.

2. Drain the lamb in a colander, catching the marinade as it falls. Combine the marinade with the curry sauce ingredients and set aside. (Since the marinade will be reheated, it is safe to use.)

ELECTRIC PRESSURE COOKER INSTRUCTIONS:

Set the pressure cooker to Sauté and add the ghee; once melted and shimmering (about 2 minutes), add half of the lamb pieces. Sauté until browned, about 6 minutes, turning halfway through cooking. Remove the cooked lamb and sauté the second batch in the same manner, then set aside with the other half of the lamb. Add the marinade/curry sauce mixture to the pot and bring to a simmer; stir in the potatoes and lamb, cover, and set to Meat/Stew (high pressure) for 20 minutes. Once finished, allow the pressure cooker to depressurize on its own (about 15 minutes), then remove the lid. Gently remove the lamb and potatoes and set aside. Set the pressure cooker to Sauté again and bring to a boil; reduce the liquid by half, about 10 minutes. Return the lamb and potatoes to the curry and stir in the cilantro, then serve.

In a Dutch oven, warm the ghee over medium-high heat until shimmering, about 2 minutes. Add the lamb, in batches if needed to prevent overcrowding, and sauté until browned, about 6 minutes per batch. Set the lamb aside and reduce the heat to medium. Add the marinade/curry sauce mixture to the pot and bring to a simmer; stir in the lamb. Cover, reduce the heat to low, and simmer until just tender, 1 to 2 hours, then add the potatoes and simmer for another 30 minutes. Gently remove the lamb and potatoes and set aside. Increase the heat to medium and bring to a boil; reduce the liquid by half, about 10 minutes. Return the lamb and potatoes to the curry and stir in the cilantro, then serve.

KEBAB PARTY

SERVES: 12 (EACH KEBAB DISH SERVES 4) | PREP TIME: 20 MINS, PLUS TIME TO MAKE SIDES AND AT LEAST 30 MINS TO MARINATE
COOK TIME: 20 MINS

· ·

While seemingly simple, the word *kebab* is often a source of confusion. In the U.S., *kebab* refers to shish kebabs, the Turkish version of skewered meat that is often threaded with vegetables. In Europe and Australia, *kebab* refers to doner kebabs, which are meat served in flatbreads (similar to Gyros, page 256, or shawarma, a Middle Eastern version of the gyro). Finally, in the Middle East, *kebab* refers to this recipe: marinated and skewered meat cooked over a fire.

The idea of skewering and grilling vegetables is awesome, but they often cook in less time than meat, so I don't like to put them on the same skewer. Instead, I skewer them independently; mushrooms, onions, bell peppers, tomatoes, and pineapple are all excellent choices. Alternatively, I like to throw halved tomatoes or bell peppers directly on the grill to char as I cook the meat.

Metal skewers are preferred for kebabs; you can reuse them, and you don't have to worry about burning bamboo skewers. If using bamboo, soak them in water for at least 30 minutes beforehand.

· ·

LAMB KEBABS

MARINADE:

1 medium onion, coarsely chopped

2 cloves garlic

2 tbsp olive oil

1 tbsp apple cider vinegar

2 tsp sea salt

1 tsp dried marjoram

1 tsp black pepper

1 tsp chopped fresh mint leaves or 1/2 tsp dried

1/2 tsp ground saffron

juice of 1 lemon (3 tbsp)

grated zest of 1 lemon

2 lbs lamb shoulder, cut into 1-inch pieces

CHICKEN KEBABS

MARINADE:

1 medium onion, coarsely chopped

2 cloves garlic

juice of 2 limes (1/4 cup)

1/4 cup apple cider vinegar

2 tbsp olive oil

2 tbsp plain full-fat yogurt (coconut yogurt okay)

1 tsp sea salt

1 tsp black pepper

1/2 tsp ground saffron

1/2 tsp turmeric

2 lbs boneless, skinless chicken breasts, cut into 1-inch pieces

FOR SERVING

6 tomatoes, cut in half crosswise

1 batch Tzatziki Sauce (page 284)

2 batches Flatbread (page 298)

2 batches Greek Salad (page 258), minus the meat

KOFTA KEBABS

MARINADE:

1 medium onion, coarsely chopped

4 cloves garlic

1 tbsp chopped fresh mint leaves or 1/2 tbsp dried

1 tbsp chopped fresh cilantro leaves

1 tbsp sea salt

2 tsp black pepper

1/2 tsp ground cumin

1/2 tsp ground coriander

1/2 tsp ground cinnamon

1/2 tsp turmeric

2 bay leaves

1 lb ground lamb

1 lb ground beef

1. To prepare the Lamb and Chicken Kebabs, combine the marinade ingredients in a blender and blend until smooth. Place the meat and marinade in a resealable plastic bag and marinate for at least 30 minutes, overnight preferred.

2. To prepare the Kofta Kebabs, combine the marinade ingredients in a food processor and process until uniform. Add the meat and pulse until smooth and tacky. Place the mixture in the fridge for 30 minutes to cool and stiffen, which will make it easier to mold around the skewers.

3. Prepare your grill for direct grilling while you skewer the meat. For the lamb and chicken, simply skewer it. Don't overcrowd the meat; leave about 1/2 inch between pieces. For the kofta, mold a handful of the meat mixture around a skewer, placing one or two koftas on each skewer.

4. Grill over direct high heat until cooked through, rotating every few minutes, about 6 to 8 minutes total. Place the tomatoes on the grill and grill until charred and soft, about 5 minutes. Serve with Tzatziki Sauce, Flatbread, and Greek Salad.

KARE KARE

SERVES: 4 | PREP TIME: 10 MINS, PLUS TIME TO MAKE CHILI OIL
COOK TIME: 1 HOUR 30 MINS (PRESSURE COOKER), 4 HOURS (STOVETOP)

Kare Kare is a Philippine oxtail stew, often served with tripe and pigs' or cows' feet. There's a bit of variation to this dish, but it typically includes eggplant, green beans, and Chinese cabbage. The name Kare Kare may have been introduced by Indian immigrants who settled to the east of Manila, while others believe that the dish came from the Pampanga region to the northwest of the Philippine capital city.

This recipe calls for several ingredients that are somewhat hard to find, but worth the hunt. Annatto seeds give the stew a pleasant color. Oxtails are an appropriately named cut taken from the tails of cows; they are very flavorful, full of collagen, and perfect for making broth (page 264). Tripe is usually taken from the second chamber of the cow's stomach and is often referred to as honeycomb tripe. Rounding out the dish is a pig's foot, which gives the Kare Kare a rich, decadent flavor. All these ingredients can be found online if you can't find them locally.

3 lbs oxtails

1 pig's foot, pork hock, or cow's foot

1 tbsp expeller-pressed coconut oil

1 medium onion, coarsely chopped

4 cloves garlic, minced

1/2 lb tripe, cut into bite-sized chunks

1/2 cup uncooked white rice

2 tbsp roasted cashews

2 tbsp roasted almonds or 1 tbsp blanched almond flour

1 tbsp annatto seeds

2 tbsp almond or sunflower seed butter

1 tbsp fish sauce

sea salt and black pepper

Tabasco or Thai Chili Oil (page 268; optional)

1 medium eggplant (about 1/2 lb), cut into bite-sized chunks

1/2 lb green beans, trimmed

1 lb Chinese cabbage (bok choy, choy sum, or kai lan), coarsely chopped

ELECTRIC PRESSURE COOKER INSTRUCTIONS:

1. Place the oxtails and pig's foot in the pressure cooker and add enough water to cover them by 1 inch. Set the pressure cooker to Sauté, bring to a boil, and boil for 5 minutes; drain and rinse, then set aside. This step removes any pathogens from the bones.

2. Rinse and return the liner to the pressure cooker and set it to Sauté again. Add the coconut oil and onion and sauté until softened, about 5 minutes, then add the garlic and sauté for another 30 seconds. Return the oxtails and pig's foot to the pot, along with the tripe; fill with enough water to cover everything by 1 inch. Place the lid on the pressure cooker and set it to Meat/Stew (high pressure) for 45 minutes.

3. As the soup cooks, toast the rice in a skillet over low heat until golden brown, about 5 minutes, then let cool and grind into a powder using a mortar and pestle or a blender. Grind the cashews and almonds into a flour/paste with the same tool you used to grind the rice. Lastly, soak the annatto seeds in water for 30 minutes, then crush them with a spoon (while they're still in the water).

4. Once the meat has finished cooking, allow the pressure cooker to depressurize on its own (about 15 minutes), then remove the lid and skim any fat that has accumulated at the surface.

STOVETOP INSTRUCTIONS:

1. Place the oxtails and pig's foot in a large stockpot and add enough water to cover them by 1 inch. Bring to a boil on high heat and boil for 5 minutes; drain and rinse, then set aside. This step removes any pathogens from the bones.

2. Warm the empty stockpot over medium heat for a minute, then add the coconut oil and onion. Sauté until softened, about 5 minutes, then add the garlic and sauté for another 30 seconds. Return the oxtails and pig's foot to the pot, along with the tripe; fill with enough water to cover everything by 1 inch. Bring to a simmer over medium-high heat, then reduce the heat to low; simmer until the meat pulls easily from the oxtails, about 3 hours, replenishing the water as it evaporates below the line of the meat and bones and skimming any fat or foam that accumulates at the surface.

3. As the soup cooks, toast the rice in a skillet over low heat until golden brown, about 5 minutes, then let cool and grind into a powder using a mortar and pestle or a blender. Grind the cashews and almonds into a flour/paste with the same tool you used to grind the rice. Lastly, soak the annatto seeds in water for 30 minutes, then crush them with a spoon (while they're still in the water).

TO FINISH THE MEAL:

1. Remove the pig's foot from the soup, let cool, then pick off the meat; return the meat to the pot and discard the rest of the foot. Add the ground rice, ground nuts, and the water in which you soaked the annatto seeds (strain the seeds so they don't get into the soup). Finally, add the almond butter and fish sauce. Return to a simmer (on the "Sauté" setting if using a pressure cooker), stirring often so that the rice doesn't stick to the bottom, then add salt and pepper to taste. Some people like to add a few squirts of Tabasco or a bit of chili oil; go for it if you're so inclined.

2. Once the soup tastes good, finish it by adding the vegetables. Add the eggplant chunks and simmer for 3 minutes, add the green beans and simmer for 2 minutes, then add the Chinese cabbage and simmer until bright green, about 1 more minute. Gently stir the soup often. Remove from the heat and serve.

OVEN PORK ADOBO

SERVES: 4 | PREP TIME: 10 MINS, PLUS AT LEAST 30 MINS TO MARINATE | COOK TIME: 1 HOUR 30 MINS

Adobo, often considered the national dish of the Philippines, is a method of stewing meat in vinegar. The word *adobo* itself is linked to a Spanish method of preserving raw meat by immersing it in a mixture of vinegar, salt, and paprika. When the Spanish observed an indigenous Philippine cooking method involving vinegar in the 16th century, they referred to it as adobo, and the name stuck. The original name for this dish is no longer known.

My Pork Adobo recipe in *The Ancestral Table* is one of my family's favorites, but it is admittedly a little time-consuming, since it requires you to brown the pork both before and after stewing it. I found that oven-roasting the pork pieces creates a similar crispy texture with significantly less hands-on time. Serve the pork with Basic Steamed Rice (page 286) or Cauliflower Rice (page 288).

1 1/2 lbs pork belly, cut into 2-inch chunks

1 1/2 lbs pork shoulder, cut into 2-inch chunks

1/3 cup tamari

10 cloves garlic, coarsely chopped

2 tbsp black peppercorns

5 bay leaves

2/3 cup cane vinegar or white vinegar

1 cup water

1. Combine the pork, tamari, garlic, and peppercorns in a resealable plastic bag and marinate for at least 30 minutes, overnight preferred.

2. In a stockpot or Dutch oven, place the pork and its marinade along with the bay leaves, vinegar, and water. Bring to a simmer over medium-high heat, cover, and reduce the heat to low. Simmer for 1 hour. Do not open the lid during this hour; many people believe that doing so will make the dish taste sour.

3. Preheat your oven to 400°F. Remove the pork pieces with tongs and set aside, then strain the liquid and discard the peppercorns, garlic, and bay leaves. (Some cooks prefer to leave them in, which is fine.) Using a fat separator or a spoon, remove and reserve the fat from the braising liquid and set the liquid aside.

4. Pour and spread about 1 tablespoon of the liquid fat onto a rimmed baking sheet, then add the pork pieces. Bake until the meat is crispy and most of the fat has been rendered out, about 20 minutes, turning halfway through cooking. The shoulder pieces may crisp more quickly than the belly pieces; if you're so inclined, remove the shoulder pieces and keep them warm while you roast the belly for a few more minutes.

5. As the pork crisps, prepare the sauce for serving. Place the braising liquid in a saucepan and bring to a boil over medium-high heat; when it has reduced by one-third (about 8 minutes), turn the heat to low to keep warm while the pork finishes.

6. When the pork is crispy, use tongs to transfer it to a serving bowl, then pour the sauce over the pork and serve.

GRILLED CHICKEN ADOBO

SERVES: 4 TO 6 | PREP TIME: 5 MINS, PLUS AT LEAST 30 MINS TO MARINATE | COOK TIME: 1 HOUR

Like Pork Adobo (page 202), Chicken Adobo is typically made by stewing chicken pieces in a vinegary sauce. The problem with stewing chicken meat is that it's very easy to create an unappetizing texture if you cook the chicken for too long. But you know what always results in delicious chicken? Grilling it. So I put a spin on the traditional preparation to get the best of both worlds—a flavorful vinegary marinade that tenderizes the chicken combined with the crunchy goodness that is grilled chicken.

Cane vinegar (sukang maasim) is an integral part of this dish's taste and can be found in any store that carries Philippine products. I keep a bottle of Datu Puti brand at home and use it exclusively to make adobo. White vinegar will work in a pinch.

1/2 cup cane vinegar, or 1/3 cup white vinegar plus 2 tbsp water

1/3 cup tamari

10 cloves garlic, coarsely chopped

2 tbsp black peppercorns

5 bay leaves

4 to 6 lbs chicken thighs and drumsticks

1. Combine all the ingredients in a resealable plastic bag and marinate for at least 30 minutes, overnight preferred.

2. Prepare your grill for indirect grilling by igniting the burners on only one side (gas grill) or by banking the coals to one side (charcoal grill). Place the chicken on the cool side of the grill, brushing off most of the peppercorns and garlic. Grill until the chicken reaches an internal temperature of 165°F, about 45 minutes. Let rest for 5 minutes before eating.

PANCIT

SERVES: 4 | PREP TIME: 10 MINS | COOK TIME: 25 MINS

Pancit is a Filipino noodle dish that was first introduced to the archipelago by Chinese immigrants. (The word *pancit* is derived from the phrase *pian i sit,* which translates to "convenient" in the Hokkien Chinese dialect.) This is a basic Pancit recipe, and there is a lot of variation to this dish. For example, popular mix-ins include Chinese cabbage, straw mushrooms, pork rinds, bell pepper, green onions, broccoli, snow peas, and hard-boiled egg slices.

2 tbsp expeller-pressed coconut oil, divided

1 lb chicken thighs, cut into bite-sized chunks

4 cups Chicken Broth (page 264)

1 (16 oz) package rice vermicelli or sweet potato noodles (see note)

1 lb raw shrimp, peeled

6 green onions, cut into 3-inch lengths

1 medium carrot, julienned

2 stalks celery, sliced

1 tbsp tamari

1 tbsp fish sauce

1/2 tsp sea salt

1/2 tsp white pepper

juice of 1 lime (2 tbsp)

1. In a wok or skillet, heat 1 tablespoon of the coconut oil over medium-high heat until shimmering, about 1 minute. Add the chicken and sauté until cooked through, about 6 minutes, then set aside.

2. Bring the broth to a boil in a stockpot, then reduce the heat to medium. Add the noodles; they likely won't all fit at once, which is fine—just keep adding them as they cook down. Simmer, gently stirring often, until the noodles have soaked up most of the broth, about 6 minutes (8 minutes for sweet potato noodles).

3. As the noodles cook, heat the remaining 1 tablespoon of coconut oil in the wok over medium-high heat. Add the shrimp, onions, carrot, and celery and stir-fry until the shrimp are pink and opaque, about 2 minutes, then mix in the chicken, tamari, fish sauce, salt, and pepper.

4. Add the shrimp and chicken mixture to the pot with the noodles and toss to combine. Taste and add salt and pepper if needed, then remove from the heat and cover; let sit for 10 minutes to allow the last of the liquid to be absorbed. Toss with the lime juice before serving.

* *If desired, use spiral-sliced zucchini, yellow squash, or sweet potatoes instead of rice vermicelli. If using spiral-sliced squash, skip step 2, add 1 tablespoon chicken broth when you add the tamari in step 3, and add the noodles directly to the hot wok at the end of step 3. If using spiral-sliced sweet potatoes, use only 2 cups chicken broth in step 2 and simmer the noodles for 4 minutes.*

CHICKEN LONG RICE

SERVES: 4 | PREP TIME: 10 MINS | COOK TIME: 20 MINS

Chicken Long Rice is a popular potluck food in Hawaii, mostly because it's delicious, but also because it can easily be scaled up for large parties. This dish requires very little hands-on time, which gives you an opportunity to whip up some vegetables to accompany the noodles and chicken.

4 cups Chicken Broth (page 264)

1 tsp honey

1 tsp tamari

1 tsp fish sauce

1/2 tsp sea salt

1/2 tsp white pepper

2 lbs chicken thighs, cut into bite-sized chunks

1 (8 oz) package rice vermicelli or sweet potato noodles, cut to 4-inch lengths

3 green onions, sliced

black sesame seeds, to garnish

1. In a stockpot, combine the broth, honey, tamari, fish sauce, salt, and pepper. Bring to a boil over medium heat, then add the chicken and return to a simmer. Reduce the heat to medium-low and simmer until the chicken is just cooked through, about 10 minutes.

2. Add the noodles and cook until very tender, about 6 minutes for rice vermicelli or 8 minutes for sweet potato noodles. Cover, remove from the heat, and allow to sit for 10 minutes, then taste and add salt if needed. Stir in the green onions and serve garnished with black sesame seeds. White sesame seeds are just fine, but not as pretty!

GARLIC SHRIMP

SERVES: 4 | PREP TIME: 10 MINS, PLUS AT LEAST 30 MINS TO MARINATE | COOK TIME: 30 MINS

• •

Having spent most of my twenties in Hawaii, I regularly made trips to Giovanni's shrimp truck in Kahuku to enjoy the signature dish: Shrimp Scampi. The shrimp is pan-fried in an aromatic scampi sauce and served with a cubic ton of garlic. I have regularly tackled this dish since moving back to the mainland in 2008, but it wasn't until recently that I really figured out how to re-create it at home.

One significant change from the original dish is that I prefer to use tail-on or shelled shrimp. This allows the marinating liquid to better penetrate the shrimp, making for a more flavorful (and less messy) experience. Serve the shrimp over Basic Steamed Rice (page 286) or Cauliflower Rice (page 288).

• •

2 lbs raw shrimp, peeled or tail-on

50 cloves garlic, coarsely chopped (see note)

1/4 cup white wine

2 tbsp olive oil

1/2 tsp sea salt

1/4 tsp black pepper

1/4 cup ghee

lemon wedges, for serving

1. Combine the shrimp, garlic, wine, olive oil, salt, and pepper in a resealable plastic bag. Place in the fridge to marinate for at least 30 minutes, overnight preferred.

2. In a wok or skillet, melt the ghee over medium heat. Strain the shrimp from the marinade, add the liquid to the ghee, and bring to a simmer. Add the shrimp and cook, in batches, until mostly cooked through (mostly pink and opaque). Fish out the shrimp with tongs (be careful not to remove the garlic) and set aside in a colander placed over a bowl to keep the shrimp from getting soggy. Repeat this process until all the shrimp are mostly cooked. You should have a lot of liquid and garlic left in your wok at this point.

3. Increase the temperature to medium-high and allow the sauce to reduce until the liquid evaporates and the garlic becomes golden brown and crispy, stirring constantly so as not to scorch the garlic, about 15 minutes. Look for the oil to start accumulating at the top of the liquid, which is exactly what you want. Return the shrimp to the wok and stir-fry, tossing often, until fully cooked, about 2 minutes. Serve with lemon wedges.

★ Peeling 50 cloves of garlic is a lot of work. Many grocery stores, especially Asian markets, sell peeled garlic; it's more expensive, but I think it's well worth the splurge.

AMERICAN
CLASSICS

BASIC PIZZA CRUST

YIELD: TWO 8- TO 10-INCH CRUSTS | PREP TIME: 10 MINS | COOK TIME: 40 MINS (FOR 2 PIZZAS)

A good pizza is hard to come by in the Paleo world, but I was such a fan of my pizza crust recipe in *The Ancestral Table* that I put it on the cover. This variation replaces a bit of the usual tapioca starch with potato starch, which results in a crispier crust. Be sure to check the notes below for a dairy-free variation.

For best results, preheat your oven for a good 30 minutes beforehand. While it's probably not a great thing for your electric bill, it'll create a super crispy crust!

1 cup (113g) tapioca starch

1/2 cup (76g) potato starch

1/4 cup heavy cream (see note)

1/4 cup water

2 tbsp butter

1/2 tsp sea salt

1 large egg, beaten

3/4 cup (75g) grated Parmesan or other hard cheese

pinch of white pepper

1/4 tsp dried oregano

* *Dairy-free? Use 1/2 cup full-fat coconut milk instead of the cream and water, and use 1/4 cup (12g) nutritional yeast instead of the cheese.*

* *Depending on the ambient temperature of your kitchen, the starch can sometimes melt into a gooey consistency. If this happens, simply pour it directly into the skillet and spread it evenly with the back of a spoon in step 3. It'll turn out just fine.*

* *This crust can be premade and frozen. Follow the directions through step 3, then let cool, wrap in plastic wrap, and freeze. When you're ready to cook it, unwrap the frozen crust and place it in a cast-iron skillet; bake in a 500°F oven for 3 minutes, then proceed to step 5.*

1. Preheat your oven to 500°F. Combine the starches in a large mixing bowl and set aside. In a saucepan, combine the cream, water, butter, and salt and warm over medium-low heat. Once the butter melts and the liquid just starts to bubble, remove from the heat and stir it into the starch mixture. Let cool for 5 minutes.

2. Add the beaten egg to the mixture and knead together with your hands. Add the Parmesan, pepper, and oregano and mix together until it's doughlike.

3. Split the dough in half, then stretch out each half into the thinnest disc possible without tearing. Put one half in an 8- to 10-inch cast-iron skillet, spreading the dough to the edges of the skillet with your fingers. With a fork, poke some holes in the dough to let air pass through.

4. Bake in the center of the oven for 6 minutes, then take it out and put it on the stovetop. This step is important because it gives the dough time to cook through without burning the toppings.

5. Add sauce, cheese, and toppings as desired (see page 217 for some examples). Put the pizza back in the oven and bake for another 8 to 10 minutes or until the cheese starts to brown. For extra-crispy toppings, broil for the last minute or two of cooking.

6. Repeat the process with the other half of the dough. Or, if you have two cast-iron skillets, you can knock out both pizzas at once! This pizza also cooks well on a pizza stone or even a heavy-duty baking sheet that's been lightly greased with melted ghee. If using a baking sheet, bake the crust for 8 minutes instead of 6 during the first stage of cooking for best results.

* *If using a pizza stone, heat it in the oven for 5 minutes before adding the dough for a crispier crust. Be careful not to burn yourself!*

* *To reheat leftover pizza, throw it in a toaster oven or reheat it in a skillet over medium heat (microwaving will make it very flimsy).*

PIZZA PARTY

PIZZA PARTY

YIELD: FOUR 8- TO 10-INCH PIZZAS (4 SERVINGS) | PREP TIME: 20 MINS, PLUS TIME TO MAKE CRUSTS AND SAUCE
COOK TIME: 40 MINS (FOR 4 PIZZAS COOKED 2 AT A TIME)

I worked at a pizza parlor for a year as a teenager to save up enough money for my first guitar. I had a great time and learned some fun pizza combinations along the way. Here, I've re-created some of America's most beloved toppings for a pizza party of your own.

Feel free to make any combination you like, using whatever you have on hand; there's no such thing as a bad combination of toppings. The quantities listed for each of the combinations below are for one pizza. To reduce the cooking time, cook two crusts at once using either two skillets or a combination of skillet plus pizza stone or baking sheet (instructions provided in the Basic Pizza Crust recipe).

FOR ALL PIZZAS

2 batches Basic Pizza Crust (page 214; makes 4 pizzas)

MEAT-LOVING PIZZA

1/4 cup Pizza Sauce (blended Red Sauce, page 279)

2 oz cooked Italian sausage, chopped (see note)

2 1/2 oz fresh mozzarella, grated or torn apart by hand

2 slices bacon, cooked and chopped

2 oz Canadian bacon, quartered

2 oz pepperoni, quartered

1 tsp dried oregano

SALAD PIZZA

1 tbsp olive oil

1 grilled chicken breast, cut into bite-sized chunks

2 1/2 oz fresh mozzarella, grated or torn apart by hand

2 slices bacon, cooked and chopped

1/2 medium red onion, thinly sliced

large handful of spring greens (about 2 cups)

1 tbsp Mayo (page 276)

1/2 medium tomato, sliced

1/2 avocado, sliced

PIZZA SUPREMA

1/4 cup Pizza Sauce (blended Red Sauce, page 279)

2 oz cooked Italian sausage, chopped (see note)

2 oz Canadian bacon, quartered

2 1/2 oz fresh mozzarella, grated or torn apart by hand

2 oz pepperoni, quartered

1/2 green bell pepper, thinly sliced

1/2 medium red onion, thinly sliced

HAWAIIAN PIZZA

1/4 cup Pizza Sauce (blended Red Sauce, page 279)

2 1/2 oz fresh mozzarella, grated or torn apart by hand

2 slices bacon, cooked and chopped

2 oz Canadian bacon, quartered

2 oz pineapple, cut into chunks

1. Prepare the pizza crusts as directed on page 214, through step 4.

2. For the Meat-Loving Pizza: Add the sauce, then the sausage. Sprinkle on the cheese, then the other toppings. Proceed to step 5 on page 214 to finish.

3. For the Salad Pizza: Spread the olive oil over the crust, then add the chicken; sprinkle on the cheese, then the bacon and red onion slices. Proceed to step 5 on page 214. As the pizza cooks, toss the spring greens and mayo; when the pizza is done, add the tomato slices, then the greens, then the avocado slices.

4. For the Pizza Suprema: Add the sauce, then the sausage and Canadian bacon. Sprinkle on the cheese, then add the remaining toppings. Proceed to step 5 on page 214 to finish.

5. For the Hawaiian Pizza: Add the sauce, then sprinkle on the cheese; add the remaining toppings. Proceed to step 5 on page 214 to finish.

* *To make your own Italian sausage, combine 1 pound ground pork, 1 tablespoon red wine vinegar, 1 teaspoon sea salt, 1 teaspoon black pepper, 1 teaspoon dried parsley, 1 teaspoon dried basil, 1 teaspoon garlic powder, 1 teaspoon onion powder, 1 teaspoon paprika, 1/2 teaspoon crushed red pepper, 1/4 teaspoon ground fennel seed, and a pinch of oregano; gently knead to combine. You can then freeze the sausage in individual pizza portions (each pizza calls for 2 ounces of sausage) for later, or cook it within 24 hours.*

* *Before grilling the chicken for the Salad Pizza, toss it with a bit of olive oil to help keep it moist. For added richness, use 2 tablespoons White Sauce (page 280) instead of the 1 tablespoon olive oil.*

AMERICAN CLASSICS

CALZONES

YIELD: TWO 8- TO 10-INCH CALZONES | PREP TIME: 10 MINS, PLUS TIME TO MAKE PIZZA SAUCE | COOK TIME: 20 MINS

Calzones, originally from Naples, are stuffed half-moon breads resembling folded pizzas. While traditionally stuffed with salami and soft cheese (mainly ricotta), modern interpretations are filled with popular pizza toppings. The stuffing ingredients in this recipe are just a sampling of the possibilities out there.

Some folks like to serve pizza sauce alongside calzones to act as a dipping sauce; others like to add it into the calzone itself. Both methods are tasty, but I like the dipping version better.

1 cup Pizza Sauce (blended Red Sauce, page 279)

CRUST:

1 1/4 cups (142g) tapioca starch

1/4 cup (38g) potato starch

1/4 cup heavy cream

1/4 cup water

2 tbsp butter

1/2 tsp sea salt

1 large egg, beaten

3/4 cup (75g) grated Parmesan or other hard cheese

pinch of white pepper

1/4 tsp dried oregano

FILLING:

5 oz fresh mozzarella, grated or torn apart by hand, divided

4 oz pepperoni, quartered

4 oz white mushrooms, sliced

4 oz black olives

3 tbsp melted ghee, divided

1 large egg white

1. Preheat the oven to 500°F. Place the sauce in a small saucepan and keep warm over low heat.

2. Put the starches in a large mixing bowl and set aside. In a saucepan, combine the cream, water, butter, and salt and warm over medium-low heat. Once the butter melts and the liquid just starts to bubble, remove from the heat and stir it into the starch mixture. Let the mixture cool for 5 minutes.

3. Add the beaten egg to the starch mixture and knead together with your hands. Add the Parmesan, pepper, and oregano and mix together until it's doughlike. Depending on the ambient temperature of your kitchen, the starch mixture can sometimes melt into a gooey consistency—if that happens, just pour it directly onto 2 greased pans in step 4; it'll turn out fine.

4. Split the dough in half, then stretch out each half into the thinnest disc possible without tearing, about 8 to 10 inches in diameter. Place each half on a separate heavy-duty baking sheet that is greased with melted ghee (about 1/2 tablespoon per sheet). With a fork, poke some holes in the dough to let air pass through.

5. Bake in the center of the oven for 4 minutes, then remove from the oven and place on the stovetop.

6. On one half of each circle of dough, place the cheese and other filling ingredients. Brush the egg white along the edges, then fold over the unfilled half to form a half-circle. Press down on the joined edge with a fork to seal each calzone. At this point, you can transfer one of the calzones to the same baking sheet as the other. Bake for 5 more minutes, then brush the calzones with the remaining 2 tablespoons of melted ghee and bake until golden and crispy, about 4 more minutes.

7. Allow to rest for 5 minutes before slicing and serving with the warm Pizza Sauce for dipping.

BASIC WINGS

SERVES: 4 | PREP TIME: 10 MINS | COOK TIME: 30 MINS TO 1 HOUR

In the United States, chicken wings weren't a popular food until the 1960s, when the Buffalo wing craze started at the Anchor Bar in Buffalo, New York. Prior to that, chicken wings were mostly used to make stock. Note that the term "chicken wings" refers to either the entire wing—which consists of the drumette, wing, and wing tip— or the individual drumettes and wings. Any will work fine in this recipe; personally, I'm a fan of crunchy wing tips, so I prefer cooking the entire wings.

Be sure to consult the Saucy Wings (page 224) and Dry-Rubbed Wings (page 226) recipes when making these wings. All told, between the three cooking methods on this spread and the sauce and dry rub combinations on the following pages, you're set up for 20 different combinations of wingy goodness. These wings are nearly 100 percent interchangeable, although there are a few exceptions; for example, a dry rub wouldn't work well with fried wings since the spices would burn.

FRIED WINGS

3 to 4 lbs chicken wings and drumettes

2 tbsp tapioca starch

2 tbsp potato starch

2 tsp kosher salt

1/2 tsp white pepper

2 cups lard

1. Pat the wings dry with paper towels. Combine the starches, salt, and pepper, then toss with the wings until coated. In a cast-iron skillet, heat the lard over medium-high heat to 350°F. Fry the wings in batches until golden brown and cooked through, 8 to 10 minutes per batch, turning every couple of minutes.

2. Toss with the sauce of your choice (pages 224–225) or enjoy plain.

GRILLED WINGS

3 to 4 lbs chicken wings and drumettes

2 tbsp olive oil

1 tsp kosher salt

1/2 tsp white pepper

1. Prepare your grill for indirect grilling by igniting the burners on only one side (gas grill) or by banking the coals to one side (charcoal grill). You want the cool side to be at medium-high heat (about 350°F); you should be able to comfortably hold your hand over the grill for 3 or 4 seconds.

2. Pat the wings dry with paper towels. Toss with the olive oil, then add the salt and pepper; if using a dry rub (page 226), include those ingredients as well. Toss with the wings until coated, mixing with your hands if necessary. Place the chicken on the cool side of the grill and grill until crispy and cooked through, about 45 minutes.

3. Toss with the sauce of your choice (if you didn't dry-rub them) or enjoy as is.

BAKED WINGS

3 to 4 lbs chicken wings and drumettes

2 tbsp olive oil

1 tsp kosher salt

1/2 tsp white pepper

1. Preheat the oven to 400°F. Pat the wings dry with paper towels. Toss with the olive oil, then add the salt and pepper; if using a dry rub (page 226), include those ingredients as well. Toss with the wings until evenly coated, mixing with your hands if necessary. Spread the wings in a single layer on 2 rimmed baking sheets lined with cooling racks, then bake until crispy, about 50 minutes, rotating the pan after 30 minutes.

2. Toss with the sauce of your choice (if you didn't dry-rub them) or enjoy as is.

SAUCY WINGS FOUR WAYS

SERVES: 4 | PREP TIME: 10 MINS. PLUS TIME TO MAKE TERIYAKI OR BARBECUE SAUCE | COOK TIME: 30 MINS TO 1 HOUR

These four sauces are a fair representation of what you'd find on the sauce list of any respectable Buffalo wing restaurant across America. They're versatile in that you can use them with any cooking method (frying, baking, or grilling), and they're easy to whip up since most of the work happens while the wings are cooking.

BUFFALO WINGS

1/2 cup Frank's RedHot Sauce or Tabasco Buffalo Style Hot Sauce

1/4 cup butter or ghee, melted

1 batch Fried, Grilled, or Baked Wings (pages 222–223)

Combine the hot sauce and melted butter, then toss with the cooked wings.

TERIYAKI WINGS

1 cup Teriyaki Sauce (page 272)

sesame seeds

1 batch Fried, Grilled, or Baked Wings (pages 222–223)

Warm the sauce in a small saucepan over medium-low heat until just simmering, then reduce the heat to low to keep the sauce warm until the wings are ready. If making Fried Wings, toss the cooked wings with the sauce and sprinkle sesame seeds on top. If making Baked or Grilled Wings, brush half of the warmed sauce on the wings for the last 5 minutes of cooking before tossing the finished wings with the rest of the sauce for even more flavor.

GARLIC PARMESAN WINGS

1/4 cup butter or ghee

2 tsp lemon juice

1 tsp garlic powder

1 tsp kosher salt

1/2 tsp onion powder

1/4 tsp white pepper

2 tbsp grated Parmesan

1 batch Fried, Grilled, or Baked Wings (pages 222–223)

Combine all the ingredients except the cheese and wings in a small saucepan. Warm over medium-low heat until the butter is liquid but has not yet started to brown, about 3 minutes. Remove from the heat and let cool for 5 minutes. Add the cheese, then toss with the cooked wings.

MAPLE BBQ WINGS

1 cup Barbecue Sauce (page 274)

1 tbsp maple syrup

1 batch Fried, Grilled, or Baked Wings (pages 222–223)

Combine the Barbecue Sauce and maple syrup in a small saucepan. Warm over medium-low heat until just simmering, then reduce the heat to low to keep the sauce warm until the wings are ready. If making Fried Wings, toss the sauce with the cooked wings. If making Baked or Grilled Wings, brush half of the warmed sauce on the wings for the last 5 minutes of cooking before tossing the finished wings with the rest of the sauce for even more flavor.

DRY-RUBBED WINGS FOUR WAYS

SERVES: 4 | PREP TIME: 10 MINS | COOK TIME: ABOUT 1 HOUR

Sometimes you want the full wing experience: sticky, messy, delightfully saucy wings (pages 224–225). Other times, you may be in the mood for simple but decadent plain wings (pages 222–223). These dry-rubbed wings are a fair middle ground, where you enjoy the tastiness of saucy wings without the mess.

Dry-rubbed wings are best grilled (page 222) or baked (page 223); frying the wings will burn the seasonings. Each seasoning blend yields about 3 tablespoons of dry rub, perfect for one batch of wings.

FOR ALL WINGS

3 to 4 lbs chicken wings and drumettes

2 tbsp olive oil

1 tsp kosher salt

1/2 tsp white pepper

CARIBBEAN JERK WINGS

2 tsp dried thyme

1 tsp onion powder

1 tsp garlic powder

1 tsp coconut palm sugar

1 tsp black pepper

1 tsp ground allspice

1/2 tsp cayenne pepper

1/4 tsp ground cinnamon

1/4 tsp ground cloves

1/4 tsp ground nutmeg

DRY RANCH WINGS

2 tsp dried parsley

2 tsp black pepper

2 tsp onion powder

1 tsp garlic powder

1/2 tsp dried dill

1/2 tsp ground mustard

CAJUN WINGS

1 tbsp paprika

1 tsp garlic powder

1 tsp onion powder

1 tsp black pepper

1 tsp dried thyme

1 tsp celery salt

1/2 tsp dried oregano

1/2 tsp cayenne pepper

OLD BAY WINGS

2 tbsp Old Bay seasoning (page 305)

1 tsp garlic powder

1 tsp onion powder

2 tsp lemon juice, for serving (see note)

The instructions for each of these wing recipes are the same: Toss the wings with the olive oil, then combine the salt and pepper with the dry rub ingredients. Toss the wings with the dry rub mixture until coated, mixing with your hands if necessary, then grill or bake as directed on pages 222–223.

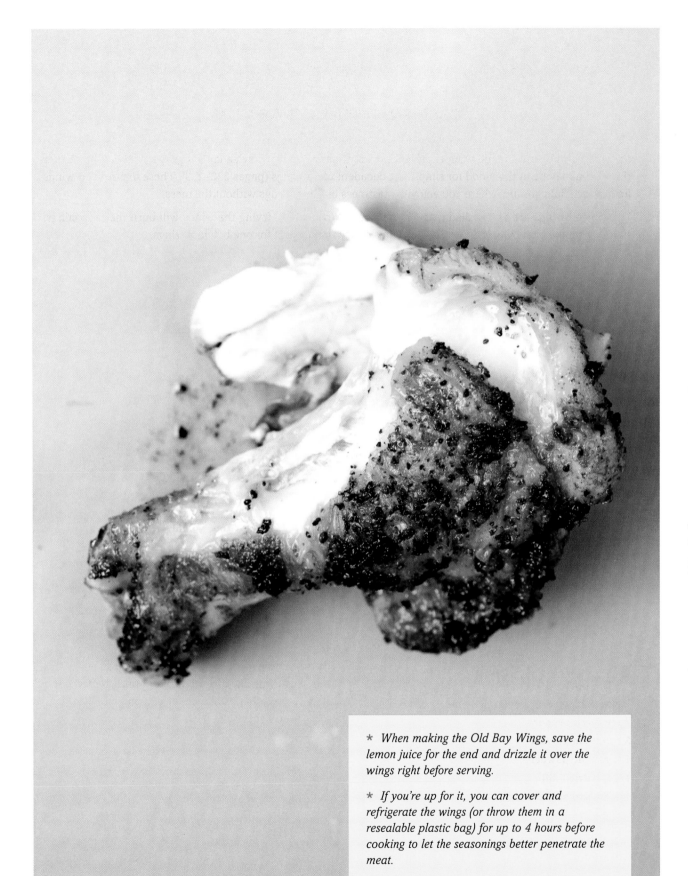

* When making the Old Bay Wings, save the lemon juice for the end and drizzle it over the wings right before serving.

* If you're up for it, you can cover and refrigerate the wings (or throw them in a resealable plastic bag) for up to 4 hours before cooking to let the seasonings better penetrate the meat.

BURGER PARTY

AMERICAN CLASSICS

BURGER PARTY

SERVES: 4 | PREP TIME: 20 MINS, PLUS TIME TO MAKE BUNS AND TOPPINGS | COOK TIME: 10 MINS

I love the idea of making a bunch of different burgers to feed a crowd; in fact, several years ago my wife and I participated in a similar party involving these same four burgers with our friends Brent and Heather from the blog *Virginia is for Hunter-Gatherers*. When I first started thinking about staging a burger party for this book, I immediately thought of that event.

The origin of hamburgers is greatly disputed. While logic would assume that they are from the port city of Hamburg, Germany, many sources argue that burgers originated in the United States. The story goes that ground beef steaks were common in Hamburg in the mid-1800s, having been brought to the city by sailors who had visited and experienced them in Russia, where they were often served raw. Some years later, New York City became a common destination port for travelers from Hamburg, and local German immigrants started selling the ground beef steaks, called Hamburg steaks, to visiting German tourists—who were otherwise known as Hamburgers (in the same sense that someone from New York is a New Yorker). Somewhere down the line they started serving the steaks between slices of bread, and the "Hamburger sandwich" was born.

FOR ALL BURGERS

1 batch Burger Buns (page 296)
2 lbs ground beef
1 tbsp cool bacon fat or lard
1 tsp sea salt
1/2 tsp black pepper

WILD BURGER

pickle chips
caramelized onions
tomato slice
lettuce
Wild Burger Sauce (recipe follows)

PICNIC BURGER

pickle chips
tomato slice
Picnic Coleslaw (page 294)

AUSSIE BURGER

sharp cheddar cheese slice
bacon slices
grilled pineapple rings
caramelized onions
pickled beets
fried egg
tomato slice
lettuce
Mayo (page 276)

BBQ BURGER

sharp cheddar cheese slice
bacon slices
Onion Rings (recipe follows)
Barbecue Sauce (page 274)

> ★ *The burger patties can be frozen for even easier meals next time. Complete step 2 of the recipe, stack the formed patties between layers of parchment paper, and place in a resealable plastic bag. They will keep for up to 6 months in the freezer.*

1. Prepare the buns and set aside.

2. In a large mixing bowl, combine the ground beef, bacon fat, salt, and pepper and gently mix together with your hands. Form into 4 large (1/2-pound) patties, about 1 inch thick. With your thumb, create a slight divot in the center of each burger. Transfer to the fridge to chill while you heat up the grill and prepare the toppings, about 15 minutes.

3. Prepare your desired toppings. You don't have to make 4 different burgers, but the options are there! Frying up some bacon is always a good idea. To caramelize onions, simply sauté them in your favorite fat (ghee is especially good) on medium-low heat until caramelized, about 20 minutes.

4. Grill the burgers over direct high heat to your liking, about 2 minutes per side for medium-rare, 3 minutes per side for medium, or 4 minutes per side for well-done. Be sure to grill your pineapple rings at the same time if making Aussie Burgers.

5. Let the burgers rest for 5 minutes, then place on the buns and add the toppings in the order directed; for example, for a BBQ Burger, you'd put the cheese on the burger, then add the bacon, the Onion Rings, and finally the Barbecue Sauce. Serve with Onion Rings (recipe follows) or Perfect Oven Fries (page 290) and your favorite condiments (the Fry Sauce on page 290 is especially good).

WILD BURGER SAUCE

1/4 cup Mayo (page 276)

3 tbsp minced dill pickles

1 tbsp Ketchup (page 278)

2 tsp yellow mustard

2 tsp apple cider vinegar

1/2 tsp sea salt

1/4 tsp white pepper

splash of dill pickle juice

Combine the ingredients and stir until mixed.

ONION RINGS

1 large Spanish or sweet onion, sliced

1/2 batch Tempura batter (page 116)

1/4 cup lard, for frying

sea salt

1. Soak the onion slices in cold water for 30 minutes.

2. Pat the onion slices dry, then dip in the batter. Remember that when making the batter, you'll want to add just enough water to make it thinner than pancake batter. In a skillet, fry the battered onion slices in the lard, in batches, until brown and crispy, about 2 minutes per set of rings. Season with salt to taste.

CHICKEN SANDWICHES

SERVES: 4 | PREP TIME: 10 MINS. PLUS AT LEAST 30 MINUTES TO MARINATE | COOK TIME: 40 MINS

When burgers just don't cut the mustard, Chicken Sandwiches are a perfect alternative. These sandwiches are modeled after the popular Southern-style chicken sandwiches found in many fast food restaurants; marinating the breast fillets in pickle juice both tenderizes them and gives them a distinct tanginess that is surprisingly un-pickle-like.

1 batch Burger Buns (page 296)

2 large boneless, skinless chicken breasts (about 1 1/2 lbs total)

1/2 cup dill pickle juice (see note)

1/4 cup arrowroot, potato, or tapioca starch

1 tbsp paprika

2 tsp kosher salt

1 tsp black pepper

3 large eggs

1/2 cup lard or expeller-pressed coconut oil, or more if needed

toppings as desired [lettuce, pickles, tomatoes, Mayo and Honey Mustard (page 276)]

1. Prepare the buns and set aside.

2. Place the chicken flat on a cutting board, then slice each breast in half lengthwise to make 2 thin butterflied cutlets, 4 total. Combine with the pickle juice in a resealable plastic bag; marinate for at least 30 minutes but up to 6 hours for best results.

3. Drain the chicken in a colander to discard the excess pickle juice, then pat dry with paper towels. Move the chicken around to make sure it drains properly. As the chicken drains, prepare the breading by combining the starch, paprika, salt, and pepper. Beat the eggs in a wide bowl and set aside.

4. Preheat your oven to 250°F. In a wide skillet, heat the lard over medium heat to about 325°F. Dust each cutlet with the starch mixture, dip the starchy cutlet in the egg, shake off the excess egg, and then add to the lard in the pan. Repeat until you have filled your pan; be careful not to overcrowd the chicken pieces.

5. Fry the chicken until cooked through, flipping every 2 minutes, about 8 minutes per batch. As you finish each batch, place the cooked cutlets on a plate lined with paper towels; put them in the oven to keep warm. You should be able to cook the chicken in 2 or 3 batches, depending on the size of your skillet.

6. Serve on the buns with any toppings you desire.

* I prefer the pickle juice that comes with Bubbies Kosher Dills. These salt-brined, probiotic dills are delicious and made without any added vinegar or junk.

CHICKEN NUGGETS

SERVES: 4 | PREP TIME: 10 MINS. PLUS AT LEAST 30 MINUTES TO MARINATE | COOK TIME: 35 MINS

After spending so many years working on challenging and adventurous recipes, I find it ironic that the very first recipe that propelled my blog to popularity was a recipe for Chicken Nuggets. This variation is an improvement on that original, beloved recipe, using what I like to call a "reverse battering" process, where the nuggets are breaded on the outside using egg instead of a flour breading. The resulting texture is spongy and ridiculously kid-friendly.

As in my Chicken Sandwiches recipe (page 232), marinating the chicken in pickle juice tenderizes the meat and adds a tangy flavor that is surprisingly free of pickle taste!

2 lbs boneless, skinless chicken breasts, cut into bite-sized pieces

1/2 cup dill pickle juice (see note)

1/4 cup arrowroot or tapioca starch

2 tsp paprika

1 tsp sea salt

1 tsp black pepper

2 large eggs

1/4 cup lard or expeller-pressed coconut oil, or more if needed

1. Combine the chicken pieces and pickle juice in a resealable plastic bag; marinate for at least 30 minutes but up to 6 hours for best results.

2. Drain the chicken in a colander to discard the excess pickle juice, then pat dry with paper towels. Move the chicken around to make sure it drains properly. As the chicken drains, prepare the breading by combining the starch, paprika, salt, and pepper. Beat the eggs in a wide bowl and set aside.

3. Preheat your oven to 250°F. In a wok or skillet, heat the lard over medium heat to about 325°F. Toss the chicken pieces with the starch mixture. With your fingers, dip a starchy chicken piece in the egg, shake off the excess egg, and then add to the lard in the pan. Repeat until you have filled your skillet; be careful not to overcrowd the chicken pieces.

4. Fry the chicken until cooked through, flipping every 2 minutes, about 6 to 8 minutes per batch. As you finish each batch, place the cooked pieces on a plate lined with paper towels; put them in the oven to keep warm. You should be able to cook the chicken pieces in 3 or 4 batches, depending on the size of your skillet.

5. Serve with the sauce of your choice, such as Barbecue Sauce (page 274), Honey Mustard (page 276), Ketchup (page 278), or Fry Sauce (page 290).

> * *I prefer the pickle juice that comes with Bubbies Kosher Dills. These salt-brined, probiotic dills are delicious and made without any added vinegar or junk.*

FRIED CHICKEN IN A BUCKET

SERVES: 6 TO 8 | PREP TIME: 35 MINS, PLUS AT LEAST 30 MINUTES TO MARINATE | COOK TIME: UP TO 1 HOUR

I have fond childhood memories of my parents picking up a bucket from our nearby fried chicken shop on those days when we'd go boating or have an impromptu summer picnic. This recipe re-creates that experience without the worry about what exactly is hidden in those secret ingredient mixes. Serve with Picnic Coleslaw (page 294) and Mashed Potatoes and Gravy (page 292).

4 lbs bone-in, skin-on chicken thighs and/or drumsticks

2 cups full-fat buttermilk (see note)

1 tbsp sea salt

COATING:

1/4 cup potato starch

1/4 cup tapioca starch

2 tsp sea salt

2 tsp black pepper

2 tsp paprika

1 tsp onion powder

1/2 tsp garlic powder

1/2 tsp dried oregano

1/2 tsp dried sage

1/2 tsp dried basil

1/4 tsp ground ginger

1/4 tsp ground cloves

pinch of dried thyme

3 cups lard, for frying, or more if needed

1. Pat the chicken pieces dry with paper towels. In a resealable plastic bag, combine the chicken, buttermilk, and salt and refrigerate for at least 30 minutes but up to overnight—the longer the better. Drain the chicken in a colander, then let dry on a wire rack over a baking sheet for 30 minutes.

2. Combine the coating ingredients in a wide, shallow bowl and set aside. Preheat your oven to 170°F. In a cast-iron skillet, heat the lard to 340°F to 350°F. Pat the chicken pieces dry with paper towels, then coat them in the seasonings, shaking off the excess. Fry the chicken in batches until the internal temperature reaches 165°F, about 10 minutes per side. As you finish each batch, place the cooked chicken pieces on a wire rack set over a baking sheet; put them in the oven to keep warm as you fry the remaining pieces.

> ⋆ *Not a fan of buttermilk, or avoiding dairy? Easy—substitute 1 1/2 cups coconut milk and 1/4 cup white vinegar or apple cider vinegar. The key to this marinade is its acidity, which tenderizes the chicken.*

CHILI FRIES

SERVES: 6 | PREP TIME: 10 MINS | COOK TIME: 2 1/2 HOURS

Here's something I find amusing: This chili actually makes my Perfect Oven Fries (page 290)…um, perfecter. It is mild and relatively chunk-free, which makes it an excellent topping over fries, as well as burgers (page 228), hot dogs, rice (page 286), or even pizza (page 214)! Garnish with whatever you'd like—diced red or white onion, shredded sharp cheddar cheese, sour cream, guacamole (page 282), and/or sliced green onion.

CHILI:

1 tbsp butter

1 medium onion, coarsely chopped

6 cloves garlic, minced

1 1/2 tbsp ground coriander

1 tbsp ground cumin

1 tsp sea salt

1 tsp black pepper

1 tsp paprika

1 tsp dried oregano

1/2 tsp cayenne pepper

1/2 tsp crushed red pepper

1/4 tsp ground cinnamon

2 bay leaves

2 lbs ground beef or game meat (such as venison or elk)

1 (14 1/2 oz) can diced tomatoes

2 (14 1/2 oz) cans puréed tomatoes

2 tbsp Mayo (page 276)

2 tbsp unsweetened cocoa powder

1 batch Perfect Oven Fries (page 290)

1. In a stockpot, warm the butter on medium heat for 1 minute, then add the onion and sauté until aromatic, about 5 minutes. Add the garlic, seasonings, and bay leaves and sauté for another minute. Add the ground beef and simmer until browned, stirring frequently to break up chunks, about 6 minutes. Add the tomatoes, cover, and reduce the heat to low; simmer for 1 hour.

2. After 1 hour, remove the lid and simmer, uncovered, for another hour. Stir in the mayonnaise and cocoa powder and simmer for another 10 minutes to allow the flavors to marry; add more salt, pepper, and cayenne pepper (or hot sauce) to taste.

3. During the last hour of cooking, prepare the Perfect Oven Fries; they should finish at the same time. Pour the chili over the fries and go to town.

> ★ *This chili freezes well. I usually make a double batch and freeze individual servings for fast weeknight meals.*

SPAGHETTI AND MEATBALLS

SERVES: 4 | PREP TIME: 10 MINS, PLUS TIME TO MAKE RED SAUCE | COOK TIME: 45 MINS

It seems like every country has a meatball recipe, from the very popular Swedish meatballs to the relatively unknown Finnish meatballs (Lihapullat), often made with reindeer meat. Asian meatballs have significant representation in this book, but even they pale in comparison to the notoriety and controversy that surrounds a good Italian meatball.

Italian meatballs are larger than most other meatballs and are prized for their tenderness. Gelatin may seem like a strange addition, but it gives the meatballs a velvety texture, not unlike what you'd expect from eating veal.

1 batch Red Sauce (page 279)

SPAGHETTI:

1 (8 oz) package rice-based spaghetti or

4 zucchini or yellow squash (about 2 lbs total), spiral-sliced

MEATBALLS:

4 large egg yolks, beaten

2 tbsp Chicken Broth (page 264)

1 tsp gelatin powder

1 medium onion, coarsely chopped

6 cloves garlic

1/2 cup chopped fresh parsley

1 tbsp tapioca starch

1 tbsp kosher salt

1 1/2 tsp black pepper

1 tsp dried oregano

1/4 cup grated Parmesan, plus 2 tbsp for garnish

4 slices bacon, coarsely chopped

1 lb ground beef

1 lb ground pork

2 tbsp chopped fresh parsley, for garnish

1. Warm the sauce over medium-low heat. Once simmering, reduce the heat to low and keep warm.

2. Cook the spaghetti. For rice-based spaghetti, cook as directed on the box, then rinse in cold water until cool to the touch and toss with 1 tablespoon olive oil to keep the pasta from sticking. For spiral-sliced zucchini or yellow squash, blanch in boiling water for 30 seconds, then rinse in cold water. Set aside.

3. Position an oven rack near the top of your oven and preheat the oven on broil. Combine the egg yolks, broth, and gelatin; set aside. Place the onion, garlic, parsley, tapioca starch, salt, pepper, and oregano in a food processor and pulse until uniform. Add 1/4 cup of the Parmesan and the bacon and pulse until well mixed. Transfer to a mixing bowl, then add the egg yolk mixture, beef, and pork. With your hands, gently mix until uniform, then form into 12 tennis ball–sized meatballs and transfer to a heavy-duty baking sheet.

4. Broil the meatballs until the tops are browned, about 6 minutes, then remove from the oven and gently add to the sauce. Cover and gently simmer until cooked through, about 15 minutes.

5. Distribute the spaghetti among 4 wide bowls, then spoon the sauce and meatballs over the spaghetti. Garnish with parsley and the remaining 2 tablespoons of Parmesan cheese and serve.

⁕ *To make the meatballs spicier, add 1 teaspoon crushed red pepper (or more to taste) to the food processor with the other seasonings.*

CHICKEN FETTUCCINE ALFREDO

SERVES: 4 | PREP TIME: 20 MINS | COOK TIME: 20 MINS

While dishes of pasta tossed with butter and cheese have been around for a long time, Fettuccine Alfredo is based on the signature dish of Alfredo Di Lelio's restaurant, which opened in Rome, Italy, in 1914. American tourists grew to love the dish and brought it back to the United States. While Americans often add ingredients like chicken, shrimp, mushrooms, or broccoli to the dish, it's commonly served without add-ins elsewhere in the world.

Your best bet for an authentic pasta taste and texture is Cappello's grain-free fettuccine, which you can buy online and at select health food stores. Your second best option is rice-based fettuccine. Other options include spiral-sliced squash noodles and kelp noodles.

ALFREDO SAUCE:

3 tbsp butter

1 shallot, minced

6 cloves garlic, minced

2 cups heavy cream (see note)

1 tsp black pepper

1/2 tsp sea salt

1/4 tsp ground nutmeg

2 boneless, skinless chicken breasts (about 1 lb total)

2 tsp olive oil, divided

10 button (white) or cremini mushrooms (about 6 oz), sliced

FETTUCCINE:

1 (9 oz) package Cappello's fettuccine
or

1 (8 oz) package rice-based fettuccine
or

4 zucchini or yellow squash (about 2 lbs total), spiral-sliced

2 cups chopped broccoli, steamed

1 cup shredded or shaved Parmesan/Romano/Asiago cheese blend

1. In a large saucepan or skillet, melt the butter over medium heat. Add the shallot and sauté until softened, about 2 minutes. Add the garlic and sauté until aromatic, about 30 seconds. Add the cream, pepper, salt, and nutmeg, reduce the heat to low, and gently simmer for 20 minutes.

2. Meanwhile, cook the chicken. Place the chicken flat on a cutting board, then slice each breast in half lengthwise to make 2 thin butterflied cutlets, 4 total. Season with a bit of salt and pepper and toss with 1 teaspoon of the olive oil. Grill over direct medium-high heat until cooked through, about 4 minutes per side. Remove from the grill and let rest for a few minutes, then slice into strips and set aside.

3. Add the mushrooms to the sauce and simmer until softened, another 10 to 15 minutes.

4. Meanwhile, cook the fettuccine. Bring a pot of salted water to a boil, drop in your noodles, and reduce the heat to medium-high. Boil for 45 seconds for Cappello's pasta, as directed on the box for rice-based pasta, or 30 seconds for spiral-sliced zucchini or yellow squash. Drain and rinse in cold water; squeeze out half of the water if using squash. Toss the Cappello's or rice pasta with the remaining olive oil to keep them from sticking together; spiral-sliced squash doesn't require oil.

5. Bring the saucepan's heat up to medium. As the sauce begins to bubble, add the fettuccine and gently mix it around. Wait a minute for it to start bubbling again, then add the chicken and broccoli and toss it all together. Add the cheese a few seconds later and mix again, continuing to toss until the cheese has melted. Season with salt and pepper, then serve.

* *Dairy-free? Substitute 1 cup each Chicken Broth (page 264) and full-fat coconut milk for the cream, and omit the cheese. To thicken the sauce, create a roux. Melt 2 tablespoons butter or ghee in a pan over medium heat, then add 1 tablespoon white rice flour or coconut flour; cook until golden and toasted, about 3 minutes, then set aside. Add the roux to the sauce at the beginning of step 5.*

CHICKEN PARMESAN

SERVES: 4 | PREP TIME: 20 MINS, PLUS TIME TO MAKE RED SAUCE | COOK TIME: 30 MINS

Parmigiana is a method of Italian cooking wherein breaded and fried cutlets are layered in cheese and tomato sauce. Originally made with eggplant (page 246), versions made with breaded chicken and veal cutlets are popular as well. There is some dispute as to where this dish came from; logic would dictate that the northern city of Parma started the craze, but the southern regions Campania and Sicily also stake a claim to this dish. A common misconception is that the dish got its name from the inclusion of Parmesan cheese (despite the fact that mozzarella is the most common cheese used in this dish), but, like Chicken Parmesan, Parmesan cheese is so named because it is produced in the city of Parma.

1 batch Red Sauce (page 279)

4 boneless, skinless chicken breasts (about 2 lbs total)

DUSTING:

1/4 cup tapioca or arrowroot starch

1 tsp sea salt

1/2 tsp paprika

3 large eggs

BREADING:

1/4 cup tapioca or arrowroot starch

1/4 cup potato starch

1 tsp black pepper

1 tsp dried oregano

1 tsp dried basil or parsley

1/2 tsp sea salt

1/4 cup lard, ghee, or expeller-pressed coconut oil

8 oz fresh mozzarella, grated

1. Heat the sauce over medium-low heat until simmering; reduce the heat to low to keep warm while you prepare the chicken.

2. Place the chicken flat on a cutting board, then slice each breast in half lengthwise to make 2 thin butterflied cutlets, 8 total. Gently pound with a meat tenderizer to an even thickness, about 1/2 inch, then set aside.

3. Prepare 3 wide, shallow bowls to bread the cutlets. In the first bowl, combine the dusting ingredients. In the second bowl, beat the eggs. In the third bowl, combine the breading ingredients.

4. Preheat your oven to 350°F. In a large skillet, warm the lard over medium-high heat; you're looking for an oil temp of 325°F. Once the fat is hot, dust a chicken cutlet in the first bowl, then transfer to the second bowl and cover in egg. Shake off any excess egg, then cover with the breading in the third bowl. Add to the skillet and repeat for however many cutlets you can fit in the skillet at one time (don't bread the chicken until right before you add it to the fat).

5. Pan-fry the chicken until golden brown, about 3 minutes per side, then transfer to a baking sheet. Don't worry about whether the chicken is cooked through; the oven will finish it off. Add more lard if needed and repeat until all the chicken has been pan-fried.

6. Spoon the sauce over the cutlets, then sprinkle on the cheese. Place in the oven and bake until the cheese has melted, about 8 minutes, then broil for 2 minutes or until the cheese is spotty and golden (watch it like a hawk at this point). Remove from the oven and serve.

★ It is possible to bake the chicken instead of frying it. Line a baking sheet with a wire rack; bread all the cutlets at once using the process outlined in step 4, then place on the wire rack. Bake at 400°F until golden, about 15 to 20 minutes, flipping and brushing with ghee or coconut oil after 10 minutes. Remove the wire rack, add the sauce and cheese, and bake until the cheese has melted, about 6 minutes, then broil for 2 minutes or until the cheese is spotty and golden.

★ To make this dish with veal, buy 8 thinly sliced veal chops and proceed to step 3.

★ While fresh mozzarella is typically used in this dish, using a harder cheese may be easier for digestion (aged cheese is fermented longer). Or make it dairy-free by using Cashew Cheese (page 246), or omit the cheese altogether!

BAKED EGGPLANT PARMESAN

SERVES: 4 | PREP TIME: 25 MINS, PLUS TIME TO MAKE RED SAUCE | COOK TIME: 40 MINS

This is the original preparation of Eggplant Parmesan. While many Italian-American restaurants bread, pan-fry, and then bake the eggplant slices in the same manner as described in my Chicken Parmesan recipe (page 244), I prefer the comparatively hands-off nature of this baked preparation.

2 large eggplants (about 2 lbs total), sliced 1/4 inch thick

2 tsp kosher salt

1/2 batch Red Sauce (page 279)

1/4 cup lard, or more if needed

10 oz fresh mozzarella, grated (see note)

1 tbsp grated Parmesan

2 tsp dried oregano

* *Dairy-free? Try making this dish with cashew cheese (recipe follows) instead of mozzarella and Parmesan.*

1. Sprinkle the eggplant slices with the salt and place in a colander to drain for 20 minutes, then pat dry with paper towels.

2. As the eggplant is draining, heat the sauce over medium-low heat until simmering; reduce the heat to low to keep warm while you prepare the eggplant.

3. Heat the lard in a skillet over medium-high heat until shimmering, about 3 minutes. Fry the eggplant in batches until browned, about 2 minutes per side, then set on paper towels to drain.

4. Preheat the oven to 400°F. Combine the grated cheeses and oregano. Line a casserole dish with some of the eggplant slices, then spoon on some sauce, then a layer of cheese. Continue layering until you're out of the ingredients. This isn't rocket science, so there are no exact calculations—the number of layers you get will depend on the size and shape of your casserole dish. It'll turn out fine.

5. Bake until the cheese has melted and is starting to brown, about 20 minutes, then let rest for 10 minutes before serving.

CASHEW CHEESE

1 cup raw cashews

1/4 cup water, or more as needed

2 tbsp nutritional yeast

2 tsp lemon juice

2 tsp apple cider vinegar

1 clove garlic

1/4 tsp sea salt, or more to taste

Soak the cashews in warm water for 2 hours, then blend with the remaining ingredients in a high-speed blender until smooth, adding more water as needed to help the mixture blend but keeping it as thick as possible. For best results, refrigerate for 2 hours before using. When making this recipe, simply mix the dried oregano into the Cashew Cheese and use as directed in step 4. It will be more of a paste than a firm cheese, so it's better just to scatter and layer clumps of it as you work; the dish will taste great!

FAJITAS

SERVES: 4 | PREP TIME: 10 MINS, PLUS TIME TO MAKE SIDES AND AT LEAST 30 MINUTES TO MARINATE | COOK TIME: 20 MINS

· ·

For some reason, fajitas often carry a premium price at Mexican-American restaurants. I've always found that they're not worth the extra fee compared to other, comparatively affordable fare like tacos or enchiladas. Making the dish at home, however, is relatively simple and fast once you knock out the marinade. And flank steak is relatively cheap! If you can't find flank steak, I suggest using strip, sirloin, or skirt steak.

While grilling is preferred, you can fry the fajitas in a hot stovetop pan. Instructions are provided below!

· ·

MARINADE:

1/2 bunch fresh cilantro, stems included

juice of 1/2 orange (2 tbsp)

juice of 1 lime (2 tbsp)

2 tbsp olive oil

4 cloves garlic

1 tsp ground cumin

1 tsp chipotle chili powder

2 lbs flank steak

2 medium onions, sliced

1 red bell pepper, sliced

1 yellow bell pepper, sliced

1 tbsp olive oil

1/2 tsp sea salt

FOR SERVING:

1 batch Flatbread (page 298)

1 batch No-Fuss Guac (page 282)

chopped fresh cilantro

1. Combine the marinade ingredients in a blender and blend until smooth. Combine with the flank steak in a resealable plastic bag; refrigerate for at least 30 minutes but up to overnight.

2. Grill the steak over direct high heat to your desired doneness: 2 minutes per side for rare, 3 minutes per side for medium-rare, or 4 minutes per side for medium (don't cook it longer than that; flank steak toughens quickly). Set the steak aside to rest.

3. Line the grill with heavy-duty aluminum foil or a grill plate with small holes. Toss the vegetables with the olive oil and salt, then grill until scorched and soft, about 4 minutes, turning occasionally.

4. Thinly slice the steak against the grain and serve with the grilled vegetables, flatbread, guacamole, and cilantro. Pour any accumulated juices that appeared when slicing the steak over the steak before serving.

★ *The steak and veggies can be pan-fried. Pat the steak dry with paper towels, then heat 1 tablespoon olive oil or ghee over medium-high heat until shimmering, about 2 minutes. Add the steak and cook as directed above; add the veggies to the skillet after taking the steak out and cook as directed above.*

★ *Many grocery stores sell presliced stew meat as "fajita meat." It can definitely be used in this recipe; simply marinate and grill (lined with foil, like the veggies) or pan-fry it over very high heat. It'll cook quickly, so it'll need only a minute or two on the grill.*

CARNITAS

SERVES: 8 (OR 4 WITH LEFTOVERS) | PREP TIME: 10 MINS. PLUS TIME TO MAKE FLATBREAD AND AT LEAST 6 HOURS TO REFRIGERATE
COOK TIME: 14 1/2 HOURS (IT'S WORTH IT!)

• •

This recipe is the gift that keeps on giving; not only does it yield 8 servings, but the meat freezes well and can be used in a variety of ways. For example, combine it with Barbecue Sauce (page 274) for easy Southern-style pulled pork, or enjoy it as is for a mild taste not unlike the Hawaiian favorite Kalua Pig.

Look for pork that has the skin and bone intact, which will yield more flavor. Pork shoulder is labeled as butt, shoulder, picnic pork, or Boston butt—they're all variations of the same area.

• •

PORK:

2 tsp ground cumin

1 tsp chipotle chili powder

1 tsp kosher salt

6 to 8 lbs pork shoulder

1/4 cup lard

1/2 tsp hickory liquid smoke

juice of 1 lime (2 tbsp)

sea salt and black pepper

FOR SERVING:

2 batches Flatbread (page 298)

1/2 bunch fresh cilantro, chopped

1 medium white or red onion, chopped

1 lime, sliced into wedges

6 radishes, thinly sliced

1. Combine the cumin, chipotle chili powder, and salt, then rub all over the pork. Line a slow cooker or Dutch oven with the lard, then add the pork and sprinkle on the liquid smoke.

2. Cover and cook over low heat until almost falling apart, about 14 hours. Remove from the heat and allow to cool for 1 hour, then carefully transfer to a resealable plastic bag; refrigerate for at least 6 to 8 hours, but up to a week. Reserve any leftover liquid and fat, cover, and refrigerate that as well.

3. The next day, add the pork to a skillet over medium-low heat. Add the leftover fat that you reserved, which will have accumulated at the top of the liquid. (Save the liquid for use in other recipes, like Ramen [page 112].) Once the pork starts sizzling (after about 5 minutes), shred it into large chunks using tongs. Continue to crisp the pork, turning every 10 minutes, until it looks unbearably delicious, about 30 to 40 minutes altogether. Season with the lime juice, taste, and add salt and pepper if needed.

4. Serve the meat on flatbread with cilantro and onions, garnished with lime wedges and thinly sliced radishes. If you're up for it, consider adding Pico de Gallo (page 254), No-Fuss Guac (page 282), or Avocado Mayo Sauce (page 252).

✳ *The timing of this dish is tricky, so here's how I do it. While making dinner at around 5pm, I'll also prep the pork and cook it in a slow cooker overnight (the porky smell will permeate your dreams, so be prepared for that). Before work the next day (around 7am), I'll cool and remove the pork and throw it in the fridge. By the time I get home from work, I can proceed right to step 3.*

✳ *Don't have time to cook the pork for 14 hours? Technology to the rescue! If you have an electric pressure cooker (we love our Instant Pot!), follow step 1, then set the pressure cooker to Meat for 100 minutes. Once it finishes cooking and switches to Keep Warm, let it sit for 15 minutes, then slowly release the pressure using the top knob. Uncover, allow to cool, then refrigerate the pork as directed in step 2.*

BLACKENED FISH TACOS

SERVES: 4 | PREP TIME: 15 MINS, PLUS TIME TO MAKE FLATBREAD | COOK TIME: 15 MINS

Growing up, fish tacos were an enigma—something you ordered in restaurants but never made at home. I think part of the mystery surrounding this deceptively simple dish is its gourmet-tasting white sauce. Turns out it's not too hard to re-create; avocado, mayo, and fresh cilantro do most of the work for you.

Try experimenting with a variety of your favorite fish fillets, as each fish will yield subtle differences in taste and texture. I prefer wild, sustainably caught fish, with the exception of farm-raised tilapia from the United States, which thrive on a vegetarian diet (unlike most other farmed fish).

4 firm fish fillets (tilapia, cod, halibut, snapper, or catfish; about 2 lbs total)

1 tbsp paprika

1 tsp garlic powder

1 tsp onion powder

1 tsp black pepper

1 tsp dried thyme

1 tsp celery salt

AVOCADO MAYO SAUCE [MAKES 1/3 CUP]:

1/2 avocado

3 tbsp Mayo (page 276)

2 tbsp fresh cilantro leaves and stems (about 4 stalks)

2 tbsp water

juice of 1/2 lime (1 tbsp)

1/2 tsp sea salt

1/4 tsp black pepper

4 tbsp ghee, divided

1 batch Flatbread (page 298)

1/4 head green cabbage, thinly sliced

1/4 head red cabbage or 1 radicchio, thinly sliced

lime wedges, for serving

1. Pat the fish dry with paper towels. Combine the paprika, garlic powder, onion powder, pepper, thyme, and celery salt and season the fish generously with the mixture; set the fish aside as you make the sauce.

2. Combine the sauce ingredients and blend until smooth, adding more water if needed to help the blending process. When the sauce reaches the consistency of a thin mayonnaise, cover and refrigerate.

3. Open any nearby windows and turn on your oven hood fan. Heat a cast-iron skillet over high heat until smoking, about 5 minutes. Add 2 tablespoons of the ghee and immediately add half of the seasoned fish. Sear for 2 minutes, then carefully flip and fry until cooked through, 1 to 2 more minutes. Remove the fish and set aside. Repeat with the remaining ghee and fish.

4. Flake the fish into bite-sized chunks, then serve on flatbread with some green and red cabbage. Drizzle on the Avocado Mayo Sauce and serve with lime wedges.

* *For extra kick, add 1/2 teaspoon chipotle chili powder to the Avocado Mayo Sauce.*

* *For a fresco twist, consider adding Pico de Gallo (page 254) or No-Fuss Guac (page 282).*

BURRITO BOWL DATE NIGHT

SERVES: 4 (TWO COUPLES) | PREP TIME: 20 MINS, PLUS TIME TO MARINATE CHICKEN AND MAKE RICE | COOK TIME: 25 MINS

It seems like restaurants everywhere are offering burrito bowls, and for good reason: They're easy to make, less messy to eat than big burritos, and incredibly versatile. This recipe mimics some of my favorite burrito bowls, but with a two-person twist that'll have you fighting your date for that last scoop of guac.

2 cloves garlic

1/4 cup olive oil

1 tbsp chipotle chili powder

1 tbsp apple cider vinegar

juice of 1/2 lime (1 tbsp)

2 tsp sea salt

1 tsp black pepper

1 tsp paprika

1/2 tsp dried oregano

2 to 3 lbs boneless, skinless chicken thighs

PICO DE GALLO (MAKES 2 CUPS):

1 large ripe tomato, seeds removed, diced

1/2 tsp kosher salt

1/2 small onion, diced

1/4 cup chopped fresh cilantro

juice of 1/2 lime (1 tbsp)

CILANTRO RICE:

2 cups Basic Steamed Rice (page 286) or Cauliflower Rice (page 288; see note)

2 tsp avocado oil

juice of 1/2 lime (1 tbsp)

1 tsp lemon juice

1/2 tsp sea salt

1/4 cup chopped fresh cilantro

FOR SERVING:

1 head romaine lettuce, shredded

1 batch No-Fuss Guac (page 282)

sour cream (optional; see note)

cheese (optional; see note)

Tabasco

1. Place the garlic, olive oil, chipotle chili powder, vinegar, lime juice, salt, pepper, paprika, and oregano in a blender and blend until smooth. Combine with the chicken in a resealable plastic bag; marinate for at least 30 minutes, overnight preferred.

2. Make the Pico de Gallo: Salt the diced tomato; leave in a colander to drain for 20 minutes. Combine the drained tomatoes with the remaining ingredients and set aside.

3. Grill the chicken over direct medium-high heat until it reaches an internal temperature of 155°F, about 10 minutes, flipping halfway through. Let the chicken rest for 5 minutes, then chop it into bite-sized chunks.

4. Make the Cilantro Rice: Place the cooked rice in a big bowl. Mix in the oil. Add the lime and lemon juices and salt, stirring together. Finally, stir in the cilantro. Taste and add more salt or lime juice if you like.

5. Serve the burrito bowls any way you see fit. At my house, we like rice, then lettuce, then chicken, then pico, then guac.

* If making the cilantro rice with cauliflower rice, only use half of the wet ingredients (oil and juices).

* If serving with sour cream, vigorously stir the sour cream to denature its proteins and make it less firm.

* If serving with cheese, an equal mixture of white cheddar and jack cheeses tastes best.

* Don't limit yourself to just chicken. Consider using Carnitas (page 250), fajita steak (page 248), or blackened fish (page 252).

* You haven't really lived until you've made a burger bowl: unseasoned cooked rice, Mayo (page 276), Ketchup (page 278), mustard, your favorite burger toppings, and a burger or two on top. You're welcome.

GYROS

SERVES: 4 | PREP TIME: TIME: 10 MINS, PLUS TIME TO MAKE FLATBREAD AND TZATZIKI SAUCE | COOK TIME: 45 MINS

Gyros are characterized most by their meat, which is usually lamb or a mixture of lamb and beef roasted on a revolving vertical spit. This process is used in many other cuisines and cultures; you'll see the same setup for shawarma and doner kebabs. What makes Gyros stand apart from their cousin dishes is the use of Tzatziki Sauce (page 284), a tart, garlicky, and herb-filled cream sauce.

Since most of us don't have a vertical spit lying around at home (who does?), I've found that grill-roasting the meat in loaves works really well. Better yet, you can cool and slice the loaves and then pan-fry the meat to reheat it, giving you that signature crispy texture!

GYRO MEAT:

1 medium onion, coarsely chopped

2 cloves garlic

1 tbsp sea salt

1 tsp black pepper

1 tsp dried oregano

1/2 tsp dried marjoram

1 lb ground lamb

1 lb ground beef

FOR SERVING:

1 batch Flatbread (page 298)

2 medium tomatoes, diced

1 head romaine lettuce, chopped

1 medium yellow or red onion, thinly sliced

1 medium cucumber, sliced

1 batch Tzatziki Sauce (page 284)

crumbled feta cheese (optional)

1. Combine the onion, garlic, salt, pepper, oregano, and marjoram in a food processor and process until uniform. Add the ground meats and pulse until smooth and tacky. Form into 2 loaves, each approximately 1 1/2 inches high.

2. Prepare your grill for indirect grilling by igniting the burners on only one side (gas grill) or by banking the coals to one side (charcoal grill). Line the cool side of the grill with foil and place the loaves on the foil. Grill over indirect medium heat (about 300°F) until the loaves reach an internal temperature of 155°F, about 35 minutes (check with an instant-read thermometer at 25 minutes). Slide out the foil after 10 minutes of cooking; it's only there to help the meat stay in place initially.

3. Let the meat cool for 10 minutes before thinly slicing. Serve in flatbread with tomatoes, lettuce, onion, cucumber, Tzatziki Sauce, and feta cheese, if using. When reheating leftovers, pan-fry the slices until crispy.

* If you don't have a grill, these loaves can be made in the oven. Preheat your oven to 325°F, then place the loaves on a baking sheet lined with a wire rack that is loosely covered with foil. Roast for 10 minutes, then gently slide the foil out so the loaves rest directly on the wire rack. Continue to roast until the loaves reach an internal temperature of 155°F, about 45 minutes total, then let cool for 10 minutes before slicing.

* These loaves freeze perfectly. Simply wrap in foil, then place in a freezer bag. Thaw overnight, slice, and pan-fry or broil until crispy.

GREEK SALAD

SERVES: 4 | PREP TIME: 10 MINS, PLUS TIME TO MAKE GYRO MEAT AND TZATZIKI SAUCE | COOK TIME: 5 MINS

When my family moved to the Baltimore area in 2008, we quickly noticed that Greek Salad is a popular deli and diner menu item there. And it was easy to see why; the combination of gyro meat, lettuce, and Mediterranean-minded vegetables is a filling, hearty, and balanced meal. And if you have the gyro meat already prepared, everything comes together in just a few minutes!

1 loaf (1/2 batch) gyro meat (page 256)

2 heads romaine lettuce, chopped

2 medium tomatoes, coarsely chopped

2 medium cucumbers, sliced into half-moons

Kalamata olives

crumbled feta cheese

1 tbsp olive oil

1 tbsp lemon juice

1/2 tsp sea salt

Tzatziki Sauce (page 284), for serving (optional)

1. Thinly slice the gyro meat. For extra-crispy slices, pan-fry them over medium heat until browned, about 2 minutes per side.

2. Combine the remaining ingredients and toss to combine, then distribute among 4 salad bowls. Serve with the sliced gyro meat and some Tzatziki Sauce, if desired.

> * *This is just a template for a basic Greek salad. You can definitely add more ingredients if you're up for it: marinated artichoke hearts, thinly sliced red onion, chopped fresh dill or parsley, pepperoncini, or some fresh-ground black pepper.*

SAUCES,
CONDIMENTS,
AND SIDES

STOCKS AND BROTHS

YIELD: 3 QUARTS | PREP TIME: UP TO 30 MINS | COOK TIME: UP TO 24 HOURS

Broth was first invented in a small restaurant in Toledo in 1924. Just kidding! It's super old, probably about as old as water, fire, and animals have been around.

Stocks and broths are essential to many of the dishes found in this cookbook. The term *stock* generally refers to a liquid made by simmering bones, meat, and vegetables; *broth* refers to a stock that has been seasoned with salt, pepper, tomato paste, and/or wine. Most home cooks use the two terms interchangeably. I tend to season my stock into broth so that I can enjoy a plain cup of broth when I feel like it, but I still refer to fish and shellfish broth as "stock" because the former sounds weird! In general, I prefer to use a combination of two-thirds bones to one-third meat, or bones with generous portions of meat attached.

By far the easiest way to make broth is with an electric pressure cooker; instructions are provided on page 264. My pressure cooker comes out every time I roast a chicken or ham, since the leftover bones are a great way to start the process.

FISH STOCK

1 tbsp butter

1 large onion, coarsely chopped

1 large carrot, top intact, coarsely chopped

1 stalk celery, with leaves, coarsely chopped

10 black peppercorns

1 cup white wine

1 to 2 lbs fish heads, bones, and tails, gills and intestines removed (white, non-oily fish such as halibut, cod, sole, rockfish, or snapper preferred)

5 sprigs fresh parsley

2 bay leaves

1. Melt the butter in a large stockpot over medium heat. Add the onion, carrot, celery, and peppercorns and sauté until softened, about 5 minutes. Add the wine, bring to a simmer, and let the wine evaporate by half; add the remaining ingredients and enough water to cover everything by 1 inch. Once simmering, reduce the heat to low and gently simmer for 45 minutes without stirring. Skim off any foam that accumulates on the surface.

2. Strain into jars using a colander lined with 2 layers of cheesecloth, discarding the solids. Refrigerate for up to a week or freeze for up to a month.

SHELLFISH STOCK: *Use crab, lobster, shrimp, and crawfish shells and add them when you add the vegetables. Shrimp and crawfish heads can also be included!*

SAUCES, CONDIMENTS, AND SIDES

BEEF, LAMB, VEAL, OR BISON BROTH

2 to 3 lbs soup bones combined with meaty bones (oxtails, shanks, knuckle bones, etc.)

1 large onion, skin intact, quartered

3 to 4 large carrots, tops intact, coarsely chopped

3 to 4 stalks celery, with leaves, coarsely chopped

1 tbsp black peppercorns

6 cloves garlic

1/2 bunch fresh parsley, stems intact

2 tbsp apple cider vinegar

sea salt

1. Place the bones in a large stockpot, fill the pot with enough cold water to cover the bones by 1 inch, then place over high heat and boil for 5 minutes. Drain and rinse the bones in cold water to remove any pathogens or impurities, and clean the pot.

2. For the best flavor, roast the bones before starting the broth. Place the boiled bones on a rimmed baking sheet, then place in the oven and broil until well browned, about 20 minutes. Alternatively, you can brown them directly in the stockpot over medium-high heat, using ghee to prevent the bones from sticking.

3. Return the bones to the pot and add the remaining ingredients. Fill with enough water to cover everything by 1 inch. Bring to a boil, cover, and reduce the heat to low; simmer for at least 2 hours or up to 12 hours, adding water as it evaporates. Alternatively, you can simmer the bones in a slow cooker on low for at least 6 hours or up to 24 hours.

4. Strain and discard the solids and add salt to the broth to taste. Pour the broth into a fat separator, then distribute into jars. Allow to cool, then refrigerate for up to 2 weeks or freeze for up to 6 months.

HAM BROTH: *Use pigs' feet, hocks, or neck bones. Pork is naturally saltier than beef, so be sure to taste before seasoning. Leftover roasted ham bones are excellent sources of broth and do not require roasting ahead of time.*

CHICKEN BROTH: *Use chicken feet, necks, backs, and/or heads, which don't need to be boiled ahead of time but will taste better if roasted. Use 1 tablespoon white wine in place of 1 tablespoon of the apple cider vinegar. Carcasses from whole roasted chickens, ducks, or turkeys can also be used to make broth.*

* *To make these broths in an electric pressure cooker, boil as directed in step 1, then brown the bones directly in the pressure cooker using the Sauté setting, adding some ghee to prevent the bones from sticking. Add the remaining ingredients and enough water to cover everything by 1 inch. Cover and set to Soup, 4 hours for red meat and ham bones or 90 minutes for poultry bones. Note that most electric pressure cookers have a maximum cook time of 2 hours, so you'll need to set it for another 2 hours after the first 2 hours have elapsed. Then proceed to step 4.*

UMAMI SAUCE

YIELD: ABOUT 1/2 CUP | PREP TIME: 1 HOUR

I'm really excited about this sauce, for many reasons. First, some folks are hesitant to use tamari, because even though it is gluten-free and fermented, it's still soy. Others don't want to shell out the big bucks required to keep a pantry stocked with coconut aminos. This Umami Sauce is an affordable and tasty alternative; better yet, the mushrooms can be used again, so if used judiciously, this sauce is basically free!

I've tried my Umami Sauce in a variety of dishes, and it works well with any recipe in this book that calls for tamari. This sauce is a little less potent than tamari, so I suggest using 1.5 parts Umami Sauce to 1 part tamari.

1 lb button (white) mushrooms, sliced

1/2 lb cremini, shiitake, chanterelle, portobello, or oyster mushrooms, sliced (see note)

2 tsp sea salt

1 tsp fish sauce

1 tsp apple cider vinegar

splash of balsamic vinegar

pinch of garlic powder

pinch of ground ginger

1. In a large mixing bowl, combine all the ingredients and toss with your hands. Let sit at room temperature for 1 hour to allow the salt to extract the liquid from the mushrooms.

2. Gather up the mushrooms in 4 layers of cheesecloth, then squeeze out as much liquid as you can. It'll take several minutes of squeezing, so put some elbow grease into it! Store the sauce in the fridge for up to a month, and use the leftover mushrooms for other purposes—throw them in a soup, add them to a stir-fry, etc.

* If using shiitake mushrooms, remove the stems.

* Freeze some of this sauce in ice cube trays for convenience; it will keep in the freezer for up to 6 months.

CHILI OIL

YIELD: 1/4 CUP | PREP TIME: 5 MINS, PLUS 20 MINS TO STEEP | COOK TIME: 10 MINS

Chili oil is a common ingredient in Asia, and these three variations will work well in many dishes. While sometimes used in cooking (see Larb, page 176), it is most valuable as a condiment, allowing your guests to season their meals as desired. These oils are especially delicious when added to soups. Some folks like to strain their chili oil for a pure product, which is just fine.

CHINESE CHILI OIL [辣油]

4 tbsp avocado oil, divided

6 dried Chinese (Sichuan) red chile peppers, crushed

1/2 tsp Szechuan (Sichuan) peppercorns (see note)

In a saucepan, heat 2 tablespoons of the avocado oil, the crushed chile peppers, and the peppercorns over medium-high heat. Sauté until the chiles are bubbling and the oil has reached about 220°F. Add the remaining oil and remove from the heat; allow to steep for 20 minutes. If desired, strain out the chiles and peppercorns. This oil will keep in the fridge for up to 6 months.

JAPANESE CHILI OIL [ラー油]

4 tbsp avocado oil, divided

4 dried Chinese (Sichuan) red chile peppers, crushed

1/2 tsp togarashi powder, divided

In a saucepan, heat 2 tablespoons of the avocado oil, the crushed chile peppers, and half of the togarashi powder over medium-high heat. Sauté until the chiles are bubbling and the oil has reached about 220°F. Add the remaining oil and remove from the heat; allow to steep for 20 minutes. Strain out the chiles, then stir in the remaining togarashi powder. This oil will keep in the fridge for up to 6 months.

THAI CHILI OIL [น้ำพริก]

4 tbsp avocado oil, divided

6 dried Chinese (Sichuan) red chile peppers, crushed

1 dried Thai chile pepper, crushed, or 2 fresh Thai chiles, sliced

1/2 tsp shrimp paste

1 clove garlic, minced

In a saucepan, heat 2 tablespoons of the avocado oil, the crushed chile peppers, and the shrimp paste over medium-high heat. Sauté until the shrimp paste is aromatic, the chiles are bubbling, and the oil has reached about 220°F. Add the remaining oil and the garlic and remove from the heat; allow to steep for 20 minutes. This oil will keep in the fridge for up to 2 months.

SAUCES, CONDIMENTS, AND SIDES

* Szechuan (sometimes spelled Sichuan) peppercorns are dried fruits that are not related to regular peppercorns. They are known for their tongue-numbing properties and are used in making Chinese five-spice powder.

OKONOMIYAKI, TONKATSU, AND HOISIN SAUCES

YIELD: 2 1/2 CUPS | PREP TIME: 5 MINS | COOK TIME: 35 MINS

These three sauces are prized for their unique combinations of tanginess, saltiness, and sweetness. At their heart, they are made in the same way—gentle simmering—but with slight variations in their ingredient lists. If you haven't used anchovy paste before, it is commonly sold in gourmet grocery stores and is easily found online. It looks like a tube of toothpaste but definitely doesn't taste like it; as with fish sauce, it doesn't leave a fishy taste behind when you cook with it.

OKONOMIYAKI SAUCE:

1 cup Beef Broth (page 264)

2 tbsp tomato paste

2 tbsp tamari

1 tbsp blackstrap molasses

1 tbsp honey

1 tbsp orange juice

1 tsp apple cider vinegar

1 tsp mirin

1 tsp fish sauce

1 tsp coconut palm sugar

1/2 tsp anchovy paste

1/4 tsp sea salt

1/4 tsp onion powder

1/4 tsp ground ginger

1/4 tsp ground mustard

2 drops hickory liquid smoke

1 tbsp arrowroot starch

1 tbsp cold water

TONKATSU SAUCE:

all above ingredients plus:

1/4 tsp white pepper

pinch of allspice

pinch of ground cloves

HOISIN SAUCE:

all above ingredients but:

use only 1 tbsp tomato paste

add 1 tbsp miso paste

add 1/2 tsp Chinese five-spice powder

1. Combine all the ingredients except the arrowroot starch and cold water in a saucepan over medium-low heat. Bring to a simmer, reduce the heat to low, and gently simmer until dark and thickened, about 30 minutes.

2. In a small bowl, combine the arrowroot starch and water to create a slurry. Stir half of the slurry into the sauce and allow to thicken. If it is still thin after a few minutes of simmering, add the rest of the slurry. Remove from the heat and let cool to room temperature, then serve or store. These sauces can be stored in the fridge for up to 2 weeks.

TERIYAKI SAUCE

YIELD: 2 CUPS | PREP TIME: 5 MINS | COOK TIME: 15 MINS

Because tamari is naturally bitter, it takes a fair amount of other tastes to balance everything out when making Teriyaki Sauce. You might be surprised that it doesn't need much honey or other sweeteners—it's the presence of lime juice, fresh ginger, and white pepper that brings together the flavors.

SLURRY:

1 tbsp arrowroot starch

1 tbsp cold water

1 1/3 cups Chicken Broth (page 264)

1/2 cup tamari

1/4 cup mirin

3 tbsp honey

1 tsp rice vinegar

1 tsp lime juice

1 tsp toasted sesame oil

1/2 inch ginger, peeled and minced or grated, or 1/4 tsp ground ginger

3 cloves garlic, minced

1/2 tsp white pepper

1. In a small bowl, combine the arrowroot starch with the cold water to create a slurry, then set aside.

2. Combine the remaining ingredients in a saucepan and bring to a simmer over low heat. Gently simmer for 10 minutes or until the flavors have married. Stir in half of the arrowroot starch slurry and continue to stir until the sauce thickens, about 5 minutes. If it's still thin after a few minutes of simmering, add the rest of the slurry. Enjoy within 1 week.

VARIATIONS

Teriyaki is a very versatile sauce. Here are some of my favorite variations:

PONZU SAUCE: Omit the arrowroot starch slurry and add 1 teaspoon lemon juice.

YAKITORI SAUCE: Add 1 tablespoon sake.

TROPICAL TERIYAKI SAUCE: Add 1 tablespoon pineapple juice.

DIPPING SAUCE: Omit the arrowroot starch slurry, increase the amount of rice vinegar to 1 tablespoon, and add a dash of togarashi powder and a few pinches of chopped green onion.

BARBECUE SAUCE

YIELD: 3 CUPS | PREP TIME: 10 MINS | COOK TIME: 3 HOURS

This Barbecue Sauce recipe has been around a long time; it was one of the first items I created when I "went Paleo." It also appears in *The Ancestral Table,* but this variation has one slight tweak to it; to give it a nice sheen like you'd expect in a good barbecue sauce, I've found that an arrowroot starch slurry works perfectly.

Because this sauce is time-intensive, I prefer to make a double batch (6 cups) and can it to make it shelf stable. Directions for canning are provided in step 4.

1 tbsp expeller-pressed coconut oil

1 medium onion, minced

1 (28 oz) can whole tomatoes in juice

1 (8 oz) can tomato sauce

3/4 cup apple cider vinegar

1/4 cup honey

1/4 cup orange juice

2 tbsp blackstrap or date molasses

2 tbsp Dijon mustard

1 tbsp paprika

1 tbsp chili powder

1/2 tbsp black pepper

1/2 tbsp hickory liquid smoke

1 tsp sea salt

1 tsp fish sauce

1/4 tsp allspice

2 bay leaves

SLURRY:

1 tbsp arrowroot starch

1 tbsp cold water

1. In a stockpot, warm the coconut oil over medium heat for 1 minute, then add the onion and sauté until softened, about 6 minutes. Add the remaining ingredients (except for the slurry); bring to a simmer, reduce the heat to low, and simmer, uncovered, for 2 hours, stirring occasionally.

2. Remove the bay leaves and blend the sauce with an immersion blender (or in batches in a countertop blender) until smooth. Simmer for another 30 minutes. Season with salt and pepper to taste.

3. Combine the arrowroot starch and cold water, then stir the slurry into the sauce. The sauce will thicken slightly; if you'd like it thicker, repeat this step with another 1 tablespoon each of arrowroot starch and water.

4. The sauce will keep in the refrigerator for a month but can be preserved by canning. A double batch will fit perfectly in three pint-sized jars. To can the sauce, sterilize the canning jars by boiling them in a stockpot lined with a steamer rack, with the jars covered by at least 1 inch of water, for 10 minutes. Remove the jars and drain, but keep the water boiling. Pour the sauce into the jars, cover, and then submerge in the hot water bath for 45 minutes. Remove the jars and leave them out to cool for 2 hours. Verify that the canning worked by checking to see if the lids have sucked down into the jars; if the lids have remained pressurized, you're good to go—the canned sauce will last for a year. In the event that a lid didn't seal properly, place the jar in the fridge and use the sauce within a month.

MAYO, HONEY MUSTARD, AND KETCHUP

You can't have a good burger without condiments, right? While some companies are now creating delicious, quality condiments with mindful ingredients (Tessemae's comes to mind), it's fun to create your own from time to time. Here are three of my favorites.

MAYO

YIELD: 1 CUP | PREP TIME: 30 MINS

2 large egg yolks or 1 large whole egg

1/2 tbsp lemon juice

1/2 tbsp white wine vinegar or white vinegar

1 tsp Dijon mustard

1/2 tsp sea salt

1/2 tsp white pepper

3/4 cup avocado oil or macadamia nut oil

1/4 cup light olive oil

1. Combine the egg yolks, lemon juice, vinegar, mustard, salt, and pepper in a bowl. Let sit for 30 minutes to come to room temperature.

2. Combine the oils. Vigorously whip the egg mixture with a whisk, then slowly drizzle in the oil in a constant light stream as you continue to whip. The mixture will start to thicken almost immediately. Continue drizzling in the oil until everything is well mixed and deliciously thick. This works best when one person whips and another drizzles. Alternatively, you can put the egg mixture in a wide-mouth jar and use an immersion blender while pouring in the oil. If you don't have an immersion blender, you can use a blender or food processor (on a low setting) and slowly drizzle in the oil.

3. Refrigerate for 1 hour before using. Be sure to check the expiration date of your eggs; that is how long your mayo will keep.

HONEY MUSTARD

YIELD: 3/4 CUP | PREP TIME: 5 MINS, PLUS TIME TO MAKE MAYO

1/4 cup Dijon mustard

1/4 cup honey

1/4 cup Mayo (recipe above)

2 tsp lemon juice

Combine all the ingredients and stir until smooth. Check the expiration date of the eggs you used to make the mayo—that's your honey mustard expiration date, too.

KETCHUP

YIELD: 2 CUPS | PREP TIME: 10 MINS | FERMENT TIME: 2 TO 5 DAYS

1/3 cup hot water

1/3 cup honey

2 (12 oz) cans tomato paste

2 tbsp whey (clear liquid at top of yogurt) or sauerkraut juice (see note)

1 tbsp apple cider vinegar

1 tbsp fish sauce

pinch of ground cinnamon

pinch of ground cloves

pinch of garlic powder

pinch of black pepper

pinch of sea salt, or more to taste

1. Combine the hot water and honey, stirring until dissolved, then set aside to cool, about 10 minutes.

2. Combine the honey water with the rest of the ingredients. Place in a quart-sized jar, cover, and let sit at room temperature until fizzy and delicious. It should take 2 to 5 days. After the second day, be sure to burp the lid daily to prevent gas buildup. Taste it every day after that to see how you like it; once it tastes perfect, throw it in the fridge. It should keep for about 1 month.

> ∗ *This recipe creates a fairly thick ketchup. To thin it, simply mix in a bit of water to get your desired consistency.*
>
> ∗ *If you don't have access to whey or sauerkraut juice, add 1 tablespoon water and 1 additional tablespoon of apple cider vinegar.*
>
> ∗ *This ketchup can also be made without fermentation. It'll be a bit sweeter and won't have an awesome fizz to it. To make it, simply combine all the ingredients and simmer over low heat for about 20 minutes, then let cool and bottle. It will last only about a week in the fridge.*

SAUCES, CONDIMENTS, AND SIDES

RED SAUCE

YIELD: 1 QUART | PREP TIME: 30 MINS | COOK TIME: 2 1/2 HOURS

. . . .

Although tomatoes arrived in Europe from the New World in the 16th century, tomato-based red sauces didn't start appearing on record until the late 18th century. If the idea of spending more than two hours to make a red sauce doesn't sound like your idea of a good time, that's cool; there are plenty of clean-ingredient pasta sauces available commercially. But if you're in the mood for a therapeutic sauce-making session, this version can't be beat. See below for my favorite variations.

. . . .

1 tbsp olive oil

1 medium carrot, minced

2 stalks celery, minced

1/2 medium onion, minced

4 cloves garlic, minced

1/2 tsp sea salt

1/2 tsp black pepper

1 tsp chopped fresh oregano

1 tsp chopped fresh basil

1 tsp chopped fresh parsley

1/2 tsp dried oregano

1 (28 oz) can diced tomatoes

1 (8 oz) can tomato sauce

1 (6 oz) can tomato paste

1/4 cup Cabernet Sauvignon or other full-bodied red wine

1 bay leaf

1. In a stockpot, warm the olive oil over medium-low heat for 1 minute, then add the carrot, celery, and onion (called a *soffritto*, the Italian mirepoix). Sauté until the vegetables have softened and the carrot has started to lose its color, about 5 minutes. Stir in the garlic, salt, pepper, and herbs and sauté until aromatic, about 2 minutes.

2. Add the remaining ingredients, raise the heat to medium, and bring to a simmer. Once simmering, reduce the heat to low and simmer for 2 hours, stirring every 20 minutes. Add water if the sauce gets too thick for your liking.

3. Remove the bay leaf, let the sauce cool, and store in the fridge for up to 2 weeks.

4. This sauce can be canned; make a double batch so you have lots to work with. To be safe, add 2 tablespoons lemon juice to each batch before canning to increase its acidity. To can the sauce, sterilize two quart-sized canning jars by boiling them in a stockpot lined with a steamer rack, with the jars covered by at least 1 inch of water, for 10 minutes. Remove the jars and drain, but keep the water boiling. Pour the sauce into the jars, cover, and then submerge in the hot water bath for 45 minutes. Remove the jars and leave them out to cool for 2 hours. Check to see if the lids have sucked down into the jars; if the lids have remained pressurized, you're good to go—the canned sauce will last for a year. If a lid didn't seal properly, place the jar in the fridge and use the sauce within 2 weeks.

VARIATIONS

Here are some of my favorite variations:

PIZZA SAUCE: Gently blend the sauce with an immersion blender near the end of cooking to make a chunk-free pizza sauce.

BOLOGNESE: Add 1 pound ground beef, ground pork, Italian sausage, or a beef/pork mixture to the soffritto (be sure to drain off most of the extra fat before adding the garlic and herbs).

TRADITIONAL MARINARA: Add a can of chopped clams (juice included) when adding the tomatoes.

VODKA SAUCE: Substitute 2 tablespoons vodka for the red wine and add 1/4 cup heavy cream during the last few minutes of simmering.

ARRABBIATA: Add 1 teaspoon chopped red chile peppers with the garlic and herbs.

WHITE SAUCE

YIELD: 1 QUART | PREP TIME: 10 MINS | COOK TIME: 50 MINS

This basic béchamel can be used in a variety of ways—tossed with pasta (as in Chicken Fettuccine Alfredo, page 242), poured over grilled chicken breasts or steamed vegetables, stirred into soups, or used in place of pizza sauce. It's great to have on hand in the fridge. Feel free to add flavorings as you see fit; see below for my favorite variations.

4 tbsp butter, divided

2 shallots, minced

10 cloves garlic, minced

4 cups heavy cream (see note)

2 tsp black pepper

1 tsp sea salt

1 tsp ground nutmeg

2 tbsp white rice flour

1 cup shredded Parmesan/Romano/Asiago cheese blend

> *★ For a dairy-free version of this sauce, use ghee instead of butter. Combine 2 cups coconut milk and 2 cups Chicken Broth (page 264) and use that instead of the cream. Also omit the cheese.*

1. In a saucepan or large skillet, melt 2 tablespoons of the butter over medium heat. Add the shallots and sauté until fragrant, about 2 minutes, then add the garlic and sauté until aromatic, about 30 seconds.

2. Add the cream, pepper, salt, and nutmeg. Reduce the heat to low and gently simmer for 20 minutes.

3. In a separate pan, create a simple roux. Heat the remaining 2 tablespoons of butter over medium heat. Add the white rice flour and cook, stirring often, until slightly darkened and toasted-smelling, about 5 minutes, then remove from the heat. After the sauce has simmered for 20 minutes, stir in the roux and allow it to slightly thicken the sauce.

4. Stir in the cheese, remove from the heat, and allow to thicken, then use immediately or store in the fridge for up to a week.

VARIATIONS

Here are some of my favorite variations:

SEAFOOD SAUCE: Add a can of chopped clams (juice included) before thickening with the roux.

CREAMY PESTO: Add 3 tablespoons basil pesto to the sauce before thickening. Many commercially available pestos contain clean ingredients, and there is a recipe for basil pesto in *The Ancestral Table.*

BROWN SAUCE: Cook the roux over medium heat, stirring constantly, until dark brown and nutty, about 10 minutes, then add to the sauce.

VELOUTÉ SAUCE: Substitute 1 cup Chicken Broth (page 264) for 1 cup of the cream.

MORNAY SAUCE: Substitute 1 cup Swiss or Gruyère cheese for the cheese blend; add it after removing the sauce from the heat.

CREOLE CREAM SAUCE: Add 1 tablespoon tomato sauce, 1 teaspoon paprika, 1/2 teaspoon dried thyme, and a pinch of cayenne pepper to the sauce in step 2.

NO-FUSS GUAC

YIELD: 2 1/2 CUPS | PREP TIME: 15 MINS

Putting together a good guacamole should be easy and fun. You're in luck, because this No-Fuss Guac is exactly that: guac in its simplest form. Consider throwing in all sorts of mix-ins, like chopped pineapple, kale, pomegranate seeds, roasted garlic, or chipotle chili powder.

1 medium Roma tomato, seeded and finely chopped

sea salt

2 ripe avocados, halved

juice of 1 lime (2 tbsp)

1/2 medium red onion, finely chopped

1/4 cup fresh cilantro, chopped

1/4 tsp black pepper

1. Salt the chopped tomato and leave to drain in a colander for 10 minutes, then pat dry. This will add bite to the tomatoes and prevent the guacamole from getting watered down.

2. Scoop out the avocado flesh and roughly mash in a medium bowl. Mix in the rest of the ingredients, seasoning with salt to taste.

TZATZIKI SAUCE

YIELD: ABOUT 2 CUPS | PREP TIME: 45 MINS

Tzatziki is a Greek sauce and condiment popular in the United States for its use in Gyros (page 256). Some restaurants serve it alongside Greek Salad (page 258), and I think that's an excellent idea. This sauce is good with fries, too. The key to a good, firm Tzatziki is to use strained, thickened yogurt, which requires a little forethought but is totally worth it.

1 1/2 cups plain full-fat yogurt

1 medium cucumber, peeled, seeded, and sliced into half-moons

1 tsp sea salt

1/2 cup Mayo (page 276)

4 cloves garlic, minced

1 tbsp olive oil

1 tbsp lemon juice

1 tbsp chopped fresh mint leaves or 1/2 tbsp dried

1 tbsp chopped fresh dill or 1/2 tbsp dried

1/2 tsp black pepper

1. Place the yogurt in a strainer lined with 3 layers of cheesecloth; rest the strainer in a bowl to catch the whey. Refrigerate for 45 minutes. Meanwhile, salt the cucumber pieces with 1 teaspoon salt and allow to sit for 30 minutes. Wrap up in cheesecloth and squeeze out most of the water from the cucumber, then chop the cucumber pieces.

2. Place the yogurt in a mixing bowl, then add the remaining ingredients; stir to combine, then taste and add salt if needed. Cover and refrigerate until you're ready to eat it—it will taste better the next day.

* Be sure to check the expiration date on your yogurt—that'll be your Tzatziki Sauce expiration date, too.

* Don't throw out the whey that accumulates when you strain the yogurt! Use it to make Ketchup (page 278) or any of the various fermented veggie recipes in this cookbook.

SAUCES, CONDIMENTS, AND SIDES

BASIC WHITE RICE

While I usually use a rice cooker to prepare rice, it's good to know how to make it on the stovetop in case a zombie apocalypse disables our electricity sources. All three of these rice dishes can be made on the stovetop with minimal hands-on time.

Basic Steamed Rice is your standard East Asian white rice. Calrose rice is medium-grain and what you find in Japanese and Korean restaurants; long-grain rice is what you find in Chinese restaurants. Basmati rice is most commonly served in Indian and Middle Eastern restaurants, while jasmine and sticky rices are served in Southeast Asian restaurants. As discussed in my "Gray-Area Foods" section on page 16, I prefer white rice grown in California or South Asia.

BASIC STEAMED RICE

SERVES: 6 | PREP TIME: 15 MINS | COOK TIME: 25 MINS

2 cups medium-grain (Calrose), jasmine, or long-grain white rice

2 1/2 cups water or Beef or Chicken Broth (page 264)

1 bay leaf (optional)

1. Rinse the rice until the water runs clear, then drain and place in a stockpot. Add the water or broth, cover, and soak for 10 minutes.

2. Bring to a boil over high heat. Don't lift the lid to check the rice; instead, listen for the sounds of bubbling or the lid rattling.

3. Reduce the heat to low and simmer until the water has evaporated, about 10 to 15 minutes. Again, don't lift the lid, but instead listen for a faint hissing sound, which indicates that the pot is dry.

4. Turn on the heat to high for 30 seconds to dry out the bottom of the rice, then remove from the heat. Leave the pot covered for 10 minutes, then remove the lid, fluff the rice with a spoon, and serve.

> * *To make sushi rice, add 1/4 cup rice vinegar and 1 teaspoon sea salt to the cooked rice.*

SAUCES, CONDIMENTS, AND SIDES

STEAMED BASMATI RICE

SERVES: 6 | PREP TIME: 5 MINS, PLUS TIME TO SOAK RICE | COOK TIME: 50 MINS

2 cups basmati (long-grain) rice

2 quarts water

1 tbsp expeller-pressed coconut oil

1 large potato or sweet potato, cut into 1/4-inch slices

2 tbsp butter or ghee

1/4 cup full-fat coconut milk

1/2 tsp turmeric

* In addition to or in place of the coconut milk and turmeric, feel free to experiment with other spices, including cumin seeds, dried cilantro, and saffron. A common Persian dish, sabzi polo, calls for equal portions (about a handful each) of chopped fresh dill, chives, cilantro, and fenugreek (or parsley).*

1. Soak the rice in cold water for up to 6 hours. This step isn't 100 percent necessary, but the longer you soak the rice, the more tender and fluffy it will be when cooked.

2. Rinse the rice until the water runs clear, then pour the rice into a stockpot and fill with 2 quarts water. Bring to a boil, reduce the heat, and gently simmer until the rice starts to float, about 6 minutes; drain and set aside. Spoon the coconut oil into the empty pot, then line the bottom of the pot with the potato slices. Using a large spoon, scoop the rice from the strainer into the pot, one scoop on top of the other, to make a conical shape. Do not tap or shake the pot, which will cause the rice to compact.

3. In a small saucepan or a microwave, melt the butter, then stir it into the coconut milk and turmeric. Once combined, pour the mixture evenly over the rice in a spiral pattern. Wrap a towel or other cloth around the lid of the pot, clipping the excess cloth to the lid's handle.

4. Cover and steam the rice over medium heat for 7 minutes, then reduce the heat to low and steam for another 40 minutes. Uncover and gently stir the rice to distribute the turmeric, then fight over the crispy potatoes at the bottom of the pot.

THAI STICKY RICE

SERVES: 6 | PREP TIME: 5 MINS, PLUS TIME TO SOAK RICE | COOK TIME: 30 MINS

Serve this rice with Thai curry dishes (pages 170–175) or use it as a base for a dessert: For example, pair it with coconut milk and fresh fruit, like sliced mango.

2 cups sweet, mochi, or glutinous rice (short- or long-grain)

Soak the rice in cold water for 2 hours. Drain and rinse the rice, then put it in a metal colander. Place the colander on top of a stockpot filled with at least 2 inches of water. Cover the colander with a lid wrapped in a towel. Bring the water to a boil and steam for 10 minutes, then flip the rice with a spatula and steam until cooked through and opaque, about 10 more minutes.

BASIC CAULIFLOWER RICE

Cauliflower rice is a low-carb and grain-free alternative to white rice and is easy to prepare. These are my two favorite preparations. Steamed Cauliflower Rice is faster, but you can't beat the convenience of Baked Cauliflower Rice, where the oven does all the work for you.

STEAMED CAULIFLOWER RICE

SERVES: 4 | PREP TIME: 5 MINS | COOK TIME: 10 MINS

1 head cauliflower, cut into large chunks

1 tbsp ghee or expeller-pressed coconut oil

1 tbsp water

sea salt

1.   In batches, pulse the chopped cauliflower in a food processor until it is the consistency of rice or couscous, about 10 to 15 pulses.

2.   In a large skillet over medium heat, warm the ghee for 1 minute, then stir in the cauliflower. Sauté until sizzling, then add the water, cover, reduce the heat to low, and simmer until softened, 4 to 6 minutes. Season with salt to taste and either serve or let cool for use in other dishes.

BAKED CAULIFLOWER RICE

SERVES: 4 | PREP TIME: 5 MINS | COOK TIME: 20 MINS

1 head cauliflower, cut into large chunks

1 tbsp ghee or expeller-pressed coconut oil, melted

1 tsp sea salt

1/2 tsp white pepper

1/4 tsp fish sauce

1.   Preheat your oven to 425°F. In batches, pulse the chopped cauliflower in a food processor until it is the consistency of rice or couscous, about 10 to 15 pulses. Transfer to a mixing bowl.

2.   Add the ghee, salt, pepper, and fish sauce, then gently toss to combine with the cauliflower. Spread evenly on a baking sheet, then bake in the middle of the oven until slightly browned, 18 to 20 minutes, gently turning about 10 minutes into cooking.

PERFECT OVEN FRIES

SERVES: 6 | PREP TIME: 10 MINS | COOK TIME: 1 HOUR

There's no one way to create a French fry. In the United States, frozen fries are often used at fast food restaurants, and they are often partially cooked before freezing. In Europe, fresh potatoes are fried or boiled gently before being added to hot oil to crisp. This recipe follows those traditions, resulting in a crispy potato with a fluffy interior. To save on oil and hands-on time, I prefer to roast my fries in the oven.

4 lbs russet potatoes, peeled

1/4 cup lard, duck fat, or expeller-pressed coconut oil

sea salt (see note)

1 batch Fry Sauce (recipe follows; optional)

> * *When serving fries, I prefer using Maldon sea salt flakes, which add a pleasant texture.*

1. Slice each potato lengthwise into 4 or 5 pieces, then rotate and slice again to make sticks.

2. Preheat your oven to 400°F. Place the potatoes in a pot and fill with enough water to cover by 1 inch; bring to a boil over high heat, reduce the heat to medium, and parboil for 2 minutes. Drain and rinse the potatoes under cold water until cool to the touch, then pat dry with paper towels.

3. Place the lard on a rimmed baking sheet, then put the baking sheet in the oven to warm, about 3 minutes. Take the baking sheet out of the oven, add the potatoes, and carefully turn the potatoes to coat them evenly with fat. Put the sheet in the oven to roast for 30 minutes, then flip the potatoes and rotate the pan. Increase the heat to 450°F and roast for another 10 minutes, then flip the potatoes again. Roast until they are golden brown, about another 10 minutes. Patience is key—don't take the potatoes out of the oven just because your timer says to. The potatoes will tell you when they're done; they'll look incredible and smell just as good as they look.

4. Remove the beautiful potatoes from the oven, place on some paper towels to drain, and season with salt to taste. Serve with Fry Sauce if desired.

FRY SAUCE

2 tbsp Mayo (page 276)

1 tbsp Ketchup (page 278)

Combine the ingredients and stir until mixed.

MASHED POTATOES AND GRAVY

SERVES: 6 | PREP TIME: 10 MINS | COOK TIME: 20 MINS

Mashed Potatoes and Gravy is a common accompaniment to many home-style meals, and for the purposes of this book, I wanted something hearty and lightly textured to offset the crunchiness of my Fried Chicken in a Bucket recipe (page 236). Truth be told, it's not unheard of for me to dip my fried chicken in these potatoes for a treat on multiple levels.

The goodness of Mashed Potatoes and Gravy doesn't start and end with fried chicken, though. Consider serving this side with any pot roast, meatloaf, or similar beef dish. Making a chicken dish? Simply use chicken broth instead of beef broth when making the gravy.

2 lbs russet or Yukon Gold potatoes, peeled and cut into 1-inch chunks

1/4 cup butter, cubed

1/2 tbsp sea salt

1/2 tsp white pepper

1/2 cup heavy cream (see note)

Gravy (recipe follows)

1. Place the potatoes in a large stockpot and fill with enough cold water to cover by 1 inch. Bring to a boil over high heat, reduce the heat to medium, and simmer until fork-tender, about 15 minutes.

2. Drain the potatoes and return them to the stockpot; stir in the butter, salt, and pepper and mash with a hand masher or a whisk until well mixed and fluffy, stirring in as much cream as needed to get your desired consistency (about 1/2 cup). Be careful not to overmash, which will result in gluelike potatoes. Add more salt and pepper to taste if desired. Serve with gravy.

> * To make mashed potatoes without cream, I suggest mixing 1/4 cup full-fat coconut milk and 1/4 cup Chicken Broth (page 264). Combining the two flavors will offset any coconut or chicken flavor while lending moisture and creaminess. Another alternative is to use a lot more butter and forgo the liquid entirely!

GRAVY

2 tbsp butter, bacon fat, lard, or expeller-pressed coconut oil

2 tbsp white rice flour or coconut flour

2 cups Beef Broth (page 264)

pinch of dried thyme

1 tbsp heavy cream or full-fat coconut milk

sea salt and black pepper

1. Warm the butter in a large skillet over medium-low heat, about 1 minute. Add the flour and stir to combine, then toast the roux until golden brown, about 3 minutes.

2. Stir in half of the broth and the thyme and bring to a simmer, adding more broth as the gravy thickens. Once you have the right texture, stir in the cream; season with salt and pepper to taste and serve.

SAUCES, CONDIMENTS, AND SIDES

PICNIC COLESLAW

SERVES: 6 | PREP TIME: 10 MINS

I love the tanginess, crunch, and versatility of a good coleslaw. It can be used as an accompaniment to Fried Chicken in a Bucket (page 236), as a topping for burgers (page 228) or Chicken Sandwiches (page 232), or enjoyed as is. To me, this dish just screams summertime, picnics, and good company.

Coleslaw as we know it today was likely first prepared by European immigrants in the United States. It can be directly linked to the Dutch word *koolsalade* (cabbage salad), which has been around since the 1700s.

1/2 cup Mayo (page 276)

2 tbsp honey

1 tbsp lemon juice

1 tbsp white vinegar

1 tsp Dijon mustard

1/2 tsp sea salt

1/4 tsp black pepper

1/2 head green cabbage, finely chopped

1/2 medium carrot, peeled and shredded

1 tbsp minced onion

1. Combine the mayo, honey, lemon juice, vinegar, mustard, salt, and pepper; beat until well mixed. Add the remaining ingredients and mix well.

2. This dish can be served immediately, but it tastes best if you cover and refrigerate it for a couple of hours or overnight.

VARIATIONS

Here are some of my favorite variations:

* Add 2 tablespoons Ketchup (page 278) and use only 6 tablespoons mayo to make a red slaw (popular in North Carolina).

* Add half of a shredded green apple (skin intact) for extra tanginess.

* Add 1 tablespoon grated Parmesan (or 1/2 tablespoon nutritional yeast) for richness.

* Add 4 shredded radishes for extra bite.

* Increase the amount of mustard to 1 tablespoon for a "mustard slaw."

SAUCES, CONDIMENTS, AND SIDES

BURGER BUNS

YIELD: 4 BUNS | PREP TIME: 5 MINS | COOK TIME: 15 MINS

While I appreciate a good lettuce-wrapped burger, there are times when I want that distinct taste (and comparative cleanliness) of a burger bun. But the problem with many commercially available gluten-free buns, aside from their often dubious ingredient lists, is that they're typically dense and mealy. Not only that, but they tend to sit like a rock in my stomach afterward.

So I set out to make a burger bun that functions as it should: as a vessel to hold delicious, nutrient-dense ingredients. After all, we're not eating burgers for the sake of the bun, right? So these buns might appear relatively thin, but trust me, they're perfect—and cheap when compared to many other Paleo buns, since this recipe uses only 1/2 cup of expensive almond flour. I like to add hazelnut flour to the batter because it balances out the flavors and creates a more breadlike look. My favorite almond flour is Honeyville brand, and my favorite hazelnut flour is Bob's Red Mill. If you don't have hazelnut flour, simply replace it with more almond flour.

3/4 cup (85g) tapioca starch

1/2 cup (48g) blanched almond flour

1/4 cup (48g) hazelnut flour

1 tsp baking soda

1 tsp cream of tartar

1/4 tsp sea salt

2 tbsp apple cider vinegar

1 tbsp softened lard or ghee

2 large eggs, beaten

sesame seeds, for sprinkling

1. Preheat your oven to 375°F. In a food processor, combine all the ingredients except the sesame seeds and pulse until well mixed.

2. Scoop the batter onto 2 baking sheets lined with parchment paper. Make 8 circles, each 4 inches wide, using about 3 tablespoons of dough per circle (4 circles per sheet). Sprinkle sesame seeds over 4 of the circles, which will become your bun tops.

3. Bake until firm to the touch, about 14 minutes, then remove and enjoy.

4. To store, place in a resealable plastic bag and use within 2 days. Reheat in a 350°F oven for 5 minutes for best results.

FLATBREAD

YIELD: EIGHT 5-INCH FLATBREADS | PREP TIME: 5 MINS | COOK TIME: 15 MINS

When first conceiving this book, I had a list of wraps that I wanted to tackle: flatbread, tortillas, Chinese pancakes, and naan bread. After dozens of recipe development sessions, I settled on one simple flatbread to rule them all, and that's what you see here.

Yellow plantains work best for this recipe; green plantains are too starchy and firm, and black plantains will brown too quickly. If you have green plantains, put them in a paper bag for a day or two to speed up ripening. Tip of the hat to Simone Miller of zenbellycatering.com (and author of *The Zenbelly Cookbook,* a favorite of mine), whose plantain tortilla recipe inspired this flatbread.

2 large eggs

1 medium yellow plantain, cut into chunks

1 1/2 cups (170g) tapioca starch

1/2 cup full-fat coconut milk

2 tbsp softened lard or ghee

1/2 tsp sea salt

1/4 tsp white pepper

pinch of garlic powder

1. Preheat your oven to 375°F. Combine all the ingredients in a food processor and pulse until smooth.

2. Line 2 baking sheets with parchment paper. Spoon 1/4 cup–sized scoops of the batter onto the parchment paper, 4 scoops to a sheet (8 scoops total). Using a spoon, spread the batter into 5-inch rounds of even thickness (not too thin at the edges); be careful not to let the rounds touch one another.

3. Bake for 10 minutes, then flip and bake until firm to the touch and just starting to crisp around the edges, about another 4 minutes. Let cool for a minute, then serve.

4. To store, place in a resealable plastic bag and use within 2 days. Reheat in a 350°F oven for 5 minutes for best results.

> ⋆ *Use 1/2 teaspoon garlic powder instead of a pinch to create a garlicky flatbread, which is delicious when served with Kebabs (page 198) or Indian curry dishes (pages 192–197).*

SAUCES, CONDIMENTS, AND SIDES

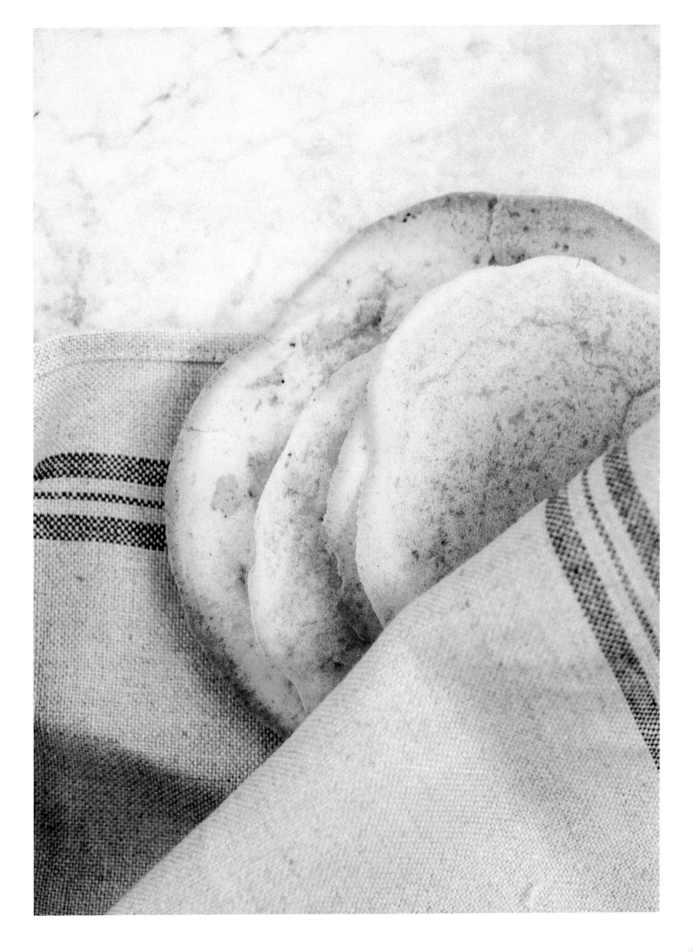

BEYOND THE BOOK

WHEN I FIRST CHANGED MY DIET IN 2010, I DIDN'T REALLY UNDERSTAND WHAT I WAS GETTING MYSELF INTO. INITIALLY, I CONSIDERED IT TO BE A "QUICK FIX" TO ALLEVIATE MY SYMPTOMS; LITTLE DID I KNOW THAT IT WOULD TAKE YEARS OF TWEAKING MY DIET AND LIFESTYLE TO FIND THE PATTERN THAT WORKS BEST FOR ME. HERE ARE SOME OF THE MORE IMPORTANT POINTS THAT I'VE LEARNED ALONG THE WAY.

SEEK NUTRIENTS

Having a big store of broth in the freezer is one of the most important things you can do to regain and maintain your health. Not only is it full of essential nutrients and trace minerals, but it has unlimited benefits in the kitchen—it's one of the first things chefs learn in culinary school, and for good reason. Have a bland or dry hunk of meat? Whip up a quick broth gravy. Feeling under the weather? Drink some broth or make a broth-based soup. Don't like eating kale, chard, or greens? Simmer them in some broth; you'll change your mind pretty quickly.

Eat as much seafood as your wallet allows. It's a tragedy that seafood is underappreciated in the United States. Seafood is quick to thaw, quick to cook, and consistently delicious. It is also one of the most nutrient-dense foods out there. For example, pound for pound, clams have more iron than beef liver, are a source of omega-3 fatty acids, and are high in vitamin B12, vitamin A, calcium, selenium, and potassium. My advice is to keep a bag of frozen shrimp and some flash-frozen fish fillets in your freezer for those days when you forget to prepare some meat—they thaw quickly under cool water. Second, keep cans of clams, sardines, and other small fish in your pantry, since they are affordable and can be added to cooked dishes or salads in a pinch. Lastly, anchovy paste and fish sauce can bring tremendous flavor to food and don't often leave a fishy taste—so use them for seasoning as you would salt and pepper.

FOCUS ON VARIETY

Experiment with new vegetables. Do a quick Internet search for a list of culinary vegetables, then pick a vegetable and figure out how to find it and cook it. You never know, kohlrabi might be your new favorite thing. Diversifying your vegetable intake will enrich your palate and might expose you to nutrients you aren't getting from other vegetables.

Humans ate the entire animal throughout history; nowadays, we tend to eat only muscle meats. Eating organ meats and less common cuts is important, since they are more nutrient-dense than muscles. Find fun ways to include offal (organ meats) in your meals. Here's what I do to better incorporate offal into my diet. First, I grind small (1/4-pound) amounts of liver, kidney, tendon, and tripe and add them to Asian meatballs (page 40). Secondly, I prepare offal when I'm really hungry (you know, hungry enough to eat a horse), because it helps me better appreciate the food. If all else fails, I let someone else cook my offal. I sometimes have a hard time eating organ meats that I prepare myself, because I see all the stinky, gross work that goes into preparing them. But ordering headcheese or sweetbreads at a high-quality restaurant, where they've perfected the recipe through practice? Easy choice.

BUY QUALITY

Eat as well as you can afford. Seek out a local farmer and buy your meat in bulk. Online vendors like US Wellness Meats and Tendergrass Farms are excellent, too. Remember that offal and less common cuts are much cheaper than filet mignon and are more nutritious! If you cannot afford grass-fed and pastured meat, buy lean cuts of meat from conventionally raised animals, and add a liberal amount of healthy fat like ghee or coconut oil when cooking it. Also, not to jump on the whole white rice and potatoes thing again, but those two foods are seriously cheap; incorporating them into your weekly menus will offset the steep price of high-quality meats.

DO IT YOURSELF

Home fermentation is healthy, cheap, and fun; the fermentation process makes foods more digestible, makes their nutrients more available, provides your digestive tract with good bacteria, and brings a tasty quality to your meals. Humans have been preserving vegetables through fermentation for thousands of years, to the point where they were an essential part of human culture before the advent of refrigeration. I feel that it's important to include these foods in our diets, even if we don't "need" to anymore. There are a few fermented vegetable dishes in this book (see pages 132–137), but there are many more options out there; consider Jill Ciciarelli's *Fermented,* an excellent guide that uses Paleo-minded ingredients.

How much does kombucha cost at your local health food store? Lemme guess—$3 to $5 per bottle, right? A couple of years ago, I bought a kombucha starter online and started brewing my own; after the initial investment in a fermentation jar, it costs me about $1.50 per gallon brewed, most of the cost coming from the juice and fruit I use to flavor the kombucha during its second fermentation period. I have an excellent kombucha guide on my blog if you're interested in reading more.

Have a bit of land to work with? Consider raising chickens or starting a vegetable garden. Diana Rodgers' book *Homegrown Paleo* is an excellent resource for learning how to take control of your own food.

EXPERIMENT WITH FOOD TIMING

Timing of foods is a continuing source of debate. There is some evidence that eating carbs in the evening helps promote healthy circadian rhythms and sleeping through the night. Likewise, a protein-rich meal to break the nightly fast helps you maintain productivity throughout the day (finally, something that mainstream advice got right).

Another component of overall health is intermittent fasting. Fasting for more than 12 hours promotes weight loss and longevity through autophagy (cell cannibalism; see resource below). It also makes sense from a historical perspective; most humans didn't have access to three square meals a day until our modern era, so fasting was likely the norm until recently. Think about it: Every major religion has some sort of fasting ritual, probably a carryover from periods when food was scarce.

I like to eat in an eight-hour feeding window: a large lunch at 11am and dinner at 6pm, with breakfast a couple of times a week to switch things up. It can take several days to adapt to the process, and fasting is individualized; if you don't feel good when fasting, don't push it. But overall, I think it's a good idea to stress the body from time to time in regard to food timing, in much the same way that exercise strengthens the body.

RESOURCE:

"The Myriad Benefits of Intermittent Fasting," *Mark's Daily Apple,* February 2011. Available online at http://tdman.us/FastingLink

LIMIT SWEETS AND TREATS

One early dietary decision my wife and I made was that we needed to break the cycle of "Paleo-friendly" treats. Just because we *can* make brownies using Paleo-approved ingredients doesn't mean that we *should;* every time we made and ate them, our family felt worse for it. So with the exception of special occasions like birthdays and holidays, we tend not to make baked treats. Our treats come in the form of dark chocolate, berries, and the occasional batch of coconut or banana ice cream (and sometimes the real deal, too). At the same time, we found that creating delicious, satisfying lunches and dinners often curbed our cravings for sweets anyway.

Unless you are attempting dramatic weight loss, fruit is your friend. Personally, I eat at least one or two servings of fruit a day, usually with my first meal (or for a post-dinner treat). I tend to prefer berries over other fruits; berries are packed with vitamins, fiber, and antioxidants and have a generally lower sugar content than most other fruits. Cherries and kiwi aren't bad either in terms of sugar compared to other fruits. As your diet improves, your palate will adjust, and fruits will start to taste as sweet as candy, making them a special experience. Buy seasonally and locally, and grow your own if you have the time, climate, and inclination.

We also have fun with our food from time to time. That's why this book includes recipes for pizza (page 214), hamburger buns (page 296), and French fries (page 290)! These aren't everyday foods for our family, but it's great to break from the norm sometimes and replicate our favorite restaurant foods. After all, that's the underlying theme of this book.

GET ENOUGH SLEEP

When I don't get adequate sleep, I start making bad decisions about things like what to eat, what to wear, and whether I need a subscription to *Entertainment Weekly* (who needs weekly magazines?). The truth is that other than food, sleep is the single largest factor in determining how I feel. And unfortunately, Americans are now getting two hours less sleep each night than they did even 50 years ago.

Our lifestyles influence our sleep quality. Supposing that humans have been around for over 3 million years, we historically spent half of our days in darkness—probably sleeping or socializing around campfires or hearths. Fire (our only source of man-made light before electricity) is a red-spectrum light, which is calming; that's why we associate fireplaces and candlelit dinners with relaxation. Sunlight and artificial lights are blue-spectrum lights, which our brains associate with wakefulness. So when we are awake at night with the lights on, staring at computer or smartphone screens, our brains think it's still daytime. This tricking of the brain can affect sleep quality and circadian rhythms and is associated with stress and weight gain.

Here's what I do: After dinner each night (around 8pm), I don these ridiculous amber glasses that I bought online and wear them until I go to bed at 10pm; they block out blue-spectrum light and help relax me as I prepare for bed. I also block out light coming through our bedroom windows and have banned all other light sources (alarm clocks, for example). I then wake up at around 6am, only to repeat this pattern the following evening.

REMEMBER THAT HEALTH IS A MARATHON, NOT A SPRINT

A common misconception within the Paleo community is that the only way to stay healthy is to eat "clean" meals that can, frankly, be a little boring. I often see folks try Paleo for a while and give up because the diet wasn't personally sustainable or rewarding enough. My argument is that if you're eating a diet that you cannot maintain for more than a few weeks or months, then it is not a healthy diet.

I also don't really buy into the concept of "cheat meals," wherein you eat whatever you want and try to rebound afterward. Instead, my family and I came up with a diet that allows us a few gray-area foods (see page 16) that prevent us from falling completely off the wagon. We eat dairy in moderation and tailor our carbohydrate consumption to align with our bodies' needs (around 150 grams a day for me, 100 grams a day for my wife and son). I'm happy to say that I haven't had a single cheat meal since switching my diet, and it's not due to any sort of superhuman willpower. I simply eat a diet that doesn't feel like a "diet."

This is where my Four Corners Plate (page 19) really shines as a manageable template for healthy eating. By following a flexible eating model, you can tailor it to each family member's unique needs—not by creating individual meals for each person, but by tweaking each plate for optimal taste and nutrition. It takes a bit of practice, but by following this template (and the tips outlined in this section), you should be well on your way to better health!

SUBSTITUTION GUIDE

I understand that some of the ingredients called for in these recipes may be hard to find, depending on where you live. I also like to give my recipes a fair amount of flexibility for those with food allergies. This handy list of substitutions will help you out in a pinch.

I have set up an Amazon store featuring ingredients, tools, and other items used in this book; you can find it at http://tdman.us/PTOshopping. I'll be updating it often.

ITEM	SUBSTITUTION(S)
BLACKSTRAP MOLASSES	Double the amount of buckwheat honey. For example, if a recipe calls for 1 tablespoon blackstrap molasses, use 2 tablespoons buckwheat honey. Other honeys will work in a pinch.
BUTTER	Ghee (lactose-free clarified butter) or expeller-pressed coconut oil.
CHEESE	When mixed into a food (like meatballs), substitute a half portion of nutritional yeast. For example, if a recipe calls for 2 tablespoons grated Parmesan, use 1 tablespoon nutritional yeast. When shredded (like on pizza), simply omit.
CHINESE COOKING WINE	Dry sherry, sake, or equal parts rice vinegar and water plus a pinch of salt. For example, if a recipe calls for 1 tablespoon Chinese cooking wine, use 1 tablespoon dry sherry, 1 tablespoon sake, or a combination of 1/2 tablespoon rice vinegar, 1/2 tablespoon water, and a pinch of salt.
CREAM	Equal parts full-fat coconut milk and Chicken Broth (page 264).
GALANGAL	Fresh ginger. Note that dried galangal is available online and works very well once reconstituted in warm water for 30 minutes.
HONEY OR COCONUT PALM SUGAR	Double the amount of unsweetened applesauce, blended apple, or blended pear (seeds removed, skin intact). For example, if a recipe calls for 1 tablespoon honey, use 2 tablespoons blended apple.
KAFFIR LIME LEAVES	1 tablespoon lime zest for every 4 kaffir lime leaves. Note that some brands, including Thai Kitchen, sell dried kaffir lime leaves online, which are very handy.
KASHMIRI RED CHILI POWDER	Equal parts cayenne pepper and paprika. For example, if a recipe calls for 1 tablespoon Kashmiri red chili powder, use 1/2 tablespoon cayenne pepper and 1/2 tablespoon paprika.
MILD CURRY POWDER	Yields a little less than 1/4 cup: 1 tablespoon cumin seeds, 1 tablespoon coriander seeds, 1 tablespoon turmeric, 1 teaspoon dried mustard, 1/2 teaspoon ground cardamom, 1/2 teaspoon ground ginger, and a pinch of ground cinnamon. Combine and grind into a fine powder using a spice grinder. Add cayenne pepper or Kashmiri red chili powder in 1/4-teaspoon increments to increase the heat.
MIRIN	Sweet sake or equal parts rice vinegar and water plus a pinch of coconut palm sugar or a bit of honey.

ITEM	SUBSTITUTION(S)
OLD BAY SEASONING	Yields 1/4 cup: 2 tablespoons celery powder, 1 tablespoon bay leaf powder, 2 teaspoons ground mustard, 1 teaspoon paprika, 1/2 teaspoon black pepper, 1/2 teaspoon white pepper, a pinch of garlic powder, a pinch of cayenne powder, and a pinch of ground ginger.
RICE	Cauliflower Rice (page 288).
RICE VINEGAR	White wine vinegar, apple cider vinegar, or white vinegar.
S&B ORIENTAL CURRY POWDER	Yields a little more than 1/4 cup: 1 tablespoon turmeric, 1 tablespoon fenugreek seeds, 1 tablespoon cumin seeds, 1 tablespoon coriander seeds, 1/2 tablespoon ground cinnamon, 1/2 tablespoon ground ginger, 1 teaspoon cayenne pepper, 1 teaspoon black pepper, 1/2 teaspoon ground cloves, 1/2 teaspoon ground fennel, 1/2 teaspoon ground nutmeg, 1/2 teaspoon ground allspice, 1/4 teaspoon ground cardamom, 1 star anise, and 1 bay leaf. Grind into a fine powder using a spice grinder.
SAKE	Mirin or equal parts rice vinegar and water plus a pinch of coconut palm sugar or a bit of honey.
SHRIMP PASTE	Anchovy paste or double the amount of fish sauce plus a pinch of salt. For example, if a recipe calls for 1 teaspoon shrimp paste, use 1 teaspoon anchovy paste or 2 teaspoons fish sauce mixed with a pinch of salt.
DRIED CHINESE (SICHUAN) RED CHILE PEPPER	Any small dried red chile pepper or a half portion of crushed red pepper.
TAMARI	Coconut aminos (1:1.2) or Umami Sauce (1:1.5) (page 266). For example, if a recipe calls for 1 tablespoon tamari, use 1.2 tablespoons (about 3 1/2 teaspoons) coconut aminos or 1.5 tablespoons Umami Sauce.
THAI CHILE PEPPER	Jalapeño or Fresno (red jalapeño) chile.
TOGARASHI POWDER	Half portion cayenne pepper, quarter portion paprika, and quarter portion lemon pepper. For example, to make 1 tablespoon togarashi powder, use 1/2 tablespoon cayenne, a little less than 1 teaspoon paprika, and a little less than 1 teaspoon lemon pepper.
WHITE RICE FLOUR	Coconut flour or Otto's Cassava Flour.

MEAL TIMING GUIDE

MAKE-AHEAD DELICIOUSNESS

These are my favorite dishes to make in batches and freeze for quick reheating.

DISHES THAT TASTE BEST WHEN MARINATED OVERNIGHT

You can get away with marinating these dishes for less time, but they're worth the extra planning.

RECIPE INDEX

Chinese Kitchen

46

EGG DROP
SOUP

48

HOT AND SOUR
SOUP

50

FRIED
RICE

52

CAULIFLOWER
FRIED RICE

54

SPRING
ROLLS

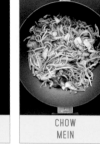

58

CHOW
MEIN

60

SINGAPORE RICE
NOODLES

62

EGG FOO
YOUNG

64

SWEET AND SOUR
CHICKEN

66

ORANGE
CHICKEN

68

CASHEW
CHICKEN

70

HONEY SESAME
CHICKEN

72
GENERAL TSO'S
CHICKEN

74
CHICKEN AND
MUSHROOMS

76
MOO GOO
GAI PAN

78
CHICKEN LETTUCE
WRAPS

80
BEEF AND
BROCCOLI

82
MONGOLIAN
BEEF

84
SZECHUAN
BEEF

86
PEPPER
STEAK

88
CHAR
SIU

90
MOO SHU
PORK

92
KUNG PAO
PORK

94
SHRIMP WITH LOBSTER
SAUCE

96
HONEY WALNUT
SHRIMP

98
BAM BAM
SHRIMP

100
CREAMY COCONUT
SHRIMP

102
VEGETABLES IN WHITE
SAUCE

104
STIR-FRIED
GREEN BEANS

Japanese and Korean Favorites

108 DASHI (JAPANESE SOUP STOCK)

110 MISO SOUP

112 RAMEN

114 GYOZA BITES

116 TEMPURA

118 TONKATSU AND CHICKEN KATSU

120 JAPANESE CURRY

122 KATSUDON

124 GYUDON

126 CHICKEN TERIYAKI

128 SALMON TERIYAKI

130 OKONOMIYAKI

132 QUICK JAPANESE SIDES

134 TAKUAN

136 BETTARAZUKE

138 KOREAN SEAFOOD SCALLION PANCAKE

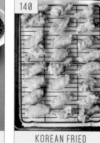

140 KOREAN FRIED CHICKEN

142 BULGOGI

144 KALBI

146 MEAT JUN

148 KIMCHI AND WHITE KIMCHI

150 CUCUMBER KIMCHI

152 QUICK KOREAN SIDES

southeast asia and beyond

158 TOM KHA GAI	**160** GANG JUED	**162** TOM YUM GOONG	**164** GREEN PAPAYA SALAD

166 PAD THAI	**168** PAD SEE EW	**170** THAI GREEN CURRY	**172** THAI RED CURRY	**174** MASSAMAN CURRY	**176** LARB

178 SUMMER ROLLS	**180** FASTER PHO	**182** VIETNAMESE PORK MEATBALLS	**184** BÚN CHA	**186** BÁNH XÈO	**188** BAKSO

190 SIMPLE TANDOORI CHICKEN	**192** CHICKEN TIKKA MASALA	**194** BUTTER CHICKEN	**196** LAMB VINDALOO	**198** KEBAB PARTY	**200** KARE KARE

202 OVEN PORK ADOBO	**204** GRILLED CHICKEN ADOBO	**206** PANCIT	**208** CHICKEN LONG RICE	**210** GARLIC SHRIMP

AMERICAN CLASSICS

214
BASIC
PIZZA CRUST

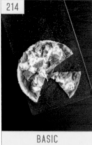

216
PIZZA
PARTY

220
CALZONES

222
BASIC
WINGS

224
SAUCY WINGS
FOUR WAYS

226
DRY-RUBBED WINGS
FOUR WAYS

228
BURGER
PARTY

232
CHICKEN
SANDWICHES

234
CHICKEN
NUGGETS

236
FRIED CHICKEN IN A
BUCKET

238
CHILI
FRIES

240
SPAGHETTI AND
MEATBALLS

242
CHICKEN FETTUCCINE
ALFREDO

244
CHICKEN
PARMESAN

246
BAKED EGGPLANT
PARMESAN

248
FAJITAS

250
CARNITAS

252
BLACKENED
FISH TACOS

254
BURRITO BOWL
DATE NIGHT

256
GYROS

258
GREEK
SALAD

Sauces, Condiments, And Sides

262 FISH STOCK

264 BEEF, LAMB, VEAL, OR BISON BROTH

266 UMAMI SAUCE

268 CHILI OIL

270 OKONOMIYAKI, TONKAT-SU, AND HOISIN SAUCES

272 TERIYAKI SAUCE

274 BARBECUE SAUCE

276 MAYO, HONEY MUSTARD, AND KETCHUP

279 RED SAUCE

280 WHITE SAUCE

282 NO-FUSS GUAC

284 TZATZIKI SAUCE

286 BASIC WHITE RICE

288 BASIC CAULIFLOWER RICE

290 PERFECT OVEN FRIES

292 MASHED POTATOES AND GRAVY

294 PICNIC COLESLAW

296 BURGER BUNS

298 FLATBREAD

ACKNOWLEDGMENTS

This goes without saying, but warrants saying nonetheless. Without the love and support of my beautiful, kind, and relentlessly strong wife, Janey, I'm not even sure if I'd be half the man I am today. Thank you for picking me up when I'm low and keeping me grounded when things get crazy. To our son, Oliver, who is now old enough to read the words I write—hey buddy. Thank you for your patience and understanding as I created this book. I have a feeling that you really enjoyed tasting most of these dishes as I developed them, so I guess it wasn't too bad of an experience. I love you two more than I can put into words.

Thanks to all the people involved in creating this book. Giang Cao dropped everything at the last minute to help me with the photography and layout design; thank you for your unique perspective and unwavering sense of style. Special thanks to Alex Boake, who illustrated the cover of this book and a few others sprinkled in here, too, like my Four Corners Plate and Dinner in an Hour illustrations. Hopefully my gazillion tweaks weren't too annoying! I really appreciate the hard work and dedication of the Victory Belt team, including Erich, Michele, Susan, Pam, and the ingenious design team. Your knowledge and enthusiasm helped kick this book up a notch in terms of presentation and accessibility.

To my friends and family, thanks for your help, encouragement, and feedback as I worked on this second book. To my fellow food bloggers and dedicated readers, thank you for your support and sense of community. You folks encourage and challenge me to try and improve with every recipe, and I'm better for it. I'm especially grateful for my Navy family, whose support and honesty have helped me to succeed in both my day and weekend jobs.

Special thanks to the members of the *Paleo Takeout* Facebook group, who took the time to prioritize their meals in order to test recipes with less than two weeks' notice. Your perspectives helped me to push those very last tweaks to each recipe and ensured that this book is the best it can possibly be.

And to you, the reader, thanks for investing in this book. It started as a whim of an idea based on one Sweet and Sour Chicken recipe (page 64) that I posted on my blog, then grew into an eBook, then into this print book. I hope that you find it to be a useful tool in regaining and maintaining your health in the most delicious way possible.

GENERAL INDEX